TAHITIAN JOURNAL

TAHITIAN JOURNAL

BY GEORGE BIDDLE

UNIVERSITY OF MINNESOTA PRESS

Printed in the United States of America at the North Central Publishing Company, St. Paul. *Library of Congress Catalog Card Number: 68-56112.* Published in Great Britain, India, and Pakistan by the Oxford University Press, London, Bombay, and Karachi, and in Canada by the Copp Clark Publishing Co. Limited, Toronto

TO H. S.

my best critic and true friend

A PUBLISHER'S NOTE ABOUT THE AUTHOR

GEORGE BIDDLE was born in Philadelphia on January 24, 1885. He attended Groton School, graduated from Harvard in 1908, and went on to Harvard Law School. He and his brother Francis, later Attorney General of the United States, both received the LL.B. degree in 1911. But George Biddle was never to practice law. He had recently become more and more interested in art and now with a profession to fall back on if need be he went to Paris and enrolled at Julien's Academy to study painting.

When the United States entered World War I he was just beginning to establish himself as an artist. He volunteered for army service and was sent to France. At war's end, like many another young man of that time, he took up residence in a foreign land. But unlike many others he had a specific goal in mind: to isolate himself for a year or two in order to devote himself to uninterrupted painting.

He chose a remote village on the island of Tahiti. There he lived with the natives, learned their language, and worked at his painting. The rich coloring of the tropics, transforming a three-dimensional world into a tapestry of brilliant colors, influenced him to turn from French Impressionism toward the flat design that became characteristic of much contemporary art.

Late in 1922 he left the South Seas, his course as artist firmly fixed. In succeeding years his work was exhibited in more than a hundred one-man shows in America, Europe, and Asia. He executed murals for the World's Fair in Chicago and fresco panels for the Department of Justice Building in Washington, the main lobby of the National Library in Rio de Janeiro, and the lobby of the Supreme Court Building in Mexico City. His work is found in the collections of the National Gallery, Metropolitan Museum of Art, Whitney Museum of American Art, Museum of Modern Art, Brooklyn Museum, Philadelphia Museum of Art, Pennsylvania Academy of Fine Arts, Fogg Art Museum, Carnegie Art Institute, Art Institute of Chicago, Colorado Springs Fine Arts Center, Portland Art Association, Omaha Art Institute, Seattle Fine Arts Center, Palace of Legion of Honor in San Francisco, Collection of Encyclopaedia Britannica, Collection of National Defense at the Pentagon, Boston Art Museum, San Diego Art Museum, Houston Art Museum, Denver Art Museum, Cincinnati Art Museum, National Gallery of Canada, Museum of Modern Art in Tokyo, University of Baroda, Kaiser Friedrichs Museum in Berlin, Tel Aviv Museum in Israel.

In the tradition of his family he has also served in government. He helped initiate the New Deal Federal Arts Projects. During World War II he was chairman of the War Department Art Committee, which sent artists to make pictorial war records at the front lines. His book *Artist at War* reflects his work in this period. (He has also published several other books, including *American Artist's Story*, *The Yes and No of Contemporary Art*, and *Indian Impressions.*) In 1950 President Truman appointed him to the National Fine Arts Commission.

At the age of eighty-two, still active as painter and writer, he turned back to the journal he kept during his months in Tahiti and prepared it for publication.

ACKNOWLEDGMENTS

I wish to acknowledge my indebtedness to my friend Donald S. Marshall, distinguished anthropologist, author of *Ra'ivavae.* I met him in the spring of 1963 when he was working on a life of Frank Stimson, whom I had known many years before in Tahiti. During our talks together I told him I had kept a diary while living there. He read it and urged me to revise it for publication. He has been most generous in correcting mistakes in Tahitian words and phrases and other factual errors.

I am also indebted to Professor Robert C. Kiste of the Department of Anthropology at the University of Minnesota for providing information on publications by Frank Stimson, E. C. S. Handy, and Percy Smith concerning Tahitian and general Polynesian culture that are cited in the footnotes and for comments on the culture and mores of primitive people.

In presenting here the journal I kept while I was living in Tahiti and, for a brief period, in New York City in the early 1920's, I have added a few short passages from memory about my American friends and I have made some observations on the island and its people which reflect what I subsequently learned. (These passages have been set off typographically, by use of the double column, from the journal entries.) When necessary I have cut or amended the original diary sufficiently to make it readable. I have also prefaced the Tahitian journal with some selections from my wartime diary of 1917–1919. Perhaps I may go as far as Baudelaire, who wrote in his *Journeaux Intimes*: "Le premier venu pourvu qu'il sache amuser, a le droit de parler de lui-même."

Croton-on-Hudson, January 1968

CONTENTS

TAHITIAN JOURNAL

THE ROMANTIC AND THE LOST GENERATION

WAR can affect us in different ways. I remember Agnes Irwin, a great lady and educator, a friend of William James's and also of my father's, telling me as a child that the Civil War left its mark on the faces of all those who fought through it. But it was not the mark of a "lost generation." Any generation of course is lost whose true direction has been warped by forces beyond its capacity to control. There was a lost generation of the young men who came of age during the Depression. There will be a lost generation – God help them – growing up in the South in the years ahead. But somehow Gertrude Stein's expression has clung to that generation, then in their twenties, who found themselves uprooted by World War I and unable to respond to the challenges of the postwar world.

I belonged to another, an earlier generation, since I was already thirty-two and beyond draft age when I went to the First Officers Training Camp at Fort Niagara in 1917. I think of ours as the romantic generation. I must say a word about our attitude toward the war: our state of mind, and thoughts, and feelings. There will never be the same response again. Perhaps it is better so.

Once our country had declared war all of us, overage or not, were anxious to get into it if one of the services would take us. And once we had our commissions we were in a hurry to get "over there" before things were finished. Using every device I could think of, I wheedled my company commander at Fort Niagara into recommending me for the first overseas contingent. In France, on account of my knowledge of French and German I was immediately ordered up to the A.E.F. general headquarters at Chaumont.

Eventually I landed on the G-2 staff – enemy intelligence – of the First Army Corps. The Corps entered line for the first time since the Civil War. It took part in the second battle of the Marne and the Meuse-Argonne offensive. With another officer and friend, Arnold Whitridge, I prepared the Infantry Assault and Artillery Objective maps for the Saint-Mihiel offensive, which were sent down as far as battalion headquarters. I was promoted to captain, and after the Armistice became acting assistant chief of staff of my section, G-2, with several hundred officers and men under my administrative command. Occasionally, not often, I was under artillery fire, night bombings, and gas attacks.

But during that year and a half overseas I could not entirely rid myself of a feeling of shame that I had not served in a line division. There was no dirtier word in the French language than *embusqué* — a word applied not just to a man who had kept out of uniform, but also to one who had kept out of the trenches.

Twenty-five years later I was with our front-line divisions for several months in Italy and Sicily. Our G.I.'s of World War II had as good stuff in them as our doughboys of World War I. But theirs was a more realistic philosophy. I remember once at officers' mess a young infantry lieutenant proposing a toast: "To the Russians — God bless them — let them do the fighting." Romance had gone out of war.

It was a bad time to have interrupted my career. I was just getting started. One of my paintings had been accepted by the jury of the Pennsylvania Academy Annual. Bill Yarrow, a young Philadelphia artist who showed great promise, and I had talked to Frank Rehn at the Milch Gallery. He considered giving us an exhibition. And then, two weeks before I received my sailing orders, I got married.

From my journal of the time:

September 7, 1917

We left Pier Number 1 at Hoboken at about 5 P.M. We are carrying 3000 to 3500 troops. They are very green. They have been drafted within the past month, largely Pollacks and Italians. I doubt if many of them are native-born. Their officers tell me they are quite without discipline, but will make good soldiers when they learn to speak and understand English! How different from the lusty Bavarian peasants I saw in Munich in August 1914 as they marched off, wild roses fastened to their bayonets; and from the young French *poilus* who used to come swinging up the road from Vernon past our cottage at Giverny in 1915 whistling the "Marche du Départ."

September 11, 1917

I had written to Fred Frieseke, my earlier counselor and dear friend, telling him my fears for my artistic future; how terrifying at times they have been. Just before sailing I had the kindest and most reassuring letter from him. He wrote me: "Your art will follow creative growth. It doesn't matter how long your work is interrupted as long as imagination doesn't atrophy." This is all that is left me now. For a long time I shall not have a chance to paint. I would that the thing in me which later may produce works of art may now continue to develop. This is one reason why I intend to keep a diary. *Je veux préciser ma mentalité créatrice.* Hitherto this has been a vague dilution of impulses and desires. An artist is primarily concerned with the concrete — the actual painting — not with the aesthetic theories which it illustrates.

All lights in the ship are out by six o'clock. The men turn in by nine. At night as I lie in the dark, waves of creative desire sweep over me.

The day before we sailed I visited Mr. Allison, one of the partners of the Keppel Gallery. I showed him my lithographs and etchings. He promised to make use of whatever I could send him and see that I get exhibitions elsewhere. What a wonderful incentive to sketch. Surely there will be opportunities. My heart kept singing all afternoon.

Passion and intelligence. Albert Besnard's definition of genius. *Une passion intelligente.* What a time to be alive. One must live with restrained, controlled, directed passion.

How can I hate all Germans? I don't hate any; or anyone. I hate vicious ideas. We are only bound together by great and pure ideas; by mutual admirations and mutual passions.

Now that I have taken the plunge all the painful moral torments that have vexed me these past three years have blown away like mist. I feel today about this mad war what I felt when I left Munich in the spring of 1915. I won't hate the Germans. But now with justification for engaging in the war I can abandon myself to the full joy of fighting in defense of France. My heart is no longer in conflict with my sense of right and wrong. And I shall always love Bavaria.

Just six years ago, this same eleventh of September, I arrived in Paris. I met Waldo Peirce at the Café des Deux Magots and we had coffee together. During my first year at the Harvard Law School Waldo and I had joined a life class, drawing from the nude, under the old landscape painter Paul Dudley Murphy. That afternoon Waldo and I signed up at the Académie Julien in the Rue du Dragon.

September 17, 1917

I kept watch on the bridge. At first the intensity of the stars seemed to throw the sky back into darkness. Soon the night melted into a lovely, luminous, pearly gray. Where a cloud lay on the horizon its edges were sharply outlined.

I slept from seven until ten o'clock and was ordered back to the bridge. The sea was a white-gray slate color, the dirty gray made by mixing vermilion, viridian green, and a neutralizing white. The surface of the water was plowed up into myriads of silver-ridged furrows, and the silver against the dirty gray of the sea was the polished surface of some old embossed and chiseled bowl, tarnished with use. Where the shadow of a cloud fell on the silver-gray sea, the most delicate gauze seemed to have been laid on it—as delicate as a mauve-colored spider's web. Beyond, the still more luminous pearl-gray of the sky was sliced with streaks of crimson and cadmium yellow.

September 18, 1917

The following notice has been posted about the ship: "Anyone who falls overboard after midnight tonight will be abandoned. No effort will be made to pick him up. We will merely throw over one of the cork rings. With submarines in the vicinity the ship's safety will not be endangered by slowing down the vessel."

Two nights ago we ran through a belt of phosphorus. I was told that it comes from the

African coast. The sky was indigo and the sea a deeper indigo. The wake of the transport could be seen for miles astern like incandescent rivers of indigo and milk. It was blowing. Each wave was a furrow of pale gold. The waves thrown up by the passage of the ship made a riot of light which lit up the bottoms of the lifeboats, swung out on the davits. Hundreds of mad snakes zigzagged from the ship's sides.

G.H.Q., Chaumont, Haute Marne, September 27, 1917

A doughboy who had seen service with Pershing in Mindanao in the Philippines, where "the niggers have knives six feet long and cut fellers in two," described to us a speech which the General had made to his troops, "'And gee,' he says, 'fellers, we want to kinder get on the good side of these Goddamn niggers. And there's no Christly reason why we shouldn't make a hit with them. That's what we're here for, boys, to make a hit.' And I said to the guy who was standing beside me: 'Well, we'd better make a hit with the bastards pretty quick, or the sons of bitches will make a hit at us.'"

September 29, 1917

As General Joffre rode by the other day a small child sitting on his father's shoulders exclaimed: "Hisses-moi, papa, plus haut. Je veux voir le père singe."

Yesterday Lieutenant Griffiths was officer of the day. During the evening he wandered down to the Y.M.C.A. cantonments. Things seemed unusually jolly. The barracks were crowded with prostitutes. The men were in excellent spirits. The Y.M.C.A. chief approached Griffiths, wringing his hands, and begged him to "get them out of here." Griffiths walked over to the most conspicuous of the tarts. Crossing his arms he accosted her with severity: "Mademoiselle, que faites-vous içi?" The lady turned around, startled. "Ah, Monsieur, que vous me faites peur!" Griffiths with increased severity inquired once again: "Que faites-vous içi, Mademoiselle?" "Ben quoi," she answered sulkily. And then, perceiving and pointing to the Y.M.C.A. chief: "Ah, c'est lui! Mais j'attends mon ami." Griffiths finally shooed the girls out. A *laveuse*, who remained on service, grumbled: "C'est sévère, ça. On travaille toute la journée, et puis on ne peut pas entendre un peu de musique."

September 30, 1917

All morning my assignment was to translate German newspaper articles filled with venomous lies and propaganda against us and the English. For the rest of the day I felt lonely and blue. I am a tiny cog in a vast machine, and my part in it becomes more meaningless day by day. I try to believe that all this is necessary to carry out a noble purpose—at the very least a necessary and a generous one. But to feel enthusiasm or emotion while part of such a machine! Never. Only weariness.

And I am helping to manufacture hate where so little exists. The other day in my incoming basket was the account of some German atrocity. Penciled on it over the initials of a G-2 staff officer: "Red meat! Feed it down to the trenches." How dirty and petty it all seems. The feeble chatter from the home front: "On to Berlin" and "We'll hang Kaiser Bill." And our own unpreparedness in this mighty industry of war.

October 8, 1917

Yesterday afternoon I rode up the canal along the Marne past Buzy. The autumn coloring was beautiful. The low hills purple. A woman in a green field dressed in black. It became a splash of indigo, and purple was in her hair. The trees, enveloped in a silver haze, shed color. Along the bank of the canal soldiers were fishing. Soon the air turned cold and bleak. All evening it rained.

HERE my journal abruptly stopped. It must have been at this time that the First Corps was organized under the command of General Hunter Liggett and that I was assigned to G-2 of its combat staff. At Corps headquarters during the spring of 1918 Captain Whitridge and I were kept busy. We knew that we should soon see action. The first successful operation of the Allies in Europe was shortly to begin. No more time for recording anecdotes of wartime France, aesthetic speculations, or my own growing misgivings and moral depression.

I found myself absorbed in the chess game of strategy: "enemy intelligence," its relation to "military operations," and the hierarchic intricacies of "chains of command." Whitridge and I soon became competent staff officers. Under the circumstances I was as happy as could be expected. There were not too many flies in the ointment.

When the Corps moved into combat I began once more to keep a journal. A turning point in history is usually presaged, or at least accompanied, by some dramatic episode such as I now took part in. This was the overthrow of the greatest military force that up to then the world had seen. It ended the five-hundred-year cycle which began with the Renaissance. A new age was dawning. Journals kept at such moments, no matter how inadequate, should reveal to some degree the mood of the participants and the mass psychology and *élan vital* that change history.

For the first time in fifty years I have been rereading these pages, notes and observations hastily jotted down at odd moments. They constitute — not in what I wrote but in what I totally omitted to record — the most scathing indictment of war that I am capable of expressing. In all the dreary hundred and sixty pages there are only five short passages of a few lines each which suggest any human emotion — hardly a physical reaction — toward what I saw, heard, and must have felt. The rest, the jargon and minutiae of a staff officer, is as dull, flat, soulless, and repetitious as the recordings of a stock-market ticker tape. Here are a few examples taken at random.

Shelling on Lucy-le-Bocage and Bois de Belleau just as we moved out. Shells fell into Dhuysy, the French 167 P.C. . . . The three divisions opposite our sector are 5 G.D. (Veuilly-

Bussiaies), 87 D (Bussiaies-Belleau), 201 D (Bouresche-Vaux). . . . Spent the day interviewing prisoners of the 401 and the 402 regiments captured last night. A very inferior lot. Quite *abrutis*. A few from Lorraine talked freely. . . . Last night on our right sector from Bouresche to Vaux a total of 21,500 shells, of which 12,000 heavy. . . . It is rumored that we have captured Bonne, Etrepilly, and the Grande Picardy farm. Advance five kilometers. Seventeen thousand German prisoners reported taken in the three days' fighting. . . . Bits of shrapnel from our own antiaircraft fell about the kitchen where we were billeted for the night. . . . Today the Second French Cavalry Corps, 4000 men, filed by, with lances set, toward the Givry-Epaux road. . . . The 167 French has been in line for 72 days. . . . According to some reports our regiments are reduced to 4000 or 5000 men. We have orders to capture Sergy before 2 A.M. We can never do it. Our troops are all in. . . . The Germans made their first serious hold on the north bank of the Ourcq, throwing in the 4 G.D. and the 6 B.R.D., both among their best divisions. The losses among our 42nd have been heavy. In one regiment all but two of the field officers have been killed. . . . Two men of the 45 Scharfschützen Abteilung were captured today by the 32 D in the French 38 A.C. to our right. They had been attached to the 216 D. . . . Our Corps is about to move. The roads badly blocked and muddy. Engineers repairing it and the sappers burying the dead.

❦ SURELY enough. It is, however, such undigested irrelevances which, when fed into the maw of war's computing machines for analysis, provide essential data for the successful conclusion of a military operation. Being something of an amateur at my job I occasionally reported observations of another nature, quite useless as army intelligence. But even in such cases I had become disciplined—conditioned—to record them in my role as a staff officer. Not as a human being. Here again are random samples: ❦

Beyond Torcy, which we skirted, we entered the Bois de la Brigade de Marines. Crossing the gully there was a strong smell of corpses. . . . Interviewed the old and feeble mayor of Beuvardes. Told us that the Germans had behaved not badly, but had pillaged and destroyed deserted houses. The last note in his diary in his trembling handwriting: "La maison de ma bonne est détruite. Ça barde. Où sont les français?" . . . The weather hot and dry. In the woods across the Brécy-Epieds road the stench of dead men and horses. . . . Along the edge of the Artois farm and down toward Beuvardes are a line of foxholes one to four feet deep, often filled with straw or an old army coat. Occasionally a roughly made roof of sticks and mud. . . . At the Meurcy farm the dead lay very thick. A line of our soldiers about twenty yards from the German trenches. . . . In one spot at Seringe near Hill 184 nine rifles with fixed bayonets. And many dead Germans in the pits, all blackened and swollen. . . . Back in the woods of Bois Brûlé, which ran steeply up the hill, were other fortified shell craters, pits, and dugouts. Several hundred dead were lying about. The corpses blackened, swollen, eaten away, blown to bits, or partly covered by earth thrown up by the shelling. German helmets camouflaged in black, green, and blue. . . . I walked over the hill south of Villeneuve. The dead had been exhumed. The freshly covered mounds smelt of phosphates and burning wool. . . . With Roland Redmond rode over the recent scene of action of July 27 and 28. The bodies had been buried, but everywhere the evidence of a hasty retreat. Little mounds marked with wine bottles, crosses decorated with roses, a helmet stuck on a bayonet. Broken chairs, blankets, mattresses, stolen crockery, empty cans, horse fodder, loaves of bread, canteens, rifles, dispatch cases, and other rubbish. I lay under a locust tree and watched the arabesque of the leaves against the sky.

August 24, 1918

I was married a year ago yesterday.

September 12, 1918

I have handed in an application for transfer to General Malin Craig, chief of staff of the Corps. Yesterday he spoke to me very kindly about it. I told him that I would have much preferred serving with line troops. But I knew that it was now too late for this. Could I go to a staff school? This was the only way to get an assignment to a brigade staff. I would be happier at the front. He told me that a staff school was by no means necessary. That I should aim directly for chief of section of a divisional staff, G-2. General Nolan often asked him for officers. He would keep me in mind.

September 24, 1918

Drove up to the advance P.C. of 28 D beyond Croix de Pierre. The woods had been gassed. Some casualties. A human corpse on a field of battle often gives the suggestion of arrested motion. A leg thrust at an acute angle from the body. Head or arm bent incongruously out of line. Do a drawing of a dead soldier, tip it upside down, and there would be a figure convulsed with movement. I think of the superb Japanese prints of the kabuki actors. But in a dead horse the feeling of weight, inertia, empty mass is truly terrifying.

October 12, 1919

So it is unconditional surrender. By the first of February peace may be signed. By the first of March I may be home.

The German government reminds me of a robber cardsharp. Having used every device until the jig is up, he coolly lights a cigarette and stretches out his wrists for the handcuffs.

Will my art, whatever creative gift I had, be dead? No one not an artist can realize the oppressive agony of that thought. Yet reason tells me that a two years' interruption cannot entirely destroy the creative will. Much may be lost. There may be some growth or gain. But what a joy to draw and paint again. What torture, too, it will mean.

October 14, 1918

A big shake-up in the higher command. Liggett goes to the First Army. Dickman will take over the First Corps. Unfortunately Colonel X remains as our chief of section. That wretched, narrow-minded, incapable, boot-licking, spineless coward has made my life miserable.

ALL civilian soldiers are emotionally disordered and overwrought. Sexually segregated, separated from their homes, family, occupation, and friends, they lose their sense of identity. More especially does this happen at the front where they are at the breaking point of physical endurance and often face death. It is natural that they should become subject to fits of depression, jealousies, rancors, and hate. Trivial incidents can break the nerve of the most normal and self-disciplined. We heard stories of enlisted men who, at the propitious moment, shot their officers in the back. In my own case my relation to my immediately superior officer, my chief of section, was hard to bear and might have caused serious trouble for me.

Colonel X was a despicable creature. Groveling toward his superior officers, bullying his inferiors in rank, bombastic, loudmouthed, and histrionic, he had neither a sense of humor nor common sense. All through the war his eyes were fixed like a hungry dog's on one objective only, the lists of temporary promotion as they came in from Washington. His relieving trait was a melodramatic buffoonery. This I can forgive him for. It heightened his sense of the imminence of disaster and death. He issued directives to the orderlies and topographical noncommissioned officers in the map room that they should at all times carry loaded side arms. Captain Whitridge and I might raise an eyebrow at these antics, upon which, almost frothing at the mouth, he would bellow at us: "I can tell you young fellows, war is a damn serious thing."

He had two other traits that might have seemed comical had they not suggested a rather unsavory pathology. He had slowly accumulated a vast collection of obscene and pornographic postcards and pictures of naked *Fräulein* in inviting postures. These turned up consistently among the belongings of the German prisoners. He kept them in a large gunny sack. The night before each major offensive – I am telling God's truth – he would call for the sack and sit by the hour, gloating over its contents and mumbling appropriate ejaculations of satisfaction or incredulity.

The other trait was an almost necrological appetite. He savored the realization that "war is hell." When on our frequent junkets to the front lines we would run across a corpse lying in a field of poppies, he would order his driver to draw up by the roadside. Sometimes he would get out and poke about the pitiful little foxholes containing handfuls of grain gathered from the ripening wheat and discarded gas masks and helmets. At other times he would sit in silence, somberly taking it all in. He was a man of blood and iron.

In retrospect I fancy that it was the sum total of all these endearing little qualities that got my goat rather than any deep animosity. But whatever the basic cause, on one occasion my feeling about him became so strong that my self-control snapped and I almost landed in serious trouble. I have forgotten what particularly asinine thing he had just said to me. But as he closed his office door I turned and announced to the full orderly room: "Colonel X is a son of a bitch." Luckily it was not this but another indiscretion on my part which came to his attention. That night at the Officers' Club, to keep the conversation going, I suggested that the German General Staff was responsible for almost all the tactical innovations since the outbreak of war. My remarks were reported back to Colonel X by a dental major as being "injurious to army morale" and "unbecoming in an officer and a gentleman." The Colonel had me in and put me on the carpet. He banged his fist on the table and trumpeted. For a while, until I realized what the charge was, it was pretty uncomfortable. Of course I groveled and apologized – after, however, having cornered him into admitting that what I had said was perfectly true.

One might suppose that the Armistice was a tremendous relief after the strain of war. This was not the case. One only heard of shell shock after the fighting was over. Then began the immediate disintegration of discipline, the crumbling of individual morale. One more readily entertains cowardly feelings when there is no longer a danger to face.

First Corps H.Q., Tonnerre, December 20, 1918

Now that the fighting is over I want to get back to my painting, to forget it all. I have time to read and think, even to paint a little. Once more, in order to clear my ideas, and to regain some serenity, I have taken up my diary. For inactivity is worse than the actual fighting. These terrible months of nervous anticipation, readjustment, doubts, anxiety. I am ill-humored, depressed. I have lost confidence in myself, in my friends, in my future. No one can realize the strain.

I drink too much, two quarts of wine a day, red and white burgundy, but it seems to have no effect on me.

December 28, 1918

For the next five years I must be patient and study. I shall probably never sell more than a few things. I may always be considered a dilettante, for my work is not clever and today it is clever painting that sells.

Frieseke once told me that he would feel satisfied if in a given city there were half a dozen people who really understood his work.

January 1, 1919

Michelangelo wrote: "If God should give me license to choose from all the gifts which he showered on mortal man the one which I should most like to have or obtain, I should ask none other – after divine faith – than the high gift of excelling in the art of painting; and perhaps even in that I should wish to be none other than I am. For this I offer many thanks to immortal and sovereign God; because in this world, vast and complex, he has proffered me this little beacon, my ambition in the noble art of painting; so unique in merit that no other gift seems to me more glorious or more worthy of respect."

Apart from his belief in "God immortal and sovereign," art was to Michelangelo his religion, and so it must be to all great artists. Today we — I am without a religious faith. But I profoundly believe that art — to a great artist of today — must be his religion. I mean that painting or any other art is to the artist a nearer expression of divine perfection — no matter what be his divinity — than anything else on earth. Love also gives us that sense of perfection which makes us think it divine. The Italian Renaissance had reverence for its art, and reverence for beauty. Without such reverence no period can be great in art; and no painter can be a great artist. And this I believe with my whole soul.

January 4, 1919

Recently I have seen much of Emile Bernard, the old friend of Gauguin and Cézanne, who lives now in Tonnerre. He has been painting a portrait head of me. It is not at all in the color and manner of his earlier Fauve period, but quite academic in the umbers and siennas of the Beaux-Arts tradition. Together we have long talks on art. He told me the other day that he considers Titian's "Christ Castigated" in the Pinakotek in Munich the finest of his paintings. Some years ago he met Zuloaga there. Together they went to see the painting. Zuloaga exclaimed: "It is finer than any painting in the Pinakotek, finer than the Rubenses and the Rembrandts. It is the finest painting in the world." They sat together in front of it all that morning, and the afternoon, and the next day.

January 8, 1919

When Titian was well on in years and ill he wrote to a friend: "I have studied, I have worked and experimented night and day to obtain beauty and perfection without ever being able to reach them; and since my earliest years I have tortured myself to arrive at some progress, according to my lights, and now that I note some little progress, death is about to snatch the brush from my hand." By the grace of God Titian lived another thirty-three years.

January 10, 1919

During the past month I have been able to draw a few hours a day. I have finished some thirty studies of heads. It was Michelangelo who said that drawing is the foundation of painting. Contemporary artists never draw enough. The artists of the past century constantly drew: Delacroix, Degas, Mary Cassatt.

January 15, 1919

I have been reading Delacroix's journal: "J'ai senti se réveiller en moi la passion des grandes choses. Retrempons nous dans les grandes et belles productions." Mary Cassatt often told me that to keep one's standards high one must study the masters. And Cézanne repeatedly said the same thing.

Delacroix writes that genius is the ability to impose on others our particular way of seeing and feeling. This is the essential. Depth of feeling and honesty are what matter.

January 22, 1919

When I visited Rodin in his Meudon studio in 1915 I noticed for the first time and was greatly inspired by the purely formal or geometric use of line in the nude studies of his superb collection of drawings, many of them highly erotic or pornographic. But a great artist or scientist discerns truth or beauty wherever it occurs. A figure might have been contained in the outline of a pear, a triangle, a shell. These thoughts were in my mind when I painted my "Model with Black Stockings" in 1916. When Frieseke saw it he was delighted and said: "It suggests Gauguin." When Arthur Carles saw it he exclaimed: "It has qualities in it better than any of Frieseke's work. It is you, not Frieseke." I had sometimes been accused of imitating my friend.

February 2, 1919

I have little sense of visual memory. Often I cannot recall the details or color of a canvas over which I labored the previous year. Yet I remember vividly the emotional *sensation* I felt standing before Titian's "Man with a Glove" or Correggio's "Rape of Danaë" seen years ago in the Salon Carré of the Louvre. And it distresses me that I cannot actually visualize my mother's face. Yet I calm myself with the realization that many of the greatest artists were dependent on models and worked directly from nature for their inspiration: Cassatt, Monet, Renoir, Cézanne, countless others.

February 6, 1919

Emile Bernard asked me if I had been drawing recently. But for the past month I have done nothing. Toward the end of December I was promoted to acting chief of G-2 of the First Army Corps. I have had little time for drawing or painting. My spasmodic attempts only filled me with revulsion. To work for an hour today and next week perhaps an hour!

February 10, 1919

The chauvinism of our allies leaves me depressed and unhappy. They are adopting the same standards of robbery and revenge for which we castigated the Germans. Our officers argue that the Germans are criminals, mad dogs, and should be manacled or destroyed. You cannot destroy or imprison 70,000,000 people. But you can stir up trouble in the years ahead. It is all dogs fighting over a bone. Yet there is idealism among many of the individual officers and soldiers who have been fighting and dying for an idea. Idealism exists in the individual. Never in the nation. Who was it that said of history "Hieroglyphics written in mud"?

February 13, 1919

From America: ". . . I have felt that you and I have made a mistake in getting married. . . . I have felt it off and on for over a year, in fact almost as soon as you left. . . . I have known the truth but been afraid to admit it. . . ."

I went directly to General Fassett, chief of staff of the Corps. I told him that I must go home at once.

THE disintegration of my morale was precipitated by the forebodings, and soon the realization, that my marriage was on the rocks. My reactions were impulsive rather than reasoned and philosophic. I was still immature.

I felt — like many other young officers and doughboys — that, in the cause of liberty, I had voluntarily made a sacrifice, closed the doors to the realities and joys of life in a long and cruel confinement. Day by day the effort to retain my morale had become more than I could bear. My sanity, courage, ideals, and faith seemed gone. Now the prison gates had opened. Beyond I could only see disillusion and shattered hopes.

February 20, 1919

I pray for wisdom. Often it is hard to know how to be wise. At all costs I must keep this thing out of my mind. Cruel thoughts come over me; anger, revenge, despair. It is hard to keep sane. Last night I was troubled by dreams.

March 19, 1919

A telegram from G.H.Q. ordering me to St. Agnan for immediate return to the States.

Before leaving I went in to General Fassett to thank him for his many kindnesses to me. He wrote in my Officer's Record Book: ". . . For the greater part of the last two months Captain Biddle has served as acting G-2 of the Corps directly under me, and in every way he has done most excellent service. He has been loyal, painstaking, and tactful. He has the necessary qualifications of a successful staff officer."

What touched me most in leaving the Corps was the knowledge that my officers and the enlisted men were almost all genuinely sorry to see me go. And yet I am a second-rate officer, because *I hate the life*. But I understand the secret of an officer's success. I look after my men's comfort and I have been honest with them. I never raise my voice with anyone in the section. I loathe and am incapable of "bawling men out." It is never necessary if one is honest. Whenever I was mistaken or did not know the answer I always admitted it. In the long run you can't fool an American soldier. When Colonel X left the section the discipline was abominable, because he was selfish, stupid, and without discipline himself.

Poor Anderson, my orderly, had tears in his eyes when I told him I was leaving.

March 20, 1919

At times I feel as if the bottom has dropped out of my life. At other moments the demons of hell are eating into the back of my brain: bitter disappointment, rage, and hate. I am in mental terror of losing my self-control. Those are happy who in moments like this can fall back on religion. I can only fall back on myself. My religion is something apart. I am my own religion.

Brest, March 21, 1919

This evening I looked through the catalogue of the third "Vente Edgar Degas." I feel such veneration for his work. I was overcome with waves of depression. I felt my own impotence. What is the use. I said to myself: "Better remain an amateur. You are written a failure."

I love women and I need them. I could never be happy without a woman's love.

I should like to go to the Hawaiian Islands for a year; a year and a half. I need to be alone to make up for lost time; to learn to be myself. Captain Taylor, chief of our topographical section, lived for a while in the islands. He used to talk to me of the mountains, the palm trees, and the reefs.

March 22, 1919

I am choked with bitterness. I should so like to feel that there is some idealism in this war. Among most of the regular army officers I have found only pettiness, jealousies, and a desire for promotion. I so need someone to help me. Yet I may always be alone. I will not become poisoned and bitter. My friends used to accuse me of taking life too easily; of being incapable of feeling. God knows in these last two years I have lived and I have felt.

March 23, 1919

All day I have been alone, reading in my room, roaming about the gray, desolate, muddy streets of windy, rainy Brest. At the Café de la Brasserie I had supper alone. I drank too much again. I watched the prostitutes who frequent the Brasserie. I am filled with repulsion and desire. I brood over my painting. I wait for the designation of a ship.

March 24, 1919

Finished reading *Jean Christophe*, which I began three years ago. Why do the French today so bitterly criticize this noble patriot? It is because he cannot hate. ". . . Et nous, ne nous voyez pas non-plus, frères d'Allemagne, qui vous disons: 'Voici nos mains. En dépit des mensonges et des haines, on ne nous séparera point. Nous avons besoin de vous, vous avez besoin de nous, pour la grandeur de notre esprit et de nos races. Nous sommes les deux ailes de l'Occident. Qui brise l'une, le vol de l'autre est brisé. Vienne la guerre! Elle ne rempra point l'étreinte de nos mains et l'éssor de nos génies fraternels.' "

These words were written in October 1912. Is there a Frenchman or German today capable of such generous feelings?

April 1, 1919

Last night a terrifying dream. I was in an American truck driven by two German prisoners. The driver was a stodgy, unattractive fellow. I opened a small sharp penknife, which recently I had taken from another prisoner. I jabbed it into both his eyes. I whittled them out as I would an oyster from its shell. Then I became fearful that he had not died and I jabbed the little penknife into his brain, again and again, until I could feel the back of his skull.

Suddenly to my horror the driver turned around and asked me for a cigarette. I knew he was still alive and I suffered agony. I saw a steep cliff which overhung the road. At that moment another German soldier fell from the summit of the cliff and his brains spattered on the ground. I seized the driver by the hand. Running and stumbling, dragging him behind me, I led him up the cliff, over trenches and through barbed-wire entanglements. Stopping, I asked those about me what it all meant. They told me that it was Children's Day. A great Movie Picture was to be staged. The trenches and barbed wire were part of the stage setting.

At the top of the cliff sat another blind German prisoner. The children were seated about him and he was reading to them from a great book spread out on his knees.

"How can you read," I asked him, "if you are blind?"

"They are my own stories," he said. "I know them all by heart, and am reciting them to the children."

"Listen," I said. "Here is a man who will read your stories to the children." And I took his hand and laid it in the hand of the man I had blinded.

And then I became frightened and ran, and ran, stumbling down the cliff over rocks and through bracken.

April 5, 1919

Arrived in Boston.

April 11, 1919

Discharged at Camp Dix, New Jersey, and returned to Philadelphia.

THE ensuing weeks were a nightmare. I did not realize then — or for many years to come — that the pain born from a "broken heart" is compounded of many feelings: injured vanity and pride, loss of faith in oneself, frustrated sexual desire — and often love itself.

Yet underneath the Victorian varnish of the romantic generation I was fundamentally healthy. I subconsciously became aware that at least a partial road to recovery lay in the relief of my sexual desires. I indulged myself generously when opportunity offered. Some guardian angel more than once protected me from the heavy price one at times must pay for such indulgence.

I knew, too, that to isolate myself from the past, from every diversion and every association, and to concentrate my entire energy and love on my art was the only road to happiness.

I left Philadelphia within a week, never to return, except as an infrequent visitor, to the scene of my happiest childhood memories and the home of my many friends

During those endless hours on the transport ship coming home I had more or less resolved to leave for some Pacific island at the earliest possible moment. In search of solitude where time is the "solvent of all things"? To forget the war? To bury forever what I believed was a personal failure in life? Or was it merely for me the most congenial place for the *recherche du temps perdu*?

In the years following World War I many other young writers and painters for more or less the same reasons sought temporary exile in foreign countries. Hemingway, Fitzgerald, Malcolm Cowley, Matthew Josephson, Harold Stearns — the great majority — chose Paris. Others headed for London: Eliot, Charles Demuth, Conrad Aiken, Ezra Pound. George Antheil and Marsden Hartley found Berlin the most stimulating city in Europe. A few of us, Hall, Nordhoff, Robert Dean Frisbie, Jerry Blum, and I, were drawn to the South Sea Islands of the Pacific. Never before had there been such a flight of young American artists in search of better feeding grounds.

Other painters and writers before this had visited the Society Islands and the Samoan group — Stevenson, Pierre Loti, John La Farge, Henry Adams, and Gauguin. I had read *Le Mariage de Loti* and *Noa Noa*. But it was definitely not the literary-romantic exoticism of the islands which weighed with me.

The very real attraction was something subconscious, more intense. In the blood, rather than in the head. The instinctive, unreasoned, magnetic pull of the tropics. Lush vegetation, brilliant coloring, dark skins. The formalized, suggestive, yet deceptive beauty of primitive races. I had first felt this attraction on the west coast of Mexico in 1909; and later among the Negroes in Bermuda where I had spent a long, hot summer painting. It is a beauty that Gauguin also felt. For he put it into his paintings only after he had visited the Caribbean, as again of course later in Tahiti and the Marquesas. And this was the principal quality that drew me to Gauguin. I had no sympathy for his neo-primitive use of line in drawing and the violent color relations of the Fauves and the German Expressionists.

There was a further circumstance that decided me. Shortly after returning to the States I heard through circumstances I have now forgotten that a younger boyhood friend of mine was then living in Tahiti. I obtained his address and wrote him, asking all sorts of necessary questions. His answer decided me. He was building a native bungalow in Tautira, some eighty kilometers from Papeete. He invited me to join him. The matter was settled.

I should have preferred leaving immediately. This was impossible. It took me a year to straighten out my personal affairs. I stayed on in New York, took a studio and painted. I held my first one-man exhibition at the Milch Gallery on West Fifty-Seventh Street.

That year Freddy O'Brien — I was to see much of him during the next few years — published his *White Shadows in the South Seas*. It was not a great book. It was a felicitous combination of adventure, romance, fantasy, tall tales, and a few libelous passages; he had a genuine storytelling gift. It was what post-World War I America yearned for, just as post-World War II America yearned for Michener. O'Brien was a far less accomplished writer than Michener but his books had the same immoderate success. For a couple of years they gave the South Sea Islands a spurious and sentimental vogue.

I often used to see George Putnam, of the publishing firm — later Amelia Earhart's husband — at the Coffee House Club. He knew I was leaving shortly for Tahiti. One day he said to me: "Why don't you keep a journal?"

Of course I was pleased and flattered. I was also a little disturbed. Above all I wanted isolation and anonymity. Not the feeling of climbing on a fashionably exotic bandwagon. But I tentatively accepted his suggestion. I gave a good deal of thought, however, to the sort of diary it should be.

I was convinced that the only honest and valid excuse for such a journal was a sober day-to-day record and description of a still unspoiled, although rapidly vanishing, primitive society. I am not a trained anthropologist. But might not an artist's journal of his experience in such a society be of universal human interest? If at the time I had read Llewelyn Powys he might have been my model. Definitely Pierre Loti and O'Brien were not. I would, I resolved, keep myself as much as possible out of the picture; as also any reference to the few white people I might run across. This approach, however, entailed an objectivity which I did not have. Nor did I realize that my relations with many of my American artist and writer friends might prove of interest in such a journal.

O'Brien's second book, *Mystic Isles of the South Seas*, dripped with the sentimentality that often satisfies the American appetite: sex, innocence, and the lush mystery of a never-never land of breadfruit trees, blue skies, and irresponsibility. The sauce was too rich and the sales dropped. What finally killed the South Sea Islands bubble was a wicked little skit, *The Voyages of Dr. Traprock*, by George Chappel, a friend of all of us. By this time I was in Tahiti. Putnam wrote me there: "Anything on the South Pacific is out for the present." This was an understatement.

Whistler once said that nature copies art. And sometimes it is true that a distant island in the Pacific can become what tourist advertisements and trashy novels have made it. I often regret that I lived in a struggling village called Tautira, some eighty kilometers from a larger village, Papeete. The two names have taken on a flavor of tourism. I am tempted to substitute the older names which still crop up in the works of Cook and Moerenhout. Hatutira or Fatutira, through some Polynesian law of phonetics, became Tautira. Vaiete, as it used to be called — today Papeete — means "water basket."

While in Tahiti I was much impressed by a chapter of Robinson's *Mind in the Mak-*

ing. He suggests, for instance, that if a man's total span on earth could be telescoped down to a life of fifty years, then we have learned to speak during the past five years; historical memory goes back two; and the use of the telephone, automobile, and airplane has developed during the past twenty minutes. Something of that sort. Our own actual acquaintance with life has occurred only during those twenty minutes. It is the unawareness of, the inability to understand the dissimilarities and contrasts of these two memories – the subconscious-racial and the personal-actual – which creates many of our social and moral problems.

I felt at the time that part of the curriculum of every boy and girl should be a postgraduate year spent in a primitive community. It would help us all to understand ourselves better. The primitive is by no means an inferior. He is merely the expression of a different civilization, a different attitude toward life. The expression of communal life and communal thought rather than the expression of the individual. His mind is perhaps as good as ours. It is differently developed. Survival in a primitive society does not hinge on logical thinking, the reasoned deductions from given premises. On the other hand his social instincts and awareness are more acute than ours. So are a child's. Each may think less. Each watches and observes more intently. The child's approach to life – because he cannot understand it – is also more subtle and devious than ours. So is that of the Bible patriarch or the Homeric warrior. All three are primitives.

For two years I lived in a native village. For long periods the nearest white man was a Corsican peasant married to a girl from Rahiroa in the Tuamotu, who had a small plantation ten kilometers away. I knew, I fancy, every one of the five hundred natives of the district by face if not by name. Of course, being a stranger, I was better known by them than they by me. My journal records I once stepped ashore from a copra freighter on a small atoll some five hundred miles from Tahiti. Two or three of the Tuamotuans nudged each other. "*Aue! tenei e Tioti* – Look! there is George."

This two years' stay, the peripheral participation in a primitive society, the daily observation of the beauty of the human body against the background of nature, would, I felt, probably develop an artist's sense of color and design. It would surely change his attitude toward life and his aesthetic philosophy.

Almost fifty years have passed. The American friends whom I knew in Tahiti in 1920 are now dead: Hall, Nordhoff, O'Brien, Jerry Blum, Frank Stimson, Frisbie, and my boyhood friend. Many of my Tahitian friends must be dead, too. I never tried to keep up with them. For several years after I left Tahiti I dreamed about the island. I had made an unsuccessful attempt to buy a small strip of land opposite my bamboo dwelling on the banks of the Vaitipiha River. I knew I would not return. I wanted to anchor my memory by this token gesture. But one cannot repeat a love affair. I have never wanted to go back. What could we now say to each other? And the memory of primitive people is short. They are happier than most of us, for they live only in the present.

Ancient District Song of Tautira

Moemoe fenua i Tautira e,	Tautira, land of revery,
O te torea iti apatoa e,	It is the little sandpiper from the south,
I te ara mau ra e.	Winging down the true path.
O te taha iti i Vairua e,	It is Vairua's narrow strand,
O te ara iti otuitui e.	The little path trembling to the pulse of the sea.
Tei Parirerire au e	I am at Parirerire
Ua moe outou i te arioi.	While you are forgotten by the noble minstrels.
Tei hea te ara i Tautira nei!	O where is the path that leads to Tautira!

My Tahitian Friends

IN NAIPU'S HOUSEHOLD (FROM TIME TO TIME): *Ueri, Timo, Teamo, Pata, and Nane; and eventually Nanai.*

AMONG MY MODELS AND (INTERMITTENTLY) MY ADOPTED CHILDREN: *Moe, daughter of old Taura; Ave; Urari, Terae Hara, and Uraponi, daughters of Arai* vahine*; Uraponi's matronly gossip, Tetuanui, and her contumacious and undisciplined boy friend, Taniera; Moerai, twelve-year-old cook, waiter, and handyman; and, during a four months' idyll, Temehau a Teae.*

RULING FAMILIES OF THE DISTRICT OF TAUTIRA: *Ori a Ori, Chief of the district when Robert Louis Stevenson sojourned in the village before settling in Samoa; his grandson Ori and the latter's sister Tetia, mother of the baby Tehiva. Tetua, widow of the beloved Chief Faanevaneva; their daughter Marai, wife of the Second Chief, Raiarii; Raiarii's sister Pihia, of the generous mouth and somber brow; Tetua's second husband Mari, foster son of Ori a Ori and present Chief of the district; his foster daughter Ave, foster son Manuri. Old More, cousin of Queen Marau, wife of Vahio and mother of Huura.*

OTHER VILLAGE NOTABLES AND LESSER FOLK: *Tetuanui,* mutoi, *village* gendarme *and letter carrier; his wife Tetuanui* vahine *and her mother Taaroa — both dying of consumption. Afereti, the schoolmaster, foster son of old Punuari, versed in the legends of the hero Pae and familiar with the vanished trails up the valleys and across the mountains of the Peninsula. Tauire the indefatigable and his wife, in whose house Naipu and I first tarried; their baby Tihoni; their adopted relative, the gentle Moo. Paea, the* orometua, *and his two charming daughters, frolicsome Teura and Toahite, demure. Pau, carpenter and* orometua, *loyal friend. Old Tafaite, crippled by God for his impiety; his wife Teata, who cooked for Stevenson; their son Matau. Old Fareau of the* feefee *legs; his son Paruparu, the Impotent; his daughter Teha Amaru, the ape-girl. Arai* vahine *and her gossips, Terei, the blonde with the golden voice, and Tamaru, buxom and harmonious; Arai* vahine's *cousin, Pepe. Temeheu, father of Ueri, wealthy in copra and vanilla though parsimonious toward his ailing son. Temeheu, father of Timo, evil and lecherous old man. Maraia, Timo's girl. Amok the Chinaman, and his children Asa, Pahero, Tapu.*

IN PAPEETE: *Queen Marau — née Salmon — widow of King Pomare V; her daughter Princess Takao; their young cousins Poma and Ina. Mau, manager of the Tiare. Johnny Gooding — Pare to his intimates — manager of the Annex. Madame Richmond, mother of Nohorae and Jeanne, foster mother of Vahine, Nordhoff's wife.*

IN OTHER DISTRICTS: *Mote Salmon, Chief of the district of Papara; his sister Hototu. Paiatua, the hospitable Chief of the district of Teahupo. Tauire, the Chief of the district of Aferehitu in the island of Moorea. Tatamata, of the Village of Temae in Moorea, who showed me the wooden spear, cast by the hero Pae from Tautira, which had descended in her grandparent's garden.*

TAHITI, MAY TO DECEMBER 1920

TODAY one no longer travels. One commutes. The commuter jumps in hours — in minutes — over the horizon. When I was young I used to feel that mystery — the unknown — lay beyond the next range of hills.

Leaving New York early in April 1920, I reached San Francisco by rapid express five days later. Today would the trip measure that many hours? I took passage on the *Marama*, a little steamer bound for New Zealand and Australia. It was due after a leisurely three weeks to drop anchor off Papeete, unload cargo, and set ashore half a dozen passengers.

Those twenty days on shipboard are blacked out. One picture comes suddenly into focus. A still, cloudless evening. On the extreme, curving edge of the flat sea I could just make out the most delicate fringe, transparent, colorless, without mass or form. It was the distant palm trees on a string of atolls of the Tuamotu, the Dangerous Archipelago.

The few passengers stood at the rail and gazed in silence. The sky and the sea merged into the grayness of the evening. And the evening into night. I was excited and felt an undefined longing.

The next evening as darkness fell — rapidly in the tropics — we dropped anchor off the docks of Papeete. There must have been a good deal of movement. Derricks rattling, the ship's lighters grinding against her sides. Sailors shouting; customs officials; Dr. Cassiau puffing up the ship's side on the rope ladder. I leaned over the rail and watched the little brown naked bodies, splashing, diving for coins, laughing to each other, chattering in the unknown tongue.

I had the same sensation Maurice Sterne describes on first visiting the Orient: that he was returning to a surrounding he had known before, something part of him, more congenial than the civilization he had left behind.

Sentimentality? Rationalization? You cannot return to something that you have never experienced and that is alien to you. Both of us were to learn this later on. Nevertheless sensations may be poignant and they are real. So is a mirage.

Tahiti is the largest of the Society Islands, or Windward group, of French Polynesia. The Marquesas group lies over nine hundred miles to the north. The most distant of the Tuamotu Archipelago stretches almost a thousand miles southeast toward South

America. There are more than a hundred islands in French Oceania. The population today is about eighty thousand.

It is now generally agreed that shortly before the dawn of the Christian era Polynesia was settled by a series of island-to-island migrations of different racial stocks from the western Pacific, primarily Melanesia. The presence of the sweet potato, which may be indigenous to South America; the voyage of Thor Heyerdahl in 1947, which demonstrated that a balsa raft could reach Polynesia from South America; and certain cultural similarities between Polynesia and ancient Peru—these have led some to suggest that there may have been migrations from South America after the earlier colonization from the western Pacific. Anthropologists today generally agree that contact between ancient Polynesia and South America did occur. Cultural, archaeological, and linguistic evidence, however, leads to the conclusion that such contact was sporadic and was initiated by the Polynesians.

Tahiti was discovered by the English navigator Samuel Wallis in 1767. It was visited the following year by Louis de Bougainville, best known to posterity by way of the lovely flowering vine named in his honor. Captain Cook, who sojourned in Tahiti in 1769, was the first to dwell on the natural grace, charming manners, pleasant physical appearance, and idyllic life of the natives. He estimated the population of the island at several hundred thousand. A few decades later venereal disease, tuberculosis, and alcohol, customary contributions of Western civilization, had reduced the population to between fifteen and twenty thousand.

The history of the island and its people during the next hundred years was not unlike that of other primitive kingdoms when they encountered more advanced and rapacious nations. England and France squabbled intermittently over the tributaries of the Pomare dynasty—some eighty atolls, the chief vegetation of which was palm trees and pandanus, and a number of small islands. In 1843 Queen Pomare agreed to a French Protectorate. Her domains were ceded to France in 1880 when her son Pomare V abdicated—with a royal, although modest, pension.

In 1920 Tahiti and the neighboring islands of the Society group had a combined population of about ten thousand natives, a few hundred Chinese, and a handful of French. Papeete was a sprawling village of three thousand.

In those days there was no hotel on the island. In Papeete there was a lodginghouse of sorts—the Annex—with half a dozen rooms. Naipu—for so my boyhood friend was universally and affectionately called; it was as near as the natives could get to an unfamiliar name—stayed there when he was in Papeete, but took his meals out. The Annex was not prepossessing. The rooms were large and empty except for a double bed with mosquito netting, a chair or two, and perhaps a bureau. The showers and toilets were on the ground floor.

My friend had not heard of the ship's arrival. I found him in his room chatting with several native boys who were squatting or lying on the floor beside him. It was a hot night. They all wore only the native *pareu* wrapped about their loins. We greeted each other with warmth. One of the boys brought

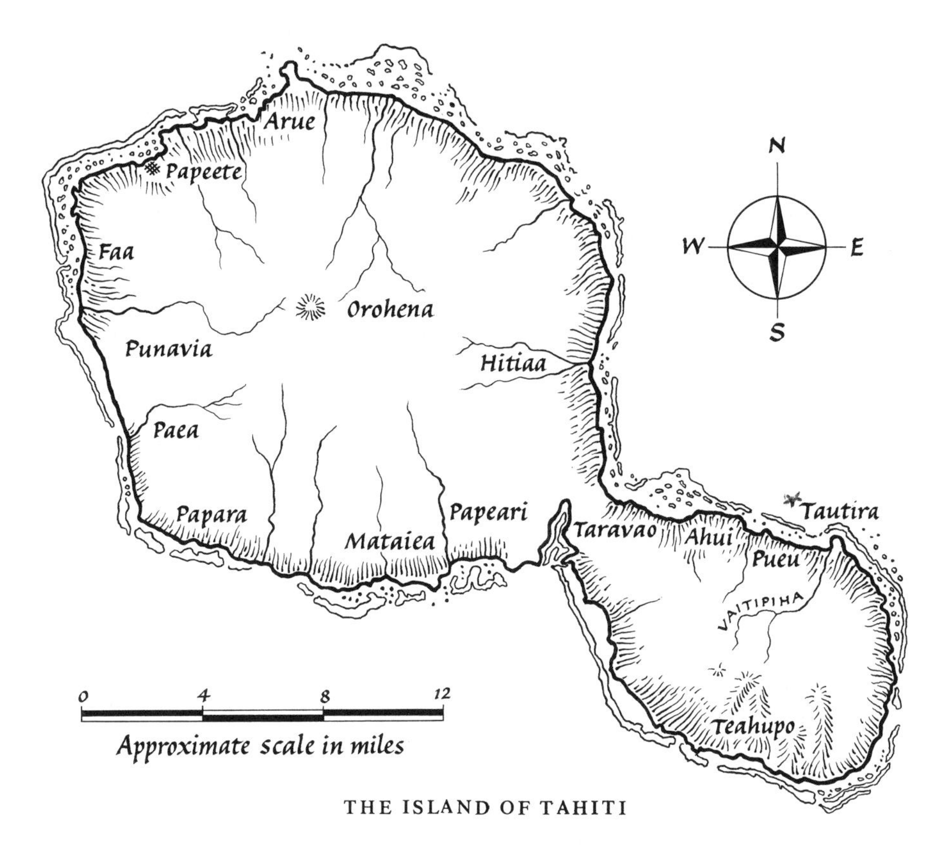

THE ISLAND OF TAHITI

us rum punches. We sat and talked. He was building his bungalow in Tautira at the far extremity of the island. Meanwhile he had arranged that we should stay with one of the natives in the village. We left together by bus a couple of days later.

Naipu was a curious mixture of many fine and likable qualities and some self-destructive ones. He had absolute rectitude, sometimes bordering on nobility – and also childish and absurd prejudices. He had idealism, a variety of interests, an excellent and well-trained mind. He had a robust sense of humor but was totally lacking in common sense. He was kind and capable of deep affections – and also unreasoned enmities. He was logical, precise, and incorruptible. But he failed to understand that others might not have these qualities. All through his life, whenever he faced a calamity, he resolutely refused to move an inch to one side although so doing might save him.

To call him quixotic or the last of the Puritans would get us nowhere in understanding him. Many quixotic persons are loved and happy. And Puritans not only survive but can be extremely useful. I think of Naipu as a modern actor in a minor Greek drama, in which tragedy must result because of the combination of certain worthy qualities of personality. I think of him, too, as essentially the "I-cannot-understand-why" character. How often have I heard dear Naipu, when a warm relation between himself and one of his native friends had been disrupted, petulantly exclaim: "I cannot understand why Ueri (or Timo or Teamo or another) behaved the way that he did." Naipu could not see that Ueri, being what he was, would under no circumstances behave differently.

There was one flaw, which need not have been too serious a frustration in his normal development and happiness, that finally drove him from the island. It was the flaw that was also the cause of his going there. He was on the edge of sex deviation, probably the result of some childhood experience. He hated his father. Months after I arrived he told me the story of how he had come to be in Tahiti.

After graduation from college he was teaching at a smart New England boarding school. One of his colleagues — he had a gift for making enemies — brought accusations against him of improper relations with the students. His approach with younger friends had always been paternal, benevolent, and Socratic. He disdainfully refused to appear at the investigation, but was completely exonerated of the charges. Rumors, however, persisted. The headmaster secured for him a better position at another school. He scornfully rejected the proposal.

Concluding his story, my friend paused. His expression was rigid and unrelenting. He said: "If this is the climate in American schools today, I should not fit into the picture. Here the standards of morality are at least free from hypocrisy."

Tautira, May 4, 1920

Naipu has left on a three-day trip to Papeete, where he will meet the northbound steamer from Australia. Mail comes in and goes out once a month. I have become happily accustomed to this feeling of isolation. The Vaitipiha River is swollen from the recent rains. Naipu was ferried across in a dugout where he met the weekly bus for Papeete.

Our cottage is typical of many on the island. It is raised on piles four or five feet from the ground. A corrugated tin roof. The interior has two bedrooms running through the house. They open on a front porch and on a narrower stoop behind. In each room is a large closet or storeroom. None of the houses in the village have doors or window casements.

In the rear is the *fare tutu* — cookhouse — built of spliced bamboo and roofed with plaited palm leaves. In front of our house — as of almost every other cottage in the village — is a small hedged-in garden. Vermilion and crimson and yellow hibiscus. On either side of the entrance is a flowering gardenia: the single gardenia, the national flower, *tiare Tahiti*, and the double gardenia, *tiare Moorea*. Above the hedge and between the stems of the coco palms lies the lagoon, maroon-colored and pale green, the outer reef, and the copper sea. And beyond the sea the purple mountains of Tahiti *nui* — greater Tahiti — the mainland, for our village is twenty kilometers from the isthmus. The mountains are almost always covered with listless, drifting clouds; but in the early morning as I walk down to the sea to bathe the summits are outlined, as by a burin, against the sky.

Tauire crossing the Vaitipiha with fei

Our host, Tauire *tane*, and his wife, Tauire *vahine*, sleep out. They drift from one friend or relative to another. There is also a two-year-old baby and an adopted relative, Moo, a shy little girl of ten or thereabouts, who carries in fresh water and has other minor household duties. They all spend a good part of the day with us: preparing our meals, continually sweeping out the house, idling on the steps or for that matter in our bedrooms. They take a lively interest in us and in all our possessions. This gives me the feeling that we belong to them, rather than they to us. It will take me some time to get used to this promiscuity. As yet the rest of the villagers leave us alone.

Our house is at the extreme edge of the village. Beyond is open country, loosely cultivated fields of taro. The grassy road, lined by flowering hibiscus, runs along the river toward the valley. It is the main artery of the village communal life. Along the path is a continual coming and going. Half-naked men, trussed in their *pareu*, pass on their way to and from the mountains, where they gather the heavy clusters of *fei* — the wild mountain plantain — breadfruit, and taro. These three constitute the bulk of their starch diet. Boys trot along, empty gasoline cans slung on poles over their shoulders, to fetch fresh water higher up the river. It is the women's job to gather the small sweet oranges which grow in the valley. Some women bear heavy bundles of wash on their heads. Their long black hair, oiled and combed, falls to the waist. The rounded, listless arms swing rhythmically at their sides.

May 9, 1920

Dearest Mother:

Naipu is back from Papeete. Determined to break down the reserve of the villagers, and at the same time to set our social position with them, we invited Mari, the district Chief, to dine with us last night. Although he had been adopted as a child into one of the great families of the district, he himself is of less good stock. His wife, Tetua, is the widow of the beloved Chief Faanevaneva, and she herself is well connected. She is tall, heavily built, light-skinned. In features she might be a handsome old Sicilian peasant. Mari is a small man, dark-skinned, heavy-browed, timid, and friendly. Since he understands only a word or two of French and does not speak it at all, we suggested that he bring with him his foster son Manuri as interpreter. Manuri has been supercargo on one of the small copra schooners plying between Papeete and the Tuamotu. He is fluent enough in French and has even a little English.

Naipu is on all occasions formal with the villagers. He deplores as I do the breakdown of the old customs and manners of the island. Out here in the country we shall discard European clothes for the native *pareu*, and following local etiquette substitute fingers and thumb for knife and fork in eating such dishes as raw fish, fried chicken, *poe*, *fei*, and breadfruit. The table had been set on the porch. In clean, freshly ironed white shirts, but barefooted and wearing our *pareu*, we awaited Mari's arrival.

He came, accompanied by his wife, Manuri, and half a dozen villagers. Mari was in

District Chief Mari and his wife, Tetua

official dress. For the occasion he had on shoes and wore a stiffly starched white drill suit buttoned to his chin. There must have been twenty shiny brass buttons on his privately designed official uniform. For a moment he looked bewildered and a little offended. But Naipu's formal manners and punctilious greeting reassured him. He asked to be excused for a few moments. Half an hour later he reappeared in his usual workaday getup.

In the districts liquor of any kind is associated with loose living, and is frowned on by the elders of the village. On this occasion a few judiciously spiked rum punches broke the ice.

Mari told us that Tautira has greatly changed since he was a boy. At that time the villagers all wore the *pareu,* except in attending church. Here trousers were prescribed by the white missionaries. The houses were uniformly built of bamboo and palm leaves. Ten years ago there was a disastrous hurricane and tidal wave. The natives fled to the mountains for safety. Every house in the district was destroyed. They were all subsequently rebuilt with wooden frames.

As a young child, Mari remembers, he saw Henry Adams and La Farge. They had stayed in the house of the old chief, Ori a Ori. Mari asked me if we had also heard of a rich Englishman, "Stevens." He had come to Tautira the year King Pomare died. That was in 1890. "Stevens," he said, "had been bedridden in England for eight years. Three months after he came to Tautira he was entirely cured. He left the island and never returned. But after his death his wife in gratitude sent a silver cup to the Protestant Church in Tautira." Stevens, Mari continued, had become very fond of him and wished to adopt him. But his foster father, Ori a Ori, would not let him leave the island. At first we had not realized that he was talking of Robert Louis Stevenson.

Mari really believes in the *tupapau,* the evil spirits of the dead. He has never actually seen them himself, but has heard them singing. Often they sing harmoniously—*mea navenave*—the old forgotten airs in the ancient language. Tahitian ghosts are evil—*mea ino.* Sometimes three successive *tupapau* will meet you in the road. The first will warn you not to pass. The second remains silent. The third will tease or bait you. He will tear open your throat or gouge out an eye. *Tupapau* look like ordinary mortals but they walk a few inches above the ground. He told me that there is an ancient idol a mile or two up the valley. About it many *tupapau* hover.

Mari is keenly interested in automatic writing and table tipping. I wonder where he has heard about this. I told him that our own ghosts were rarely malevolent, although they liked occasionally to play tricks. He kept shaking his head and said again that Tahitian spirits are evil and that it is best to leave them alone.

I paddled down the stream this afternoon in a dugout and around the spit of land where the river joins the lagoon. It is here that my friend is building his bungalow. To the right are the coral reefs. In front of me the indescribable mountains, rising from the line of palm trees like an operatic fantasy of Bakst. Inside the reef the water is nowhere deeper than five or six feet. The bottom is covered with all sorts of coral fern. Little blue and pale green fish dart in and out of the amethyst and lavender of the coral.

I came back and read a little of Gogol's *Dead Souls* and the *Voyage of Marco Polo.* Naipu has brought out with him a really fine library. The books are at present in partly unpacked crates, some in Tauire's house, some in the one spacious room of his unfinished bungalow. Apart from this there will be his cookhouse and sleeping quarters, both native style.

Your ever loving son.

May 10, 1920

Attend morning church. There are two churches in the village, Catholic and Protestant. The majority of the village are Protestant. The reason I prefer the service of the latter is that their singing is pure Tahitian music, quite different from anything I have ever heard before. At eleven o'clock I accompany Mari, the Chief. His wife has preceded him. On many occasions men and women go their separate ways.

Under the spreading branches of a royal poinciana behind the pink-walled church the men are already gathered. As new arrivals approach they gravely shake hands with those already there. They solemnly exchange greetings: "*Ia ora na oe i te atua* – May you prosper in God," or the less formal "*Mea maitai outou?* – Are you all well?" They seat themselves on the grass, smoke and gossip.

The women are already here. All are dressed in long black flowing garments, caught in just below the breasts, somewhat *à l'empire.* Some wear their hair in braids. With others it falls in profusion, oiled and perfumed, over their broad shoulders. They smoke cigarettes and spit not infrequently. All behave with the utmost decorum. Groups compose themselves under the poinciana tree. Some stand. Others gather their long dresses about their bare and well-fleshed legs, sit or squat. A few fan themselves with the leaf of a breadfruit tree. From the pink-walled church drifts the haunting rise and fall of the children's choir.

The church gong sounds for the third time. We all enter together. The service is informal. Men chat with one another from aisle to aisle. Dogs wander in and out. A mother loosens her dress to nurse her child. A new native missionary is to be chosen. The pastor says a few words. Someone rises from the back of the church to answer him. Others speak without rising. Occasionally something is said which raises a laugh. But although I understand nothing I have the impression of measured oratory. Finally the matter is put to vote by a showing of hands.

Throughout the service there is a great deal of singing. The music is quite indescribable. A group of men and women form a *himene,* a trained choir. One woman will take up the main musical theme. After a note or two the other women join in counterpoint. Other parts are woven in by the men sitting in the pew immediately behind. I do not recognize any of our intervals – the dominant, tonic, or thirds. And there must be many quarter tones. It is not at all like any Eastern or Arabic music which I know. Much closer to our own Negro spirituals or Negro church music as I have heard it in the South, where the thematic line is taken up, embroidered, and played on by other voices. In this Tahitian music the several parts seem to mingle, rise and fall, intertwine in such perfect and pulsing rhythm that I can almost feel the building vibrating. It both stirs me and leaves me restless and nervous. I think how certain sounds will make a dog howl. I recall the vibration of the cicadas' song on a hot summer's night. I used to listen to them as a child and wonder whether two insects were singing or a thousand. I would try to localize and separate the sounds. I would become confused. It was as if the whole world were shaking in a crescendo rhythm.

Church is over. We drift back to our separate dwellings. Tauire has prepared for us a lunch of sea centipedes and raw fish marinated in lime juice. This we dip into the *miti haari*, a most excellent sauce made of coconut cream, squeezed through a wringer from the tender flesh of young coconuts, and judiciously mixed with salt water and lime juice. The main dish is suckling pig, baked in the native oven between leaves of the *purau*, an indigenous tree of the hibiscus family; there is also baked *fei*, taro, and breadfruit.

The coffee was roasted this morning in a frying pan, greased with butter. About a pound of the fresh ground is poured into an old stocking, the circumference of which has been stretched and sewn about a small wire hoop. Over this is poured boiling water taken directly off the embers of glowing coco husks. I have never tasted a better or a stronger brew.

May 17, 1920

Squalls and rain. The occasional tremor of a slight earthquake. All day a small two-masted schooner, fifty feet in length, lay at anchor inside the reef two hundred yards from the shore. She had put in to load and take on water. Manuri is sailing in it for the Tuamotu. The ship will carry sixty passengers. How can they all squeeze in? A horse is tethered on the deck. Clusters of *fei*, bananas, and taro and sacks of oranges are tied to the rails or encumber the decks.

In a shed on the beach a dozen natives are gathered about a fire. An old woman peels the orange-vermilion skin from a *fei*, baked in the cinders. In a cauldron over the fire more *fei*, bananas, and taro roots are boiling. In the corner of the shed a young girl crouches. With long, slender fingers she dips into a bowl of raw fish and *umara*—the native sweet potato. Her heavily browed eyes are dark and gentle. Her jaw slightly protruding; her lips full, upcurved. I covertly watch her adolescent, well-fleshed figure under the tattered white dress. Among the older women the breasts assume enormous proportions. They hang on the upper abdomen in careless abundance.

May 18, 1920

Recently I have been painting flower pieces and landscapes with small figures. I think of these in comparison with more serious compositions as exercises in color, since I do not have to bother with drawing and composition. Later on when I am more familiar with the language and become better acquainted with the villagers it will be easier to get models. Already the men are losing their shyness, are friendlier and curious; quite eager to be painted. They stand about me as I work, utter cries of approval: "*Aue, te mea nehenehe!* — My, how beautiful!" They speak of me as "*Tioti, e taata papai hohoa* — George, the man who draws pictures." The women are more bashful. The children are the loveliest and most enticing I have ever seen. But they are apt to run when they see me coming. Some of them even cry at Naipu's approach, but I think it is his beard.

May 19, 1920

I have been taking lessons in Tahitian with Afereti, the schoolmaster, who speaks passable French. I use the grammar-dictionary by Monseigneur Tepano (Stephan) Jaussen, printed in 1898 at the Belin Press — as it is stated in the Tahitian foreword: *Neia i te nenei raa no Belin.* I also use the Tahitian Bible, translated long before that by the London Missionary Society. The language is so utterly different in structural concept from any Indo-European language that I despair of ever learning more than a series of words and phrases. It is a mistake to think of a primitive language as a less effectively organized syntax of words and phrases than ours for the communication of ideas. It is merely the expression of a different — a primitive — civilization. Actually Tahitian is more closely knit than modern languages. Its architectonics is as strictly constructed as Latin or Greek, although on a totally different grammatical order. Generally speaking, the uniting element in an Indo-European sentence is the verb. Since one of the most important traits of modern man is the concept of time it is natural that the verb complex in our languages — including of course Latin and Greek — is subtle and highly developed in its conjugation. The primitive, however, has little sense of time. One can almost say that the stability of a primitive culture is contingent on its refusal to act upon a "yesterday" and a "tomorrow." On the other hand the concepts of space — nearness, distance, position — are of great concern to the primitive. The Tahitian language is full of many particles of speech having to do with such relations — near, far, that between us, at a great distance, etc. Such particles, attached to the verb stem, designate the present, future, and past.

How beautifully the pattern of a primitive language is fashioned to the needs of its particular culture! Oliver Wendell Holmes once observed: "The growth of the law is not logic but experience." It is equally true of language. The primitive is too intently preoccupied with the concrete facts of life to indulge in abstract speculation. I was often surprised at the poverty of conceptual or psychological words in the language. I would ask Afereti: "What is the word for jealous, cruel, selfish?" "*Mea ino* — bad" was the only word he could think of. A striking example of the difficulty the primitive mind has in grappling with an abstraction is the Tahitian circumlocution for the simple word "if," a conjunction which introduces, not a statement, but hypothesis. *Mai te mea e* means more or less "like the fact being that."

There are other little quirks about the language which fascinate and bewilder me. The words for "what" and "no" seem to be verbs, since they can only be properly used with the little particles denoting past, present, or future; and the words for yesterday — *inanahi* — and tomorrow — *ananahi* — are seemingly the past and future of a nonexisting word for today!

In the designation of personal and family relations, however, the language is far more precise and particularized than ours. There are, for instance, different words for the younger sister of a sister or the younger brother of a brother — *teina*; the sister of a brother — *tuahine*; and brother of a sister — *tuane*. The personal pronouns have not only dual and plural forms, but also inclusive and exclusive forms! *Taua* — we two but not the others; *maua* — we two (there are no others); *tatou* — we, all of one group, but not the others; and *matou* — we, all of us. I have never before realized how indefinite our word "we" is!

Many other words and phrases charmed me as the poetic symbols of a civilization so different from ours, that of a people knowing only islands in a vast sea. A villager asked the location of a certain house would not answer: "Go north for a certain distance and then turn to the right." He would reply, "Go up the trade wind and then turn toward the mountains (or toward the sea)." The language is rich in metaphor and the concrete word, and re-creates the haunting beauty of a vanished civilization.

To quote at random from Monseigneur Jaussen's French-Tahitian dictionary: vent, *matai*; vent de terre la nuit, *hupe*; vent de terre le jour, *matai no uta mai*; vent tourbillonant, *matai puahiohio*; coup de vent, *rofai*; vent du nord, *toerau*; vent du nord-est, *faarua*; vent d'est, *maoae*; vent du nord-ouest, *parapu*; vent d'ouest, *aine*; vent du sud, *arueroa*; vent fort du sud, *ahuri moana*; vent du sud-est, *maraamu*; vent du sud-ouest, *uru*; vent fort du sud-ouest, *anahoa*; vent par violentes secousses, *toa huri*; vents qui se recontre, *tauhoani*; vents impetueux, *atoatoa*; vents suivis de pluie, *tuououvai*; vent qui s'établit, *tuaaoa*; vent qui souffle doucement, *puihauhau*. Many of these Tahitian words have now gone out of use. It is the language of a race of mariners whose lives and culture were circumscribed and fashioned by wind and sea.

There are seven of the more important different Polynesian island groups, some of them separated from each other for hundreds of years before their discovery by Western navigators in the eighteenth century. Each island group developed a different language-dialect and different traits. One of the characteristics of the Society group was the greater ease with which they assimilated foreign customs and relinquished their own religion, dress, and manners. On the other hand, their speech — Tahitian — has remained comparatively pure. It borrows words from other languages less readily than we do. Confronted by a situation alien to their past experience, Tahitians incorporate words from their own modest vocabulary to indicate a new object or experience. Where we have borrowed from Greek and Latin for "automobile," Tahitians with as much science and more poetry combine the words meaning "wagon" and "lightning" — *pereoo uira*. When the island was first discovered the only indigenous mammals were rats and pigs. The word they have since coined for horse is *puaa horo fenua* — the pig that runs on the ground. A cow is *puaa toro* — the pig with horns; the minah bird, *amu tutua puaa toro* — the eater of fleas of the horned pig.

May 30, 1920

Tafaite, the fat cripple, sits all day at his window and smiles at the passers-by. I am told that once he was the strongest and handsomest man in the village. In his pride he tattooed the name of God — *te atua* — on the sole of his foot. God humbled him for his impiety and paralyzed him below the waist. But he remains proud and vain. In the daytime he will not leave the house but gossips with the villagers from his open window. His wife, Teata, lean, toothless, and ravaged, as a young girl cooked and waited on Stevenson when he was a guest in the house of Ori a Ori.

May 31, 1920

We have become very fond of Paruparu — the Impotent. He is powerfully built from the waist up, but his feet are slightly paralyzed. He says that they became infected when he was a child. More probably he had a mild case of infantile paralysis. He walks slowly, flapping his feet ahead. Yet he is a splendid swimmer and the head man at the nets, diving below to free the strands of the net from coral branches. Often after the catch he stops by and presents us with a string of fish. Yesterday he brought Naipu a chicken, a gift from his father. Of course we had to give him something in return. It would cheapen our social standing to offer him money. We decided that a bottle of rum would be a suitable *quid pro quo*. We were overpaying him and he showed us his satisfaction.

June 2, 1920

Paruparu led us up the Valley of Ataroa to show us the *tii* — stone idol. It is an hour's distance from the village, a moss-covered slab of soft reddish-brown stone, about three feet high and a foot in diameter. Paruparu told us that formerly the features had been more distinctly marked, but that they had been mutilated. I am sure his explanation was due to shyness. Obviously the stone is a phallic organ, a symbol of fertility. Although crude, the carving is realistic rather than conventionalized. Subsequently the Chief told me that I was right. Such idols are rare today in Polynesia.

June 3, 1920

This morning little Ave, the three-year-old foster daughter of Mari, sat naked on her father's veranda. I went over to make a sketch of her. Usually she is wild — *mea oviri* — but today she sat demurely, combing her black hair and examining her little round belly. Tahitian chil-

Timo beside the idol in the Valley of Ataroa

dren have no dolls or other toys. Very young their play instinct becomes an imitation of the activities of their elders. The little girls are forever combing their hair and weaving for themselves garlands of flowers. They are adept, too, in making cat's cradles, a game which Captain Cook found popular among them when he first visited the island in 1769.

We invited Raiarii, the Second Chief, and his wife Marai to supper. They opened the conversation by saying that they would find me a *vahine* — wife. Later we wandered over to the *himene* at the house of the family of the old Chief, Ori a Ori. Two or three times a week designated groups foregather and sing religious songs. These are ostensibly rehearsals for church singing, but actually occasions for chamber music of a musically gifted race. The words are from the Bible, but the music is genuinely of ancient Tahitian intervals. On the way we passed two girls in white silk shawls. They buy these at the Chinese stores and will pay as much as fifty francs for one. Raiarii nudged me. "*Rave oe ia na* — Go take her," he encouraged me, smiling.

The members of the *himene* sang from the porch. I lay on the grass below, looking up at the stars. Above me three black coco palms and the stripped, checkered leaves of a banana plant. I watched the burnt gold of the moon drifting through pale clouds. Under me was the warm damp earth.

June 4, 1920

I have some difficulty accustoming myself to the promiscuity of the village. Friends or strangers walk up our steps, sit down on the porch, and wish us good day. They linger. The boys whom we know better, Paruparu and his crowd, join us in our bedrooms after supper, sit about on the floor, and chat together as if they were in a village clubhouse — often as if unaware of our presence. It is impossible in a primitive community ever to be or feel oneself alone. They have a fundamental need of "togetherness" — mental as well as physical.

Everyone dresses and undresses in public. This bothers me less. Tahitians are essentially modest and their dexterity in slipping from one garment into another could not embarrass anyone. The women come down to the river to bathe, bringing along their freshly ironed dresses. They go swimming in the old dress. No bathing suit. Later, standing on the bank, they will wriggle out of the wet dress and into the dry one, gossiping, gesticulating, and laughing together. It is an incredible act of sleight of hand.

When Naipu and I first bathed with a group of boys they were surprised and somewhat shocked by our unconcern with our own nakedness. It is not that they themselves wear anything, but as a symbol of propriety they cover their private parts with one hand. They would think it indecent not to use this convention.

June 5, 1920

Strachey in his essay on Racine defines classicism as the effort to create the most intense aesthetic emotion with the least extravagant means but with the most judicious and evocative selection of word or metaphor. Romanticism — Shakespeare — on the other hand creates its effect by the accumulation of figures of speech, the brilliance rather than the harmony of the colors. All this is true of music, painting, and sculpture. Greek art and the eighteenth century are classic in approach. El Greco, modern art, are romantic. In the very great periods of Indian and Chinese art there is both expressive passion and formal restraint.

Shock and rhythm — the "inevitability and order" of which George Moore speaks — what I think of as controlled emotion.

In Jean Jacques Rousseau's "Essay on the Origin of Language" he observes that "Every sense has its own peculiar field. The field of music is time, that of painting is space. To multiply simultaneously sounds or to make colors follow each other in a single file, is to change their economy; to put the eye in place of the ear and the ear in place of the eye." Gauguin must have had the same idea in mind when he remarked in one of his writings that painting is the only art the effect of which is immediately perceived. Whereas in the other arts — such as music, dancing, poetry, or drama — one's aesthetic emotion is suspended, and never completely satisfied until the final note, rhythm, or word. Rousseau goes on to say that "colors are effective in virtue of their permanence, and sounds through their successiveness. . . . The field of music is time, that of painting is space."

But in sculpture, although we may get one complete effect instantaneously, we must move around a statue to obtain the continuing and successive profiles, each one of which may contribute to the completed aesthetic emotion. Sculpture, then, exists both in the field of space and in that of time. In this sense it is, in a curious way, closer to the movies than to any of the graphic arts.

Can an artist working directly from nature create as freely as he does when he has turned his back on it? I think not, although nature must always be the source of his inspiration. The effort to copy or imitate must to some degree interfere with creative imagination. One is an intellectual, the other an intuitive process. In painting my landscapes or flower pieces I always finish them in my studio. Then I am only concerned with modifying color relations, with simplifying or rearranging patterns and lines. At such moments I have forgotten that what I have painted is a transcript from actuality. It has become a formal abstraction.

Recently I have become intrigued in finding graphic symbols for different aspects of nature. Will such conventions in color and line give my interpretation of nature additional meaning? I have always believed that painting is the interpretation of nature in line, color, and design. Should not the weighted leaf of the banana plant, the shadowed depth of the lordly mango, the feathered terror of the waving palm tree each have its different linear convention? Its identifying color tone?

Such symbolization of nature through formalized line and color was carried to its greatest perfection in Chinese art. My own earliest art influence was the great ukiyo-e school of Japanese printmakers of the eighteenth and early nineteenth century.

Can such symbolization of nature add philosophic or poetic significance to art? Nature is the background, the scale, which gives man's activity a spiritual meaning. I have in mind those noble prints of Hokusai, the series of the waterfalls and "Fuji in a Storm." Man's puny struggle and the immensity of nature—static, sublime, terrifying. Has nature a meaning, purpose, soul? Perhaps. But without desire or participation.

June 11, 1920

In the evenings I continue to study Tahitian and can now talk it more fluently. I still understand little unless my friends speak to me in what they call *Tahiti tinito*—Chinese Tahitian, an expression like our "pidgin English"; that is, native words strung together in what they assume is a foreign syntax. Tahitians have a very true ear and a childish delight in mimicry. With a straight face they will talk to each other in front of a foreigner, imitating his accent. Mimicking the French "r," the Chinese "l" for "r," and the long American vowel dragged into a diphthong gives them particular pleasure.

June 13, 1920

Many of the healthiest of the villagers suffer from yaws and other running sores on their legs and feet. Infections spread rapidly in the warm, damp climate. It is probably some contagious germ in the air or salt water. The least cut, unless immediately treated, will develop in a few days into a nasty sore. These sores are hard to get rid of. For the past week both Naipu and I have been troubled with them. Luckily the sore on the sole of my foot is healing. As a precaution I always carry with me a lemon with which to cauterize the merest scratch.

June 15, 1920

The sores on my legs have become much worse and are running with pus. Our solution of permanganate which I have been using has had no effect. Thoroughly frightened, I determined to see Dr. Cassiau in Papeete. This morning at an early hour I took the little steamer for the capital. Once a week it skirts the island, stopping every few kilometers to pick up dried copra, *régimes* of *fei*, bananas, and sacks of oranges. I counted fifty-two passengers. There was hardly room to sit. All afternoon men and women sang together. We reached Papeete long after dark.

FOR a month I had to remain in Papeete and here I met James Norman Hall and Charles Bernard Nordhoff. During the next two years I saw much of them. Thereafter we met infrequently on their rare visits to America. Our relations, as long as they both lived, remained unaltered. How can I describe these two good friends? They were conventional in manner and appearance but highly individual. They were stubborn and courageous, yet shy and fearful of life. They were chivalrous, romantic, loyal, and incorruptible. At the same time they were suspicious of people, of the world, of the future of civilization. I would guess that Nordhoff was an open-eyed and healthy pessimist. Hall was by nature a dreamer. He was deeply spiritual and I am sure felt intuitively that there would be salvation for man and perhaps some sort of an afterlife. Both were idealists, adventurers, and escapists. This identical approach to life on many levels must have helped to cement their friendship. But how different each from the other.

Norman Hall was a small man; dark haired with fine brown eyes; wiry, graceful, low-voiced, and courteous. I think of him and William Faulkner as of the same breed. Hall was a poet and a mystic. He had graduated from Grinnell College, Iowa. He played on the football team although he weighed only a hundred and thirty pounds. He had smashed his nose in a scrimmage. This slight facial defect confirmed the impression of purposefulness and dignity.

It was characteristic that the first job he found for himself in Boston after his graduation from Grinnell was as a social worker for the Society for the Prevention of Cruelty to Children. He saved up his holidays and was on a cycling trip in Britain when the war broke. He promptly enlisted, giving his nationality as Canadian, was trained in the "First Hundred Thousand," and came through unscathed as a machine gunner till early in 1916 when the British discovered his origin and sent him back to the States.*

Here he wrote *Kitchener's Mob*. It was a best seller. Later in 1916 he enlisted in the French Foreign Legion. When the United States joined the war he volunteered for the Lafayette Flying Corps, better known to its members as the Escadrille Lafayette. He was officially credited with three German planes. He himself never talked about his war experiences. He probably would have thought it braggadocio and in bad taste. Neither would Nordhoff for that matter. Both belonged to the romantic generation.

Hall was finally captured when he was shot down behind the German lines, coming to earth on the branches of a tree. In the fall he broke an ankle and his nose for a second time. He was hospitalized by the enemy but finally made his escape.

Nordhoff's grandfather had founded the town of the same name in the Ojai Valley in Southern California. I had also spent a year there in 1901, and I understand much of what went into the youthful experiences of Charley Nordhoff and John Steinbeck. It was the old California, tinged for a boy with the romance of Mexico: cattle *rodeos* on unfenced ranches of fifty thousand acres, *vaqueros* with leather "chaps," silver inlaid spurs, and braided rawhide *riattas*; summer roads with a four-inch blanket of powdery dust and the roadless wilderness of the coast range.

Nordhoff had followed me by a few years at Harvard. We had mutual friends who were devoted to him. When war broke out he joined the American Ambulance Service in France. Later he enlisted in the Foreign Legion. In 1917 he was detached to the Escadrille Lafayette. There he and Hall probably

*I am indebted to Edward Weeks, editor of the *Atlantic Monthly*, for giving me much of the material included in this paragraph and for other factual corrections. Mr. Weeks was long a devoted friend of both Hall and Nordhoff.

met. They became lifelong friends, the only true examples of Damon and Pythias I have known. I never heard them address each other by their first names. Though they both had a deep current of feeling neither one was demonstrative.

After the war they were commissioned to write the history of the Corps. Thereafter with rare exceptions they worked in collaboration. I never asked them why they chose to make their home in Tahiti. Like many of the "lost generation" they were in search of serenity, security, escape.

In Papeete I was stopping at the Annex, the same little rooming house where I had spent my first night on the island. Johnny Gooding was the manager. He was a nephew of old Lavina, the well-loved half-caste proprietress of Papeete's only boardinghouse, the Tiare. She had died a few years previously in the frightful influenza epidemic that carried off a third of the island's inhabitants.

With a penchant for the exotic and picturesque, Johnny preferred being called by his Tahitian family name, Aina Pare. Pare was white-skinned, short and plump. He had a delicately shrill voice, powdered himself profusely, and used eau de cologne and perfume in excess. He was proud of his stilted French, which he spoke with a heavy accent. He spoke Tahitian with polished elegance, never stooping to the corruptions of *Tahiti tinito*. He had an untarnished reputation for his rum punches, flavored with vanilla bean and powdered with grated nutmeg.

It was here that I ran into Hall and Nordhoff. They also had rooms at the Annex. At first and for a month or so until I broke down their aloofness I was hurt by the indifference they showed me. I knew they were both devoted to Naipu. I would have welcomed conversation and the chance to get acquainted with Naipu's two friends of whom I had heard so much, especially since I was chafing at inactivity. Dr. Cassiau was a strict disciplinarian. He kept me in bed or lying with my legs on a chair to decrease the circulation, and he had me bathe my sores every couple of hours in a solution of permanganate. My meals were brought to me in tin receptacles from a Chinese cookhouse. The heat was suffocating. When Hall and Nordhoff did stop at my room they stayed for only a few minutes. Nordhoff seemed stiff and reserved. He rarely smiled, although when he did, his eyes had a look of boyish innocence. Hall seemed more friendly, but he never lingered when his companion rose to go.

As time went on and I saw more of them I realized that their formality and seeming indifference was characteristic deportment, perhaps an unconscious shield to protect themselves from everything that was distasteful to them. They disliked vulgarity. I had a feeling that most Americans must have seemed to them aggressive and pretentious. They were excessively manly themselves. They might have been the product of an English public school. Yet they did not insist on such qualities in their friends. They were appreciative rather than disturbed by Pare's obvious homosexual mannerisms and by Naipu's eccentricities. They were tolerant of the occasional beachcombers who settled in the island. They never condescended to the natives and had many friends among them.

Once they had realized my own involvement in Tahiti, my affection for the natives, and my happiness in solitude they gradually accepted me and eventually we became warm friends. But they could not understand — and never did — that I should wish to return to civilization and had come to Tahiti merely because it seemed to offer the best environment to develop my painting. When Nordhoff, every few years returning to the States, had to spend a couple of days in New York, he would take a room in the Harvard Club and never venture out until he left the city. His feeling about me was not so much sorrow that I had betrayed my loyalty to Tahiti as sheer bewilderment that I wanted to return to America.

In many ways Hall and Nordhoff seemed throwbacks to an earlier period, that of Burton, Livingstone, Leigh Hunt, and the other grand nineteenth-century romantics. It was part of their charm. In literature and art neither had any interest in or understanding of current movements. Hall once told me that Robert Louis Stevenson was his ideal as a writer and his constant inspiration. Naipu, on the other hand, was thoroughly familiar with the significant literary names of the day — Joyce, Proust, Dreiser, and the earlier French Symbolists. I can't recall Hall or Nordhoff ever mentioning any of them. They appreciated my paintings only, I suppose, for the subject matter, just as they would have enjoyed Gauguin's paintings for the same reason. Naipu may not have had any intuitive response to art, but he was intellectually interested in what was going on in Paris and New York.

Hall and Nordhoff, however, were fine professional craftsmen. And they had that one essential gift for the novelist: they knew how to tell a whopping good story. In the collaboration it was Nordhoff who pressed the story forward as the born narrator, and Hall who slowed it down and gave it pause for the big lyric scenes. It was Hall who did the research on the British navy in the eighteenth century. Nordhoff, through his marriage with a native girl and through the knowledge he acquired when fishing with his father-in-law, was responsible for the intimate details of Tahitian life.*

Nordhoff had collected a good library on the island: Henry Adams' life of old Queen Pomare, and the works of Cook, Bligh, and Moerenhout. Although he was shy about talking Tahitian, he knew all the native words for their many different sorts of fishhooks, spears, and other implements. In the early novels the work was fairly evenly divided; in the later, when Nordhoff had begun his steady drinking, Hall was responsible for more than seventy-five percent of the work but would never disrupt the partnership.

Though Nordhoff was scrupulously faithful in his documentation, his willingness to believe what he had read or been told was generous. His imagination was soaring and unbridled. It was always a delight to listen to the bits of island lore he had dug up from talks with his native friends. He spoke slowly but with conviction, never overemphasizing a point, his cool gray-blue eyes expressing a mere hint of the new wonder.

*Here, too, I am indebted to Mr. Weeks for these comments on the collaboration of my two friends.

I remember once he told us of the primitive, aboriginal race that the Polynesians found inhabiting the island and had conquered and driven back into the mountains centuries ago when they came in their great war canoes on the age-long migration from the Malay Straits and through Melanesia to the eastern islands.

"And today," continued Nordy, "many believe that these dark little men are still here." His voice became softer, his words more precisely spoken, his clear eyes compelling. "No one knows how they live. For it is up among the highest peaks of the mountains quite inaccessible even to a Tahitian. I only know that many say they have seen them. Not close. High up among the topmost cliffs. Some say they walk like flies up the perpendicular face of a rock." He paused to let it sink in. But he would not overstate his facts. "I don't know. Perhaps such a feat is impossible. But you have all seen a native boy walk up the stem of a coconut palm, holding the trunk at arm's length as he goes up like a monkey. Of these small, dark mountain people I can only report what they tell me."

For several days it all seemed real to me. I was not sure whether I believed him or not.

I used to play on my old ebony flute to Nordy's accompaniment on the guitar. He was a wonderful companion. When we had become friends it was a pleasure to see his serious, resolute face light up with a look of boyish affection.

Nordhoff drank heavily. Never, as far as I noticed, to excess. Alcohol seemed only to give his talk and his flights of fancy a little more assurance. He was always full of fresh ideas, tall tales, and speculations. And he lived his romance, too. At one time while Hall was away on one of his lonely periodic treks – perhaps to Iceland – Nordhoff was very hard up. He supported himself fishing along the reefs in his little dugout, selling the fish for a living.

Nordy married a native girl. In a subsequent *Who's Who* he gives her name as Pepé Tearai. We knew her then as Vahine. She had white blood and was intelligent. She understood French well. He never spoke Tahitian with her. I think it was, subconsciously, to keep up "face." Like Faulkner he had the innate pride of the born aristocrat. He never in the slightest degree "went native." She bore him six children, Sarah, Margaret, Jane, Charles, Mary, and James. Many years later, coming back from a trip to the States, he found out that she had had an affair with a native. He divorced her immediately. He told me all this when we met by chance in Pacific Palisades in California in 1941. He mentioned it in his customary dry, matter-of-fact manner. Without actually saying so his tone implied that no other course was open if a man's honor had been tampered with. He had just remarried, a charming, much younger girl. They seemed very happy and congenial together. He said that of course he would stay in California, although Hall was still living in Tahiti. During the twenty years since I had first met him he had not noticeably changed. Only in the evening he needed a good deal more whiskey.

I never saw him again. A few weeks after our meeting the Japanese dropped their bombs on Pearl Harbor. I received a telegram from Henry Allen Moe, director of the

Simon Guggenheim Foundation, asking me if I would spend a year in Brazil with the Inter-American Committee on Cultural Activities. Passing through Grand Central Station in New York before boarding the southbound steamer I ran into a Harvard classmate of Nordy's. He told me that Nordy had also gotten himself some sort of a war job. It was inevitable. Shortly after peace was declared he died very suddenly. Had drink caught up with him?

Hall was a far less complicated man than Nordhoff. For that reason perhaps less interesting. There was nothing about him very arresting or unusual. His mind, sense of humor, conversation, tastes, and deportment were all quite average. He was all of a piece. The only really unusual thing about him was the absolute consistency of all that made him charming. I think of him what someone once said about Franklin Roosevelt: "He was the most wholesome man I ever knew." He was in all things the *preux chevalier*, straight out of the *Mort d'Arthur*. Today that may not sound normal at all.

There were just one or two little cracks in the sunny and controlled façade that gave an inkling of what must have been dormant beneath. As I said, Hall was a poet and a mystic. Every so often he felt the need of escape. To be alone on the mountain peak or in the desert. He said to me once: "When I go on a month's cruise on a copra freighter to the islands, I climb into the crow's nest and stay there all day. It isn't that the native sailors get on my nerves. But I need to be by myself with the sky and the horizon." And once twenty years later in answer to some word of congratulation on a recent publication he wrote me describing the little house and property he had bought in Arue, the neighboring district to Papeete. He told me that often he would climb to a lonely spot overlooking the sea. He would sit there for hours. He described the feelings of mystic happiness which enveloped him. He would feel so in tune with the "all" of life that he seemed at once to absorb and melt into the universe. And he knew that all things were right and that he was part of it. No one who has ever felt these moments of ecstasy is in need of the dogma of religious faith to fall back on.

With women Hall was always polite, friendly, and a little shy. Once at an *arearea* — a merrymaking — of a few of us and some of the native youths, Hall was dancing with a young Tahitian girl. I thought her very beautiful. Obviously she was not particularly attracted by him and she was a coquette. He suddenly pressed her to him roughly and kissed her with violent abandon and brutality. That one moment he had shed his cool reserve. I now understood that his was the self-imposed discipline of a passionate nature. ❦

June 26, 1920

How I loathe Papeete. It is a vast slum of dingy, crowded, tin-roofed shacks, pressing in on the few fine old buildings of this small island capital. I feel at once drawn and repelled by its lush depravity. It perverts me and corrodes my will. I lie around the Annex in the sweltering heat. In the evening I drink rum punches by myself at the Tiare.

July 13, 1920

The beautiful June and July days slip by. I have accomplished nothing. Dr. Cassiau ordered me to lie all day in a chair, my legs bound up and stretched out on another. But the poultices and permanganate seemed quite ineffectual. He finally burnt out three of the largest sores with a white-hot iron.

The others are now getting better. In the evenings I walk along the quays under the avenue of mangoes. Women everywhere. They flit by in the dark; sleep on benches; gossip by the water edge. In my loneliness they fill me with desire. I long for the districts, cool in the trade winds; the palm trees trembling on the edge of the copper-colored lagoons; the villagers, men and women, moving slowly about in the happy ritual of their daily tasks.

Last evening I walked to Arue, a few kilometers beyond the town. The road skirts the sea. It is lined on either side by purple-shadowed mango trees. At Arue King Pomare V lies buried in a small pink-walled chapel. Above the entrance of the shrine are inscribed the words *Fetia poipoi ataata* — Bright is the morning star.

This afternoon I visited Government House and chatted with a friendly old official. He told me that he had often seen Gauguin and had occasionally exchanged a few words with him. He spoke of him as a beachcomber and described him as "farouche." "Il ne fréquentait pas le monde." Once he had seen a canvas of his, in which all the natives — "les kanaques" — had been painted green. He could have bought it for a few francs. He never understood how such trash fetched so much money.

Tautira, July 17, 1920

The eighty-kilometer bus ride from Papeete to Tautira little by little washed away the grayness and slime that lay heavily on me. My spirits rose. In the districts all seems wholesomeness, purity, and beauty. The little villages with their now familiar names slipped by: Faa, Punavia, where Gauguin painted, Paea, Papara, the home of the Salmon clan, Mataiea, where Rupert Brooke wrote his verses, Taravao on the isthmus, Afaahiti, Pueu, Ahui, and Tautira. The Vaitipiha was too swollen by the rains for the bus to attempt a passage. I waded across carrying my suitcase. Naipu was waiting on the opposite bank.

July 19, 1920

I paddled ten kilometers up the coast with Afereti, the schoolmaster, in his wooden dugout. Much of the time it rained. The villagers own small parcels of land in the *fenua ahieri* — the outlying rural areas beyond the village, the "districts." Here Afereti's old mother cultivates a small holding and Afereti goes often to visit her. The old lady gave us breadfruit and two large baskets, woven from strands of the palm leaves and filled with oranges.

July 21, 1920

After supper I often go up the river with Tauire *tane*, our host, and Raiarii, the Second Chief, to spear shrimp and eel. A couple of kilometers from the sea the Vaitipiha narrows to a fast, clear stream. After the rains it is a swollen torrent. Even in dry weather there are pools three and four feet deep. Large shrimp lie along the bottom in eddying pools and eel hide under the bank or in the shadow of a stone.

Tauire has made me a shrimp spear. He hammered down the heads of three-inch steel nails, sharpened them with a file and drove five or six of them, forming a ring, into the tip of a wooden shaft. The eel spears have a forked iron shank about eight inches long. Even a small, two-foot eel is strong, slippery, and vicious. A shrimp spear would never hold him. Tauire and Raiarii truss up their *pareu* high around their loins. They show great skill in spearing the shrimp which are hard enough to see under the eddying water. They dart away at the least disturbance on the surface. But the timing of the men's thrust is perfect. They appear to pick them out of the fast current. I am happy if I get a dozen in an evening, while they will fill the pouches slung over their shoulders.

July 23, 1920

Several nights ago I lay on the porch of the Chinaman's store. There was to be an *arearea*, dancing and singing. A chimneyless kerosene lamp flickered at one end of the porch. A boy had gone to fetch a mouth organ – *upaupa*. The girls had not yet come. They are shy and always the last to join the merriment. Gradually they appeared in twos and threes.

A girl slipped out of the darkness. She squatted alone in a corner of the porch and smoked. Her upper lip was delicately curved and caught a shadow from the low flame of the lamp. I thought at first she had a thin line of mustache. Her smooth brow was contracted in a frown. Her eyelids drooped and her eyes were sullen. The boys goaded her with frequent and mischievous sallies. "*Haavare* – you lie" was her only answer. Her voice rasped, throaty. Her name, I am told, is Ave.

The next evening I persuaded Paruparu's sister, Teha Amaru, to fetch Ave as a model. I had several times made drawings of Teha Amaru, who is far from shy and joins our evening gatherings. In looks she is typical of the dark, low-caste Tahitian. One often sees a strain of the Melanesian among the natives. Teha Amaru has heavy black eyebrows over a low brow. Her nose is flattened and negroid, her jawbones protruding. Her body is barrel shaped and her limbs round and firm. When she walks and laughs she resembles a great, playful ape. But her eyes, especially in repose, are beautiful. And this is true of all Tahitians. They have Mediterranean eyes, large, gentle, and grave.

Ave arrived with Teha Amaru and a following of boys. At first she was timid and hid behind a bush. I could not coax her to join us on the porch. Paruparu remarked with unconcern that it was hardly worth my while making a drawing of her. "She is not beautiful. She is dark. She comes from the Tuamotu." I asked Ave if it were true. "*Haavare,*" she answered in her sullen, throaty voice.

Since then she frequents our gatherings after supper. Her looks fascinate me. There is a distinguished perversity in the animal purity of her features. She is sixteen years old and has a bad reputation. They tell me that she is living with a boy of the *taurearea*. The word means "youth" but also designates the *jeunesse dorée* of the village — our American equivalent: the drugstore counter loafers.

July 25, 1920

Seven canvases under way or finished. But I have continual difficulty with my models. They are all eager to pose and do so courageously for an hour or so. Then they become bored. I use every blandishment but it is useless. Now when I introduce small figures into a landscape I do it without using a model, or from sketches. I have become more and more interested in the use of color as a distinct element of the design — even at the expense of fine drawing.

The villagers show a genuine and unaffected interest in my painting. Yet I am sure they have no understanding of color or drawing. It would be impossible that they should. They have never had the means of expressing themselves in such art media. It is true that before Europeans discovered the islands they showed originality and a marked sense of design in their crafts. But the impact of Western civilization has entirely obliterated such creative aptitudes. Although in music they are sensitive and gifted this does not give them an understanding of the graphic arts. However, their music and poetry, both religious and profane, are part and parcel of their daily activities, of the life of the village. They do not, as we civilized nations do, separate art from life. So they accept any art form as natural and reasonable and worthy of interest. Their philosophy is instinctive and unreasoned. They have neither an inclination or the word mechanism for theoretic speculation.

July 27, 1920

All day it rained. In the evening Paruparu arrived with others of his gang: Teamo, Timo, Pata, and Ueri. The conversation again turned on the *tupapau*. Paruparu's eyes narrowed, his back stiffened, and his voice faded to a whisper. He told us what he had himself experienced, and what was also common knowledge of the spirits of the dead.

He has never himself seen a *taata tupapau* — a human ghost. But he once saw an *uri tupapau* — a dog's ghost — and a *puaatoro tupapau* — a steer's ghost. The dog had formerly belonged to relatives of his and therefore would not injure him. It even recognized his voice. Although incapable of barking it whined in anguish. The *puaatoro tupapau* was of a reddish color. Its horns were four feet long and twisted down to the ground. It walked along the strip of land where Naipu is building his bungalow.

This bit of land, Paruparu says, was formerly a *marae* — burial plot. The villagers feel that this is an omen of bad luck. Anyone who builds on it will eventually be stricken with *feefee* — elephantiasis. He will catch it from the corpses that were buried here. The *tupapau* hover about the *marae*. He himself would never venture there alone after dark.

Ueri also spoke of the spirit of a red sow which lived by the edge of the sea where she bore her litter.

Human spirits, unlike those of the animals, are always evil. They have tongues three feet long and are playful — *hauti*. A gun or a lantern is no protection against *tupapau*. They will tear a man's face to threads, whipping at it with their long tongues. If you scream at them or throw a stone they will make for you and disembowel you. They are one and all *taata mea ino* — evil beings. But if you rub two bits of bamboo together the *tupapau* will vanish and you can cut off their navels with the bamboo stick. *Tupapau* are seldom seen by daylight; most often they appear when the moon is full or at the exact moment when it rises above the lagoon.

Bligh, Stevenson, Loti, and other writers all dwell on the Polynesians' dread of evil spirits and on their universal apprehension of the night. This is strange in a physical environment so gentle and friendly to man. In Tahiti there are no dangerous wild beasts, no snakes or frogs, and little bird life. One can sleep in the open all the year round without a covering. And nature is provident. *Fei*, breadfruit, oranges, coconuts, fish, and other seafood provide an ample diet. A coconut, split in half, serves as bowl or dish. Water can be boiled in the segment of a bamboo stalk. The leaf of the *purau* is a satisfactory substitute for dish or napkin, and its bark or that of the *auti* (our "croton") can be pounded into a durable fabric. In such felicitous surroundings one might expect a communion of harmony and confidence between man and the spirit world of his creation. Yet beneath the surface gaiety of this race of sunny, carefree children is a strain of pessimism and a belief in the pervading presence of a malevolent spirit world.

July 29, 1920

Above our door Tauire has hung a twig of a tree called *tohuno*. Its odor collects butterflies of a certain variety. All day they circle in a black and silver cloud about the dried leaves or hang clustered, intoxicated by the odor.

July 30, 1920

I have been reading Lt. Bligh's *A Voyage to the South Seas*, published in 1772. On page 178 he writes: "They said, when a man died in Otaheite, and was carried to the *tupapow,* that as soon as night came he was surrounded by spirits, and if any person went there by himself they would devour him; therefore they said that not less than two persons together should go into the surgeon's cabin for some time. [The surgeon had died on shipboard. His body was laid out in his cabin.] I did not endeavour to dissuade them from this belief, otherwise than by laughing and letting them know that we had no such apprehensions." Bligh further relates that during the burial of the surgeon "many of the principal natives attended and behaved with great decency. Some of the women at one time betrayed an inclination to laugh at our general responses; but, on my looking at them, they appeared much ashamed."

This passage is revealing. It shows how little the social behavior of this lovable race has changed. They quickly forswore their own beautiful religious myths in exchange for the stern Biblical code of retribution and vengeance taught them by the missionaries. Yet their sunny dispositions remain unaltered. The greatest charm of Tahitians is their extreme social sensitivity combined with innate friendliness and gaiety. They have both the dignity of the American Indian and the warmth and jollity of the African Negro. They have an urge to please but are easily offended. Like all primitive people and like children they suffer more from the boredom of life than from its tragedy.

Cook and Bligh introduced into Tahiti sheep, cattle, roses, oranges, and cats. Of all these gifts the cats were the most welcome. The island was infested with rats. It still is. In addition to the rats the island had in great abundance the breadfruit tree, the coco palm, yam, taro, banana, *fei*, hogs, and chickens.

In another passage Bligh remarks: "I was much delighted in this walk with the number of children that I saw in every part of the country: They are very handsome and sprightly and full of antic tricks. They have many diversions that are common with the boys in England; such as flying kites, cats' cradle, swinging, dancing or jumping in a rope, walking upon stilts and wrestling."

Bligh mentions the fact that in meeting or parting from each other their salutation was, as he spells it, *"Yourah no t'Eatua* – May you prosper in God." This is still the common salutation today (the current spelling would be *Ia ora na oe i te atua*). Then, however, it referred to their own Tahitian deity; now, I suppose, to the foreign importation. The word "missionary" is derived from the Latin *missus* – sent or given. But to destroy the faith of a nation and substitute for it an alien belief has always seemed to me less a gift than a rape – of course rape with the best intentions and highest motives.

August 2, 1920

Dearest Mother:

Meetia is a rocky island, two kilometers in length and lying about seventy kilometers east of Tahiti. The island is uninhabited but there is much game on it: wild goats, pigs, and fowl. It rises like a sugarloaf from the sea. Once a year the villagers visit the island. They stay there for a week to gather the coconuts. They split them open, dry them out in the sun and ship them back to the market in Papeete.

The men own shares in a small auxiliary sloop. It is a rickety old craft, far too small to sail in safety with so many people. But it has a gallant name, *Tamarii Taravao* – The Lads of Taravao.

Before we put off, the men and boys prepared themselves a feast. Armed with stones they crept into the bush after chickens. There was a lively chase. The chickens are never cooped up or fed and are quite wild. They linger round the houses to pick up whatever is thrown away. In the evening they retire to the bush, where they roost high up in the branches. The villagers seem to know, however, which chicken belongs to whom. The particular delicacy of the birds is the six-inch-long centipedes. Chickens are immune to their poison, just as pigs are to a rattlesnake's bite. And the centipedes are well fleshed and juicy. The boys showed surprising skill with their missiles. The birds flew screaming through the bush in every direction, but in a short time a dozen were slaughtered.

The native oven – *ahimaa* or *himaa*, as they usually call it – had been prepared. Round lava shingles were heated. *Fei* and generous portions of chicken were wrapped in leaves of the *purau* tree. These were covered with the red-hot shingles. Earth was shoveled over the stones and the earth covered with banana leaves. The leaves were weighted down with larger stones. The food baked for a couple of hours.

Other banana leaves were laid out at the edge of the sea. Each guest was provided with a bowl of *miti haari*. Two or three *purau* leaves were laid beside each bowl. Tahitians are fastidiously clean. They not only use a napkin but wash their fingers in a basin of water before and after eating. We squatted down, each before his individual pile of chicken and *fei*, dipping the food with fingers and thumb into the *miti haari*. Partly to get at the succulent sauce between the fingers but also in polite appreciation of the food, men and women sucked in noisily as they gulped down the dripping morsels. Not a word was spoken. Enormous quantities of food were consumed.

It began to rain and all afternoon the rain continued. I lay inside a bamboo shack and played with the children.

At eleven o'clock at night the rain let up and we paddled out in the dark to the *Tamarii Taravao*. The engines were started. Ten minutes later we grounded on a coral reef. Again the rain came down in torrents. I was chilled to the bone. It took them half an hour to warp the boat off the reef and work her through the narrow passage to the open sea.

Now the wind blew very strong. A heavy sea was running. The captain had lowered the sails and we were moving under power. The boat was pitching heavily. I don't think I ever passed a more miserable night. I went below to get in from the weather. All the women were crowded into the cabin and most of them were sick. Three of them were nursing babies. The stench of the vomit was pretty bad. I became sick myself. I was so fatigued that every moment, standing up, I dozed off, only to be lurched into consciousness by the pitching of the boat.

By four o'clock in the morning the sea was running really high. A sudden squall caught the awning and almost capsized us. The men scrambled up on deck and managed to get the awning down and pull it in. The captain hoisted a storm jib. This somewhat steadied us. By now all the women were sick, but they behaved very well. I didn't hear one complaint.

A nursing baby of eight months, who had also dined to its full on baked *fei* and hardtack, slept through it all peacefully.

The captain was thoroughly frightened. He put the boat about and we ran before the wind on her storm jib. We made the opening in the reef into the lagoon of Vaitoto. It was now morning. I was told we were fifteen kilometers from Tautira, which we had left eight hours earlier.

A meal was again prepared. A pig was caught and slaughtered. At ten o'clock we settled down to breakfast on roast pork, *fei*, breadfruit, taro, and coffee.

I could not tell how soon the wind and heavy sea would abate. I didn't want to spend more time away from my work. A friendly villager loaned me a little red pony. Together we rode home bareback to Tautira.

I love these excursions with the natives. I only wish I had more time for them.

Your own loving,
G. B.

THE Polynesians are among the world's greatest navigators. By the time or shortly after Columbus discovered America, they had traveled thousands of miles across the Pacific. There is some evidence from their recorded songs that they even penetrated to the edge of the Antarctic Ocean. Using a coconut shell filled with water as a quadrant, they learned to take angles on the sun and the stars. But they had no chronometer. And they never learned the dynamics of wind on a closely hauled sail and the resistance of water to a deep keel. For motor power they had only long, narrow paddles and elbow grease. To this day they are the world's most incompetent sailors. But they had an intuitive understanding of the elements: wind, waves, and currents. They learned to guide a clumsy wooden craft through hidden openings in coral reefs or to steady it on the crests of formidable breakers. They rank high among the greatest mariners and explorers of all time.

August 3, 1920

I am really happy with the five flower pieces which I have finished during the last few weeks. They have helped me immensely. There is a better organization of line and color. In my landscapes, too, I am searching more consciously for a simplification and abstraction of the background and figures. I find myself less concerned with atmospheric effects and more attracted toward flat two-dimensional design. My last summer's work in Bermuda which I exhibited at the Milch Gallery summed up all I had gotten from *plein air* Impressionism. Now I see a new direction in my paintings.

August 5, 1920

In the evening to a *himene*, this time in the church. I sat outside on the steps, playing with some children. Gossiped with Marai, Raiarii's wife. Like her mother, Tetua, she is light of

Raiarii, the Second Chief, and his wife, Marai

skin, not particularly pretty, and has lost a couple of front teeth. But she is vivacious and friendly. She tells me that Tahitian women are sensitive and proud. Because of this they are more timid with Europeans than are their men. The girls consider the Chinese storekeepers their social inferiors. They make fun of them and love to mimic their singsong manner of of talking. But the Chinese treat them well, never beat them, and successfully court them with silk shawls and other presents.

Marai tells me that she is not at all shy with the *popaa* — Europeans — probably because her father, Faanevaneva, entertained many of them in his position as Chief. She added that her stepfather, Mari, is unpopular in the village. He is vain and lacking in generosity.

She asked me why I had not taken a *vahine*. Tahitians, like children, have a disarming candor in satisfying their curiosity. After a while she left me and joined her husband, with whom she stood whispering. She then came back and asked me if I should like to take Pihia, Raiarii's sister, to live with me. "If Pihia does not go to you she will end up with a Chinaman. Do you think that would be preferable?" I had to agree with her. The suggestion was not unpleasant.

Pihia is a pure Tahitian type. She is about sixteen years old, shy, and strictly brought up. She speaks only a few words of French but appears to understand it moderately well. She is beautiful rather than pretty. Tall and straight, dark-skinned, with the characteristic heavy jaw and low brow. Her lips are full and generous. Her grave, shadowy eyes are a little sad and wistful. There is something unusually straight-backed and severe in so young a girl.

Raiarii and Tauire are more than friendly neighbors. I think of them as true friends. Both are superb physical beings with the perfection and grace of fifth-century Greek sculpture. Often in watching these godlike men and women I feel that they must look on us *popaa* as pale, deformed, and slug-like vertebrates.

Both Raiarii and Tauire were conscripted during the war and saw action in France. Both agree that one of the worst discomforts at the front was the necessity of wearing shoes and stockings. Raiarii was decorated with the *Croix de guerre*. I asked him in what engagements he had been. But he is as modest as Hall. He smiled and shrugged his shoulders. "Finie la guerre" was his only comment. He added, however, that the Germans were "*Taata mea ino roa* — very evil people" — because they were the enemy; but that the French were also evil, because they made the Tahitians fight. A very philosophic attitude toward war.

Raiarii is a big man. Always in the mountains after *fei*, out on the reefs at night with a lantern and eight-foot spear, or supervising the hauling of the big net. He is gay and smiling like an overgrown boy. Having been a couple of years in Europe he justifiably considers himself a man of the world. Together we converse and exchange information about our so different countries. The other evening as he and Marai passed I called to him to join us on our veranda for a glass of rum. The idea pleased him, but not Marai. Stooping, she picked up a stone, scowled at him, and made a threatening gesture. He smiled sheepishly at me and shook his head. An interesting comment, I thought, on the marital relations of Polynesians.

Tauire is smaller, lighter in color than Raiarii, but with the same bodily perfection and grace. He is reserved, dignified, without humor, and a little shy. But his quiet self-possession conveys the impression of honesty and friendliness. He is a dynamo of energy. In repose he suggests a tightly coiled spring. His wife is a relative of Marai. She is friendly, gay, and also a little toothless when she smiles.

August 6, 1920

I am working on a figure piece of two little girls, Uraponi and Tetuanui. They are about eight years old. Tahitians never know their exact age. Uraponi is the rare type of Polynesian blonde — *rehu* or *pupure*. Her hair is a dull red gold, a gold with the shine taken out and more copper added. Her skin is the color of her hair. Her eyes are brown. She has charm and the disposition of an evil, diminutive witch. She has a will of her own and an inclination to taste life to the full. Between poses she smokes one of my cigarettes. When I chide her she covers her mouth with her hands and her body squirms in vexation. If I tease her she thrusts out her lower lip, her eyes cloud, and she glowers at me, more to intimidate than in fear.

Tetuanui is as good as Uraponi is naughty. She is plump and matronly. She arrives washed and combed. She perspires with shyness and excitement. When I coquette with her she does not thrust out her underlip but her large dark eyes moisten in embarrassment. Her dress is freshly starched and her behavior exemplary. Uraponi runs wild in the bush and climbs trees like a monkey. Her dress is a dirty torn rag.

Uraponi and Tetuanui arrive together an hour before the appointed time. They constantly run to my mirror between poses to comb their hair. They make use of my talcum powder and douse themselves with my hair tonic. When they are so humored they sing for me Tahitian *ute* — ribald songs or improvisations about their neighbors and friends. They also sing a few French rhymes which they have been taught in school. They sing these in parts very accurately. It is remarkable that such young children without any training can sing unfamiliar music in close harmony. It is evidence of the musical sensitivity of this people.

August 7, 1920

Dearest Mother:

Ten days ago a young archaeologist, Dr. Edward S. C. Handy,* who is waiting for a schooner to take him to the Marquesas, came out here with Princess Takao. She is the daughter of old Queen Marau, the widow of Pomare V, whom the French pensioned off after her husband's death. Marau is a member of the Salmon family. She therefore has white blood. The Salmon clan are all descended from a certain Solomon, a Jewish trader, who

*A monograph on field work in Tahiti in the 1920's was published by Dr. Handy in the Bishop Museum series of publications. A book describing his early work in Tahiti and the Marquesas, *Forever the Land of Men*, was published in 1965 by Mrs. Handy.

Uraponi

settled in Tahiti and married a native several generations ago. The Salmons established themselves in Papara where Stevenson and La Farge visited them. Mote is the name of the present district chief.

Takao is a woman of dignity and intelligence. Her father was a French naval officer who became one of Marau's many lovers. She was educated in Paris. She speaks French perfectly but with a charming soft drawl, the *voix trainante* of Tahitians. She is interested in art and unlike most Tahitians of mixed blood is proud of her ancestry and the legends and folk art of her people. In features she is quite European. Her hair is long, thick, and beautiful. It falls well below her waist.

I asked her about the choral singing at the Fourteenth of July celebrations in Papeete. She was scornful of much of it as being derivative of European music. "The words were trivial and often indecent. A few years ago they would have been jeered and shouted down. But the singing of the Papara chorus was all ancient music and the songs of historic legends, the best of Tahitian poetry."

She showed an interest in my paintings. Particularly liked some of my silverpoint drawings of the children. She wants me to do one of a relative, perhaps a child. This pleased me.

Sunday I walked the forty kilometers to Taravao on the isthmus and back without getting overtired. During the entire walk mountains and palm trees to one side, palm trees and the copper-blue sea on the other; and through the pale lavender stems of the palm trees ahead of me the purple distance of the mainland, Tahiti *nui*.

At Taravao I lunched at Butscher's. He is an Alsacian, long settled here and married to a fine old native woman. At present he is pearl fishing in the Tuamotu Islands. The old lady has a reputation as an accomplished cook, but she needs a couple of days' notice. However, she served me a substantial meal: shrimp and *langoustes*, followed by sea centipedes, steak, *fei*, taro, fried bananas, wine, and coffee. Madame Butscher told me that if she had had warning that I was coming she would have speared some young devilfish on the reefs the night before and stewed them for me in coconut sauce.

After lunch she put her bedroom at my disposal for a siesta. Lying on her couch I could see the women on the veranda washing the naked babies. For an hour I read Moore's *Confessions of a Young Man*. He writes: "All except an emotional understanding is useless in art." He is talking about the novel. How true it is in painting, too.

On the way home an old couple called out to me from their little *case* of bamboo, thatched with palm leaves: "*Haere mai na, Tioti, tamaa*—Come in, George, and eat." The natives know me now within twenty kilometers of Tautira. I joined the old couple, seated cross-legged on a mat in front of their humble dwelling. Their fare was simple, raw fish and baked *fei*. They broke open a coconut for me. It is the most refreshing drink I know, notwithstanding the slight suggestion of fermentation.*

*I only realized several weeks later that such an invitation to come in and eat was often merely an expression of good manners, not to be taken literally; the equivalent of the Spanish *Aqui está su casa*—

The old people here have such dignity and self-possession they seem a different race from the younger generation. I mentioned this to Takao and she asked me what was the quality in the old people that attracted me. I could only answer: "C'est peut-être que les vieilles gens tahitienes sont toujours des vieilles gens sympathiques." You remember the particular quality of Grandmother Robinson's or Aunt Agnes' charm? Well, every old Tahitian woman has just that. You feel that they are from an old family *de race*. Their behavior is so simple and engaging, yet they are always self-possessed. I love to watch them spit. They do it with the dignity with which royalty might wipe her mouth or blow her nose in the corner of a scented lace handkerchief.

Again: Try to visualize an old woman, in a tattered black gown and wearing a black straw hat, sitting with her bare legs crossed and dipping raw fish with fingers and thumb into a bowl of coconut sauce. You can see her. But can you imagine her doing it with the poise and grace of Grandmother Robinson sipping her mid-morning glass of sherry?

The young women and girls are shy and self-conscious. A pity, for they are most attractive. Has the younger generation lost something? Or is it simply that they are not yet old Tahitian women?

I wish you could see your way toward coming to France with me for a couple of years when I leave Tahiti for good. Reading Moore's *Confessions* so brought back to me my own one perfect year in Paris as a student in 1911 that the tears nearly came to my eyes with a *mal du pays*.

Your own loving,
G. B.

August 8, 1920

I have started a large canvas, sixty by fifty inches, with three figures in it, the woman in the center holding her baby, Paruparu standing beside her. Banana leaves in the background repeat the perpendicular lines of two of the three figures. I think it is going well; but Moe with her baby has left for Papeete. I am in a sweat lest she fail to return. Today and yesterday I painted in the background. None too well, but I think I can pull it together when the figures are in.*

Here is your home. The old couple carried off the situation, perhaps embarrassing to them, with the innate breeding of their race. Little by little I corrected some of my social blunders. On another occasion I asked a couple of girls where they were going. "*Haere taua tatahi* – We are going to the sea" they answered without showing the least concern at my curiosity. We Europeans stumble from one euphemism to another in awkward efforts to avoid mentioning by name one of the simplest and most satisfying physical functions of life. "Going to the sea" is not a euphemism but a simple statement of an intention to evacuate. How sensible these people are. Can any toilet be more effectively flushed than by the full power of the tides? Can any john have a more relaxing and lovelier setting?

*This painting was subsequently purchased by the Pennsylvania Academy of Fine Arts.

August 9, 1920

Two or three times a week when the weather is favorable the villagers cast the nets from the long, narrow stretch of beach that runs between the Vaitipiha and the lagoon. The heavy outrigger, hollowed from the trunk of a *purau* tree, carries the nets. It is paddled over from the village and lies offshore. Thirty or forty of the villagers — men and women with their babies and the boys and girls of the *taurearea* — gather on the beach to help haul the nets and string the fish. These are divided up and distributed among the families who assist in the catch.

High up in the nest of a palm tree a couple of men scan the surface of the water. Sometimes there is a long wait before the fish work in close enough to the shore for the men to drop the nets. The elders gossip in the shade of the palm trees. The young bucks of the *taurearea* exchange salacious remarks about the girls. The latter respond in kind. But if their admirers become too audacious, they will not hesitate to pick up a stone or chase them with a stick.

I love to participate in these homely village rituals. The setting is a tapestry woven in purple and gold. The deep shadows of the palms tremble with splashes of orange and cadmium yellow, as the breeze ripples through the leaves. Silver and gold quiver over the cooler tones of the lagoon. The torsos of the men are copper-colored, but when they move into the sun their shoulders are bathed in pure vermilion, in contrast to the scarlet and ultramarine of their *pareu*.

The net is owned by Owen Carbuth, a half-caste from Papeete. If there is a heavy catch the fish are kept fresh in a great ten-foot basket until he arrives in his truck. He will drive them to Papeete and sell them on the open market. As owner of the nets he will take a third of the proceeds from the sale. He will take another third for the use of his truck. The remainder is divided among the families who have participated in the catch. On a good day's haul a man will make between forty and seventy-five francs.* When the fish are running well the villagers may cast the nets three times in a week.

Yesterday I took time off from my painting, swam across the river, and joined the gathering on the beach. Later I helped haul in the net. The big outrigger had made a wide circle from the shore about the school. The fish churned, leaping from the water. The men waited until they quieted, lest they break the net. Then smaller nets were dropped within the larger one. The men speared a young female shark among the fish and dragged it to the beach. It was about five feet in length. The boys cut her open and four of her young were taken out of the sack in her belly. They were thrown back into the water. The children played with them as they swam awkwardly in the shallows. I borrowed a pair of sea glasses from Paruparu. Eight or ten of the men swam about the perimeter of the net as it was hauled in. They dove below to see that it did not get entangled among the stones and coral.

*Up to four dollars, as I remember the current rate of exchange.

August 10, 1920

The Chief's wife is no longer young, for her daughter Marai is in her twenties. But she has just given birth to a baby boy. She is resting at her husband's place in Ahui, the next village to Tautira. I walked over there this afternoon to offer them my congratulations. They were obviously touched and insisted on my kissing the nine-day-old baby. Mari poured me a tumbler of rum and offered me the makings of a cigarette. Later I walked on another five kilometers to Pueu and made a call on Pietri, the old Corsican peasant, and his Tuamotuan wife. His two daughters read French and occasionally borrow books from Naipu. I brought them over George Sand's *Mare au Diable.*

August 11, 1920

About three weeks ago Naipu moved into his new quarters. Teamo, Timo, and Ueri have joined his household on the understanding that they will assist in the cooking, wash the dishes, and keep the place in some sort of order. The four of them room together in the sleeping shed — *fare taoto.* This is the customary arrangement on the island. Often a wealthy villager will buy a shiny new cast-iron bed in Papeete and install it in the main room of his house. But it is merely an ostentatious display. He prefers the comfort of a pandanus mat stretched on the ground in his cool sleeping shed to the more elegant bedroom, sweltering under the tin roof of the main building.

Naipu's new household arrangements leave little room for me. I shall continue to sleep at Tauire's but will take my meals with Naipu. This way I get the benefit of his cooking and can keep up my relations with Tauire, whose company I find more relaxing than the adolescent chatter of the boys.

One of the chief characteristics of adolescence, the world over, is the desire to conform, the herd instinct to hunt with the pack. Diversification of tastes and individuality usually appear only in the adult man — and not always then as the recent war has shown. Since one of the chief traits of primitive people is this emphasis on conformity, ritual, and deep conservatism, I am not surprised to find how much alike Naipu's boys are. All three are good-natured, friendly, and willing. Like Italians they have an urge to smile and to be smiled at. And what an endearing quality this is! They are all easily bored, and equally easily entertained. They are warm and affectionate; rather forgetful and occasionally not to be trusted. As I get to know them better, however, I become aware of the little differences which make each an individual, not just a type.

Timo is the most doggedly faithful and dependable of the three. He has less physical looks and less intelligence than the others. At times he has not quite enough intelligence to distinguish what belongs to him and what belongs to Naipu. In a Tahitian household such distinctions are less sharply defined than with us. Much of the property is communally shared, whether by the household, the family, or the village. It would seem quite proper to any of Naipu's boys to appropriate his pocketknife or shrimp spear without asking per-

Naipu's bungalow

mission, just as a household guest with us makes free use of the family refrigerator. On the other hand Timo knows that he must not pour himself a drink out of Naipu's demijohn of rum or take his money or camera without permission. But there are those vexing borderline cases which confuse poor Timo.

Teamo is the gentlest, the sunniest, and the handsomest of the three. He has a *dolce far niente* grace and languor that belie his strength. Ueri is quiet, observant, and intelligent. He shows qualities of leadership. He invites his friends in to listen to Naipu's phonograph, but will also discipline them if they forget their manners. His charm is a dry and somewhat sardonic sense of humor.

August 12, 1920

I have noted that there are several words in Tahitian for brother – there are actually four – where we have one. May not this greater precision in primogeniture and consanguinity attest to the economic structure of a primitive society whose only wealth was land acquired through proof of blood kinship? Many of the old Maori songs that have been recorded in New Zealand are nothing more than genealogical recitations, such as occur in the thirty-sixth chapter of Genesis. These songs of an illiterate and seafaring race, constantly shifting from island to island, were their only title to establish land claims. In their society land was the sole wealth. Land and sea provided generously. But two hundred years ago the islands were densely populated. Productive soil was restricted to a narrow fringe girdling precipitous mountains; or often among the atolls rings of sand and coral circling inner seas.

These two inherited traits have still survived among these wanderers of the deep: the rootless drifting from island to island and the immemorial claim to land through proof of blood relationship – often transferring nothing more than the right to gather *fei*, breadfruit, and oranges in some remote and narrow valley and the use of a plot of ground on which to erect a bamboo dwelling.

Recently a young man from the island of Raiatea stopped over on his way to the Tuamotu in a copra schooner. He was able to offer proof of kinship with one of the villagers and was invited by the family to visit them. During his stay he became attached to a young Tautira girl and set up house with her on his cousin's land. Here the young couple are now permanently installed, and settled in our village.

Although there are four words in the language for brother there is no precise designation for father or mother. The word for father – *metua tane* – may also refer to uncle or any male kinsman of the father's generation. And *metua vahine* – mother – has the same loose connotation. This linguistic ambiguity is, at first view, hard to reconcile with the necessity of proving consanguinity in order to inherit wealth.

Tahitians love their children and take great pride in them. But their sense of paternity is based on a very different concept from ours. There is parenthood *de jure* as well as *de facto* – a legal status as well as a physical fact. An adopted infant is as dear to a Tahitian as is one of his own flesh and blood, and according to age-long custom, the unwritten law of the island, he has the same legal rights. Often the child is more attached to his *metua vahine amu* — literally, the female parent that feeds — than to the *metua vahine fanau* — the mother that conceives.

It may seem inhuman to us that parents should be willing to relinquish control over their children. Our own attitude toward "in-laws" will help us understand this double paternity. American and European parents are proud and happy if their daughters marry into wealthy and distinguished families. A Tahitian mother feels the same satisfaction if her child is adopted by a family which will be responsible for its upbringing and enhance its social standing in the community. Godparents are another example of this double parentage, although here the attachment is more tenuous. In neither of these cases do the parents feel that they are relinquishing their child; rather they feel that they are increasing its well-being in giving it a second social status.

This double parenthood colors the whole fabric of Polynesian society.

More than among any other people I have known, Tahitian children are independent of their elders. A child of eight or ten will flit from one parent's household to the other's without so much as a "goodbye" or a "thank you." Sometimes out of pique or merely for a change of air. One and all treat adults as their equals. Not always even that.

As with many primitive people adoption into the family or tribe is a mark of esteem, given in gratitude or to confer honor. It has, however, its practical side. As elsewhere the woman rules the house but much of the work is done by the children. There are no servants. In the districts the conception of domestics is unknown. And there is much more work to be done in Tahitian households than with us where we have built-in help. Preparing breakfast coffee may take a couple of hours. The beans must be roasted and ground, and cream pressed from the flesh of a young coconut that grows forty feet above the ground. Naipu enjoys cooking but he is quite as lazy and incompetent in keeping house as I am. To run his establishment he had either to find a girl or to adopt several boys. The former alternative would have been more economical. A girl would be happy without additional company to entertain her. But Tahitian boys are easily bored alone and thirst for gaiety and chatter. A minimum of three seemed the necessary requirement. Naipu has made his choice and perhaps it is a wise one.

With the same blunt common sense Polynesians have solved other social problems that have vexed our "civilized" societies. Primitive people are rarely hypocritical. I have never known any stigma attached by them to a child born out of wedlock. This seems natural enough where child adoption is so common. In a land-poor economy a fine healthy baby is a welcome dowry. Eight- or ten-year-old children can fetch water, tend the babies, help dry the copra, gather oranges, or string the fish at the hauling of the nets.

In a society like Tahiti's where illegitimacy does not leave a scar the young girl has great sexual freedom. She enjoys it. As with the French, the whole Tahitian nation sings her praise. But I believe that her moral code is as principled as ours and certainly more sensible. The elder women's deportment is unquestionably more dignified. A married woman would think it not in good taste, and certainly irrational, to behave like a courtesan without being one.

The Tahitian girl never confuses sexual intercourse with either love or marriage. With her it may be desire satisfied, unabashed flirtation, or idle curiosity. But it is also a rational process in the selection of a mate. Her code teaches her that marriage is consummated when she settles down in a man's house and cooks his supper for him. Once she is thus committed her standards are exactly the same as ours: those of strict monogamy.

How faithfully do they live up to these standards? This is always an interesting question but subject to speculation. Theirs is the open society, and one of "togetherness." They hate and sometimes fear being alone. They cannot, as with us, pull down the blinds and lock the doors. My guess is that Tahitian women are at least as faithful as ours. Perhaps more so.

There is another sexual problem, the cause of unhappiness, frustration, and tragedy, which Europeans have never solved. We seldom discuss it without bias and sometimes are afraid even to mention it by name. I am speaking of course of homosexuality.

The Tahitian word for a "pansy" is *mahu*. I first heard the word at the Fourteenth of July celebrations in Papeete. The Papeete dance chorus was led by an old retainer of Queen Marau's — her butler and majordomo. The performance of the dancers was at times ragged and uninspired. The old fellow ran up and down the line of the dancing girls, urging them to greater efforts. If a girl fell slightly out of line, if the fury of her movements slackened, he did not hesitate to switch her legs with a bamboo twig. His function reminded me of that of the drum majorettes at our football games. The dancers responded to his exhortations with redoubled frenzy. The crowds broke into a happy roar of approval: "*Aue te mahu e! Mirimiri i te mahu!* — Hurrah for the *mahu*! Just look at the *mahu*!"

Let me describe a typical *mahu*. He may be a pansy, but the word has not necessarily the ugly connotation of our "homosexual." It designates a social type.

In Tahiti some of the work and social functions are carried out jointly by the entire village — men, women, boys, and girls. For instance the hauling of the nets, or the *himene* and church choral singing. Gathering clusters of *fei* high up in the mountains, manning the outriggers and the lighter dugouts, spearing fish, or setting up a house is a man's work. There are other occupations that are exclusively women's: washing and ironing the linen, the continual ritual of sweeping the house, and gathering oranges up the valley. I do not understand why this last should not also be a man's job. I am tempted to think that there may be some long established *tapu* connected with it. Men and boys, however, would feel as shy joining the girls to pick oranges as they would with us in knitting stockings. The girls play at juggling three or four oranges without letting one drop. A Tahitian boy would blush with shame if he were seen indulging in such a sissy pastime.

Pua is an attractive young *mahu*, sixteen or seventeen years old. He has a thin treble voice, sways his hips coquettishly when he walks, and snatches for a broom at the slightest pretext. He accompanies the girls when they set off up the valley after oranges. He is adept, too, at juggling them and can keep four or five in the air at once. Nor does he truss up his *pareu* about the loins; he wears it becomingly like a short skirt an inch or two below the knees. When he grows older he will doubtless let his beard grow like old Marau's retainer. With the exception of the *mahu*, and occasionally the missionaries, Tahitians always shave.

But the *mahu* is not necessarily a sex deviationist. He could better be defined as a third sex, with the emphasis on the social functions which he fulfills. In our own society – probably in every society – there is such a need. But only in Polynesia and other primitive cultures is the *mahu* openly accepted and distinguished by a different manner of dressing. With us he is the cotillion leader, the fellow who can always strum out a tune on the piano, make any party a success. He is the confidant of men and women, because he understands the problems of each. He can help a girl with her knitting, or a man in the selection of a tie. He is the middleman and broker of the arts. Throughout the ages he has been witch doctor, priest, and prophet.

Perhaps all of us have at bottom a little of the *mahu* in us. I should like to think so. A hundred percent man or woman is a very trying person and I don't think quite fits into our modern world.

When Naipu came out to Tahiti he brought with him a small set of homeopathic pills, a first-aid kit, and many simple remedies for colds, fever, or upset stomach. Several times a week the villagers come to him for consultation. He successfully administers soda mints or a dose of castor oil. They reward him with a chicken or a string of fish. He has achieved a standing of deference and authority in the village.

About a week ago Pua came to visit my friend in great distress. Naipu found somewhat to his surprise that the boy had contracted a severe case of gonorrhea. He had been living with Ave, my former model, the Tuamotuan girl with the sultry charm and dubious reputation.

Primitive civilizations have successfully adjusted their social manners to their economic problems. Their art, their mores, and their communal economy are better integrated than in our Western civilization, where they too often seem at war with each other. But we cannot imitate their manners any more than we can blindly accept the solutions of their social problems. That would be accepting the expressive symbols of a civilization alien to our own. We can, however, sympathetically study the reasons and behavior which seem to clothe with beauty their way of life. A primitive civilization is always old. One trait of ancient man was his hostility to change. Perhaps that is also the reason why the pattern of his life has attained such an all-round symmetry and form.

Our civilized, modern world shows the growing pains of youth. Adolescence, if not sick, is often unattractive. Yet it is better to grow, experiment, and desire rather than to have attained the beauty that only comes with age and precedes death.

August 15, 1920

This morning finished another flower piece, twenty-five by thirty inches. Exhausted but exhilarated with the efforts of the last two days. A real step forward. I have definitely escaped from Impressionism and there is no influence of Gauguin.

Thank God I can stay out here as long as I choose. But I expect I shall return to New York in December or January for a short visit, and if possible to arrange an exhibition.

How I have grown to love Tahiti, the people and the language. I would like to be part of the blood of Tahiti, to mingle with the blood of this blessed island.

August 18, 1920

Olsen, a friend of Naipu's, has been visiting him for the past few days. During the flu epidemic in 1918 he drove about the island distributing medicine to the natives. They have never forgotten him and whenever he stops in a village they heap his car with fruit, chickens, or a young pig.

In a neighboring island, which he visited, a district chief even offered him his daughter as a mark of gratitude. When she was left alone with him the girl burst into tears. He reassured her that he would not touch her and lay down beside her to sleep. In the middle of the night she wakened him and told him to proceed with his business. "If you do not take me now my father will feel insulted."

"Yet it would have been worse than discourtesy," Olsen added, "to seduce or have an affair with my friend's daughter or sister unless she had been offered to me."

That afternoon he and I walked to Ahui to visit Mari and his wife. As we passed a bamboo shack the owner, who remembered him, came out with his two sick children to beg his help. The sight was pitiful. Their faces, the palms of their hands, their fingers, and their feet were covered with syphilitic sores. The older boy will surely die. The poor man seemed utterly distracted. His gratitude and absolute faith in Olsen are deeply touching.

August 22, 1920

On the steps of the Catholic Temple. Black rain clouds gather and drift slowly overhead. The heat is insufferable. Timo's sister, Maria, toothless, crouches behind me. Her legs are repellent with sores. Raiarii has warned me that I should avoid having relations with her. His admonition is superfluous. Playfully, she switches my back with a sprig of hibiscus. From within the church the intoned Bible readings by the elders alternate with the plaintive, intoxicating throb of the *himene*. But it seems that the chorus is not in form. Old Fareau, Paruparu's father, calls out to me that the singing is not harmonious—*aita mea navenave*. A dog wanders into the church and curls himself among the sleeping children and the babies, rolled up in bedspreads on the floor. Uraponi and Tetuanui have settled down beside me. They make furtive efforts to get a peep at my phosphorescent wristwatch. They giggle at each unsuccessful attempt. The *himene* is over. I wander back with Teamo and the others. It is nearly midnight. The heat is stifling. Soon the rain clouds will break.

August 29, 1920

For many days I have been planning a walking trip around the trackless and almost impassable peninsula to Teahupo. From here the road continues along the coastline to Taravao on the isthmus. There is only one man in the village who has been over this route, now long forgotten, old Punuari, a relative of Timo and foster father of Afereti. I have persuaded Raiarii to accompany me. If we cannot get Punuari, who is now out in the *fenua ahieri,* to guide us he can at least indicate the way.

We started a little after daybreak. Eight or ten kilometers beyond the village we reached Raiarii's small plantation. His sisters and their men were stopping here to dry out copra. The women were resting in a bamboo hut. One of them was suckling a baby. Pihia sat in a corner. She was dressed in an orange blouse with an old red *pareu* bound about her hips. She shyly scratched among the pebbles which served as a flooring with her long slender fingers. She kept her head averted and would not answer my greeting.

The *taata mata ore* — the man without a face — lay on a pandanus mat dying of the flu. His face had been eaten away by congenital syphilis. He cannot talk but the natives understand the noises which he makes through the awful cavity which was once a mouth.

We pushed on. By eleven o'clock we reached the end of the road, which had by now thinned out into a hardly discernible path. Here Afereti's old foster parent dwelt. But he had gone on to gather *fei* and breadfruit. We did not stop to rest. We constantly lost and found the path along the sand beach, under the coco palms, among the piles of lava stones, and through the jungle of pandanus and giant ferns.

About one o'clock we came across the *fetii ruau* — old kinsman. He was sitting naked in a stone basin under a waterfall, rubbing his withered chest and arms with a small round stone. Beside him was a heavy load of *fei* and breadfruit. He refused to accompany us since it was getting late, but he explained the way as best he could.

"*Faaitoito* — Make way with courage," he called after us, the customary God's speed among the natives.

The way wound up and along the edge of a precipice which overhung the sea. Slipping in the mud, covered with dust and sweat, clinging to the serrated stems of the pandanus, the giant ferns and the roots of the *mape* trees, the Tahitian chestnuts, we struggled on.

From the summit of the cliff we gazed toward Meetia, lying cone-shaped in the haze, sixty kilometers out to sea.

Perpendicularly we shot down under the giant ferns and through the bracken. Looking overhead through the broad pandanus leaves and the tall spires of grass we could catch a glimpse of the sky. Peering down between ferns and pandanus we could make out patches of blue and copper that were the sea. Far below us a woman shouted.

By three o'clock we had reached the foot of the cliff. Here are the legendary caves of Te Pari. The caves open on a narrow beach closed at either end by a wall of rock and facing an opening in the reef. Here were camping a dozen natives who had paddled over from Tautira to work copra. "*Faaitoito*," they called to us. It was getting late and we could not afford to tarry.

For three hours more we crawled on over rocks with the surf boiling a few feet below us, up to our waist in water, picking our way over the red, slippery coral; scrambling once more over mud and rocks. Raiarii found a young sprouting coconut. He cracked it open on a rock. We ate the tender, juicy, coagulated flesh.

About six o'clock we came across three naked boys spearing fish on a reef. They told us that before reaching Teahupoo we would have to swim across a gully. Here the cliffs descend sheer into the boiling surf. We continued on our way. Now we met other natives who pointed out to Raiarii a path up into the mountain which would avoid the gully. Once more we set our backs to the sea and climbed as best we could, pulling ourselves up the side of the cliff. Darkness had fallen but later the moon came out.

By ten o'clock we reached Teahupoo. We asked our way to the house of Paiatua, the Chief. Warned beforehand, this hospitable man had waited our arrival. Fortified by generous portions of rum, we dined on soup, fish, chicken, *fei*, sweet potato, and tea. We finished eating at midnight.

Four months ago Paiatua's little boy upset a pot of boiling water. His back was horribly scalded. Since then the poor child has been forced to lie on his stomach on a pandanus mat. Over him is stretched a crude wicker frame, covered with cloth to protect him from the flies. He is attended by a native doctor who soothes his suffering with liniments brewed from herbs. He will probably recover but it will take another three or four months before a new skin grows over the raw flesh.

There are two French doctors in Papeete who look after its three thousand inhabitants. The doctors are too busy ever to leave the capital. The seven or eight thousand natives in the districts of Tahiti and Moorea are without medical care. The French government, which has assumed responsibility for the islands, does nothing to alleviate the diseases which the white man has brought with him: tuberculosis, largely resulting from the European dress prescribed by the missionaries, dental trouble, and venereal diseases.

When Queen Pomare agreed to a French protectorate she insisted that the natives should never be taxed on their land. They can at least live on its yield. Otherwise their lot would be pitiable.

August 30, 1920

We slept our full. At two o'clock another feast had been prepared for us: suckling pig, *fei*, *umara*, and red wine. Paiatua refused to take any recompense in return for his hospitality. At four o'clock, a little footsore, bloated with our gargantuan meal, relaxed and happy, we trudged on barefoot another ten or twelve miles to Taravao. We refreshed ourselves again at Madame Butscher's: soup, omelet, boiled shrimp, and a couple of bottles of wine.

Mari had sent on a boy to fetch us home in his crazy two-wheeled rig. I can never forget that drive. To our right rose the dense impenetrable shadow of the mountains. On our left the mirror of the sea. The moon was full in our faces. Against it like filigree work by Aubrey Beardsley were patterned the silhouettes of the trees whose native names I have learned to love. The great many fingered leaves of the *uru* (breadfruit), the leafless branches and plum-shaped fruit of the *vavai* (kapok or cotton tree), the delicate fernlike tracery of the poinciana, the flowering plumage of the lordly *vi* (mango), and the swaying, feathery fronds of the *tumu haari* (coco palm). The gentle night breeze, heavy with the cloying odor of the drying copra, caressed our faces. At midnight we splashed through the shallows of the Vaitipiha. Naipu had stayed up to welcome us.

August 31, 1920

From Naipu I have the recent village gossip. Pau, the native missionary, a good friend and trustworthy man, has cautioned him against his boys' incompetence. He has suggested that he take Moe as a *vahine*. Moe – the word means lost or forgotten – has just returned from Papeete. She is sorrowing for her Chinese lover who was ordered by his old father to leave for the island of Rurutu in the Austral group on a business venture. She is a sweet and responsible girl and promises to continue posing for me with her baby.

Item 2: Pihia told Marai that if she came to me and later I should return to America it would not be seemly. It could only end in a *peapea rahi* – a great sorrow. I am sure she is right. Pihia is no light-o'-love.

Item 3: Pau has also told Naipu that he will advise him from time to time which of the village girls are rumored to be diseased. Gossip spreads.

Item 4: Teamo told Naipu that he first contracted *opi* – gonorrhea – at the age of fourteen. His mother gave him the local cure: complete rest and a diet of coconut water. For a week no other food.

Item 5: Naipu thinks that he may have a case of *opi* himself. At any rate he intends to spend a week in Papeete. He has asked me to take charge of his household while he is away.

September 1, 1920

There has been a wave of influenza. The villagers flock to Naipu for remedies. Daily he dispenses purgatives, aspirin, and hot tea. Yesterday little Tihoni, the Tauires' fat smiling baby, the pride of the family, the joy of the little girls, was taken desperately ill. His large brown eyes were lusterless. All night he choked and moaned. Paruparu, who loves little Tihoni as we all do, rocked him in his great arms but could not quiet his sobs. He took him to the kitchen outhouse where it is cooler. Here a dozen women carrying their own babies had gathered to offer their condolence. Tauire was distracted with grief and hardly understood me when I spoke to him.

The next day Tauire drove Tihoni twenty kilometers to Paea to visit the native doctor. The doctor diagnosed his illness. He prescribed poultices and hot compounds of various roots, leaves, sugar cane, and coconut juice. Tihoni has passed the crisis.

September 10, 1920

Naipu has not yet returned from Papeete, where Dr. Cassiau has been treating him. There is still a great deal of flu among the villagers. For the past few days I have been laid up with it myself. This morning I visited Naipu's household. I was shocked by the filth, untidiness, and pilfering that has been going on. During his absence and contrary to his strict orders the boys have invited in their friends, Matau, the son of old Tafaite the cripple, Nane, and others of the *taurearea*. All day long they lie about playing the gramophone. They have helped themselves generously to his canned foods and butter, cigarettes, and wine. Matau is also down with the flu. He has made himself comfortable on a couch in the living room, where his mother comes to nurse him with native cures.

Distracted with the filth and continued chatter I decided to take my meals with Tauire and work there until Naipu returns.

September 11, 1920

Notwithstanding my reproaches, angry scolding, and the warnings of what would await them on Naipu's return, I hear from Tauire that the boys and their friends are still merrymaking. I felt weak with the flu but thought it advisable to take matters resolutely in hand. In the evening I returned to Naipu's house. Here Teha Amaru, the jolly ape-girl, was cooking a meal for a dozen of the *taurearea*. Cans of meat, tripe, vegetables, and soup had been opened. Teamo reclined on a couch, a towel wrapped about his head. Tui — I suspect his girl friend — was massaging his stomach with some of Naipu's hair oil.

I was in a rage and sent the whole lot packing. Matau, apparently feverish and also suffering from a case of *opi*, was carted back to the house of his father Tafaite. I also ordered Teamo home. Later on I relented and sent him some soup and castor oil, for he is obviously ill. I have closed the house until Naipu's return. It is a symbolic cloture, for his bungalow like the other houses in the village has neither doors nor locks. But I believe it will remain "off bounds." Ueri and Timo, the most reliable of the lot, are to sleep there to see that my orders are obeyed. I have given them a spare allowance of tea, bread, and cigarettes.

September 12, 1920

Thank God Naipu is back from Papeete. He gave Timo and Ueri a fatherly dressing down, offering them the choice of dismissal from his household or physical chastisement. They were of course repentant and chose the latter punishment. I never had the heart to inquire if it was carried out. It would have hurt their pride and Naipu's own self-esteem as a strict disciplinarian.

He explained to me that he could have forgiven their untidiness, filth, and excessive depredations into his larder—the canned foods, butter, cigarettes, and wine. Such paltry misconduct was perhaps due to their immaturity and native upbringing. In his eyes their chief transgression was in not ordering people off the place while he was away. This had been his peremptory injunction to them. It was direct disobedience.

How quixotic he can be! He continues to treat the native boys as if they had the discipline of a New England boarding school and the code of honor of the Ivy League. He refuses to recognize that if a villager sees an acquaintance pass his door it is unseemly and rude not to greet him with a "*Haere mai na tamaa*—Come in and eat." And it may be more than a formal greeting.

I cannot help taking a detached interest in his efforts to educate the boys. He has been a teacher by training and by nature is a philosopher and moralist. My own instinct under similar circumstances would have been to lock up the rum and other perishables. He insists, however, that the boys are his adoptive friends. He will continue to treat them as his social equals, as he would Americans of the same age. Not to trust their honor and veracity would be an insult to their friendship!

September 13, 1920

Naipu has brought back with him from Papeete Frederick O'Brien, author of the *White Shadows in the South Seas*, and a friend, Dr. Malcolm Douglas. O'Brien is a rather unattractive looking, little, middle-class Irishman in his fifties. But he is good company. To my surprise he seems less familiar with the island than I was after a week's stay. His knowledge of Tahitian is limited to two phrases: *maitai* and *ia ora na oe*—fine and may you prosper. His *White Shadows* was an enormous success and he has come back for a month or two to write another best seller. He likes Tautira. He will stay here to do a chapter on our village. I have arranged with Ori to board him and his friend.

September 15, 1920

The more I see of O'Brien the better I like him as a human being and the less I respect him as a writer. He is quite a character. A boon companion, warm, generous, merry, irrepressible. A wonderful storyteller in his cups—and almost illiterate. Dr. Douglas is a quiet, gentlemanly New York clubman. He worships Fred. He is a Boswell to the latter's Johnson. One is a perfect foil to the other.

I had them both to dinner with Tauire and the Chief. O'Brien regaled them—I interpreting—with his adventures in the Marquesas, the Tuamotu, the Hawaiian Islands, Java, and the Philippines. Tauire and Mari listened politely but seemed unimpressed. After they left he read us some of Rupert Brooke's poems written during Brooke's stay in Mataiea. Tomorrow he will give a farewell party before leaving for Papeete.

September 16, 1920

O'Brien's *arearea* was held under the mango trees on Naipu's spit of land where I painted my large canvas. For a tablecloth banana leaves had been spread on the ground; for seats, pandanus mats. Some seventeen guests in all. Princess Takao, her two young cousins, Poma and Ina Salmon, Mote, the Papara Chief, and his sister Hototu drove out together from Papeete. Norman Hall brought his two half-caste girl friends, the Richmond sisters – Nohorae, demure; Jeanne, lovely and provocative.

We reclined on the pandanus mats. Punch was served. We helped ourselves from generous bowls of boiled shrimp, raw fish, sea centipedes, *maoa* – a shellfish – gathered on the coral reefs, fried chicken, and baked *fei*. A young pig had been roasted on lava stones while we finished the preliminary dishes. The tender meat, cut into suitable portions, was piled on *purau* leaves at convenient intervals. The boys poured red wine.

After the coffee some slept in the shade of the mangoes. Others of us bathed and sported in the river. At six o'clock we gathered again for supper at Ori's house.

Later in the evening, Takao, O'Brien, Hall, and I wandered over to the Temple to listen to the *himene*. After a few moments Takao spoke to them quite sharply. She upbraided them for singing with so little spirit; told them she had expected a better performance in Tautira. I was a little surprised at such a scolding while the service was going on. But she spoke with great self-assurance and simplicity. Her words were a royal command and galvanized the *himene*. I never heard such singing. The different groups competed with each other. The men seemed hypnotized. They leaned forward behind the women: their eyes closed, their heads thrown back, their chins supported on a hand. Their bodies swayed to the rhythm. One daring tenor broke into a free melodic solo accompaniment. The women embroidered improvisations on the main theme.

September 17, 1920

This afternoon Takao, Poma, O'Brien, and I walked up the valley of the Vaitipiha to see the idol. The green trunks of the *mape* trees were ribbed like the members of a gothic column. Parasitic plants and ferns hung luxuriously overhead. The branches of the *purau* trees stretched their horizontal trunks and branches in defiance of the laws of gravitation. The sun never penetrates the depth of a tropical forest. The green light had the artificial and shadowy coolness of Boecklin's "Toten Insel."

We crossed and recrossed the shallow basin of the river. The girls wreathed garlands of woodferns for us. Takao's long hair hung almost to her knees. It is her great beauty. Her cousin Poma has a thick mass of dark brown hair which she rubs with coconut oil perfumed with the petals of the gardenia. It frames her golden skin and dark red-brown eyes. She is only sixteen years old but has the ample form of a woman of thirty. Like many Tahitians she has beautiful hands with long tapering fingers. Her arms are round and firm. She is a strong swimmer and in the river frolics like a sleek young seal.

September 19, 1920

Yesterday quite a to-do. The French Governor was out here on his annual visit. He was entertained by Mari and the three other civic functionaries of the village salaried by the government: Raiarii, the Second Chief; Tetuanui, the *mutoi* (local policeman and letter carrier); and Afereti, the schoolmaster. The Governor left for Papeete about three o'clock. Then the Chief brought out more rum. The four of them finished off a quart apiece on Mari's porch.

Tahitians are as a rule sober. The majority of the natives never touch alcohol. But when they drink they are apt to overdo it. Afereti and Mari soon passed out. Their respective wives in due course got them home. I walked by the Chief's house about five o'clock. Marai had come in her cart and was with some difficulty loading her husband into it. I saw them safely off and stopped for a few moments to chat with Tetuanui. He seemed a little high but I thought no more about it and left.

After supper I went to visit O'Brien and Dr. Douglas. Raiarii had come to and was again drinking with O'Brien. He was holding his liquor well but his face was a dull scarlet. He talked with deep emotion. Tetuanui, he said, had just been killed by his wife. Enraged with his appearance when he returned home, "she had hit him from behind with a stone. When he fell she clubbed him over the head with a stake and killed him. This all happened at four o'clock."

"But I saw him at five o'clock myself," I cried.

"Then it must have happened just after you left," said Raiarii. "He did not immediately die. He collapsed opposite the house of Temeheu, Timo's father. His wife shows no sorrow or compunction for her crime. She is still enraged with him for his drunkenness. She has left their home and is staying with her parents. I have written to the *mutoi rahi* – the chief of police – in Papeete. She will get twenty years' hard labor in the penal colony at Nouméa."

I was horrified. I had spoken to him just a few hours before and I was fond of both the *mutoi* and his wife. Tetuanui *vahine* has the appearance of a gentle and well-behaved little woman. She is serious, hard working, and has the tranquil beauty of a Luini madonna. The *mutoi*, too, had always seemed good-natured and he had a reputation for sobriety.

Neither O'Brien nor I could believe that this gentle and beautiful little creature could have murdered her husband without provocation in such a brutal manner. I determined to do what I could for her the next day.

Meanwhile Raiarii, who had seen Tetuanui's corpse, had dispatched a letter to the French *gendarme* in Taravao. He expected that she would be arrested the following day. She was sitting, he said, with her family and showed no signs of repentance. He told us that she has a reputation for being a scold. This is a quality that no Tahitian will tolerate.

The next morning I went to see Afereti. He had just awakened and knew nothing of the calamity. What most distressed him was that the crime was provoked by the drinking bout of the four highest functionaries of the village and only a couple of hours after the Governor's departure. We went immediately to the house of Tetuanui *vahine*'s parents. They told us to our great amazement that only an hour before they had seen Tetuanui bathing in the river. This we verified. Apparently he had lain unconscious for several hours. The whole village had believed him dead. We returned to Raiarii with the news. At first he would not believe us. Luckily the letter which he had written to the *gendarme* in Taravao had not gone off. This was due to the fact that Tetuanui himself was the mail carrier!

What struck me most in this incident was the callousness on the part of Tetuanui's friends a few moments after they thought him dead. Mari, Raiarii, Afereti, Marai, and the others discussed the affair with as much detachment as if it had been some irrelevant newspaper scandal. The primitive is more emotional and volatile in his emotions than we are. But, like the child, he can remain detached and indifferent about the suffering of others if it does not directly affect him.

September 23, 1920

There is a very beautiful word in Tahitian which has no exact equivalent in any other tongue. *Aroha* means to sympathize with someone in sharing his grief. Our word "sympathize" has lost the sense of the Greek *sympatho* from *pathaino* — I suffer. A people who in their sympathy grieve or suffer themselves, even though the pain may be symbolic rather than real, are far from callous or insensitive.

September 26, 1920

Three days ago I went into Papeete to see O'Brien off. Poor fellow. He was in despair. He told me that several of the characters in his last book were modeled on some of his drinking companions at the French Club, the Cercle Bougainville, and he was being sued for libel. One old sea dog, Captain Joe Winchester,* a trader, swore that he would horsewhip O'Brien if he should catch him in the streets. Another let it be known that if he met him he would break every tooth in his head. Poor Freddy stuck to the Annex and had his meals carried to him from the Chinese cookhouse. He was sick with worrying and unable to find a lawyer to represent him. It was in fact rumored that the plaintiffs in the libel suit had secured the services of the only lawyer on the island. This proved not to be the case. O'Brien has now found someone to represent him. But he has been bound over under heavy bail until the case is settled. I put him safely on board the *Marama*, a whole, a wiser, but an unrepentant man.

October 10, 1920

For three days Tetuanui nursed his anger and threatened to divorce his young wife. I argued with him that he had been partly to blame. But I felt that the sympathy of the village was with him. However, youth, beauty, and — as O'Brien more pithily remarked — sex have triumphed over conjugal squabbles. The quarrel has been patched up. The *mutoi* and his wife are once more living harmoniously together. Yet they are dogged by misfortune. The girl's

*Norman Hall subsequently married Captain Winchester's daughter Sarah.

mother Taaroa is in an advanced stage of consumption and will not live more than a few months. Tetuanui *vahine* has caught the same horrible disease, the scourge of the islands. Her husband has taken her into Papeete to consult Dr. Cassiau. The good man has given up his position as *mutoi* and found himself a job in Papeete where she can get medical care. It is seldom that a native is sufficiently patient with or confident in a European doctor to submit to a long and expensive course of treatment. On this score at least he need have no anxiety. Dr. Cassiau is the only Frenchman I have yet seen who cares for the natives and will sacrifice his time and his money to help them.

October 16, 1920

I have been reading J. A. Moerenhout's *Voyages aux îles du Grand Océan*, which Nordy loaned me. It was published in 1837. Its author, the indefatigable explorer-merchant-scholar, transcribed many of the religious epics from the native priests a few years after the first missionaries reached the islands. There was of course no written language. Like Cook and Bligh before him Moerenhout had to improvise a phonetic spelling. Tahitian, owing to its poverty of consonants and runs of successive vowels, is an extremely difficult language to spell correctly. It takes a very sensitive ear to spell phonetically such a word as *maoae* — east wind, or to distinguish the difference between *mataū* — to fear, *matău* — fishhook, and *mătau* — to be accustomed. In Tahitian there is no one accented syllable as in English, merely an almost imperceptible lengthening or weighting of the vowel. To train my ear I would ask our boys to pronounce one or another of these three words, but was rarely able to guess the correct meaning.

Some of the ancient myths which Moerenhout has transcribed in French are so beautiful that I made an effort to translate them into English. In doing this I consulted Afereti the schoolmaster. I relied on his judgment, as much as on Moerenhout's version, for the proper meaning of obsolete and hieratic words.

"Mais écoutons le vieux prêtre, mon respectable instituteur," writes Moerenhout in his introduction to these ancient myths. "Voici comme il s'explique sur la cosmogonie, l'éternité de la matière, l'imortalité de l'âme et la vie future, ainsi que sur la théogonie de ses compatriotes."

CONCERNING TAAROA, THE GOD CREATOR

Parahi; Taaroa te ioa.	He existed; Taaroa his name.
Iroto i te aere.	He existed in the void.
Aita fenua; aita rai.	No earth; no sky.
Aita e tai; aita e taata.	No sea; no human being.
Pii Taaroa,	Taaroa called aloud,
Areara aita roa.	But none answered.
Ona ae iho toreira e ua riro oia i te hoe noa.	He alone existed at that moment.
Te tumu Taaroa.	Taaroa, the foundation.

Te papa.
Taaroa te one.
Oia o Taaroa iho tona ioa.

The rocks.
Taaroa, the sands.
Taaroa his very name.

Taaroa te ao.
Taaroa tei roto.
Taaroa tei oteo.
Taaroa tei raro.
Taaroa tei tai.
Taaroa tei paari.
Faunau i te ao,
Te ao rahi e te moa,
Ei paa no Taaroa,
Te ori, ori ra fenua.

Taaroa, the universe.
Taaroa, the innermost center.
Taaroa, the germ of life.
Taaroa, he below.
Taaroa, the oceans.
Taaroa, the ruggedly wise.
He gave birth to the universe,
The great and sacred universe,
As a shell for Taaroa,
That the land should dance and sing.

THE CREATION

E te tumu, e te papa,
E te one,
Matou teie.
Haere mai outou tei hamani i te fenua.
Pohia. Popohia. Aita e farerei.

You foundations, you rocks,
You sands,
It is we.
Come hither you who shall create the land.
He urges them. He urges them again. They will not assemble.

Taaroa ona i te hitu rai ei hamani i te tumu matamua.
Fanau ai te rai.
Pau te po.
Ua itea pauroa hia.
Te maramarama raa iropu i te ao.
Ua maere te atua i te ite raa.

He, Taaroa, built the seven heavens as the first foundation.
He created the sky.
Darkness was dispelled.
Everywhere there was light.
In the center of the universe there was light.
The God marveled at the sight.

E pau te hauti raa.
E pau te afai parau.
E pau te orero raa.
E faa i te tumu.
E faa i te papa.
E faa i te one.
Ua ohu te rai.
Ua tetei te rai.
Ia hohonu.
E pau te fenua i hamani hia.

His efforts have ceased.
His words have been carried.
The talk is over.
The basic foundations are fixed.
The rocks are in place.
The sands are strewn.
The sky revolves.
The sky hangs above the sea.
The sea lies in its depth.
Finished the creation of the earth.

THE BIRTH OF GODS AND MEN

Taoto aera Taaroa i te vahine o Hina.
Atua tai te ioa.

Slept then Taaroa with the woman Hina.
Goddess of the Sea her name.

Fanau aera ana i te ata poiri,	She gave birth to the black clouds,
E ata uouo e ua.	The moist clouds and the rain.
Taoto aera Taaroa i te vahine atua uta te ioa.	Slept then Taaroa with the woman, Goddess of the Earth her name.
Fanau aera ana	She gave birth then
O te aa i toro i uta.	To the roots beneath the soil.
Heemaira imuri te tupu ra te fenua.	Was born then that which grows above the ground.
Heemaira imuri te ohutiatia moua te ioa.	Was born then Mist of the Mountains her name.
Heemaira imuri o aito te puai te ioa.	Was born then the hero, the Strong One his name.
Heemaira imuri te vahine unauna, haamea te ioa.	Was born then the bedecked woman, Pleasure her name.
Taoto Taaroa i te vahine o Hina, atua nia te ioa.	Slept then Taaroa with the woman Hina, Goddess of the West Wind her name.
Fanau aera te anuanua te ioa.	Was born then Rainbow was her name.
Heemaira imuri te marama te ioa.	Was born then Moon was her name.
Heemaira imuri te ata uteute,	Was born then the Red Clouds,
E ua toto.	The Blood Red Rain.
Taoto aera Taaroa i te vahine o Hina atua raro te ioa.	Slept then Taaroa with the woman Hina, Goddess of the East Wind her name.
Taoto aera Taaroa i te vahine ovaa utu.	Slept then Taaroa with the woman, Ends of the Earth her name.
Fanau mai i te mau atua imuri nei:	Gave issue then to the following Gods:
Etono te Terei e moa ia.	Gave birth to Terei, ordained a God.
Etono te Fatu e moa ia.	Gave birth to Fatu, ordained a Goddess.
Etono Rouanoua e moa ia.	Gave birth to Rouanoua, ordained a God.
Vevetia te vahine ati faoao.	The woman gave birth to all that she contained.
Haere mai ai i rapai to roto.	There issued forth all that she contained.
Maoae.	The East Wind.
Tua.	The Angry Sea.
Tua matai.	The Angry Wind.
Tua roa maru.	The Calming of the Tempest.
O Roo te afai vea.	Roo who dispatches messengers.

DIALOGUE BETWEEN FATU AND HINA, GODDESSES OF THE EARTH AND THE MOON

Parau atura Hina ia Fatu:	Spoke then Hina to Fatu:
Faaora oe i te taata.	Let man live again.
Parau atura te Fatu:	Then spoke Fatu:
Eita vau e faaora.	I shall not let him live again.
E pohe te fenua.	The earth shall perish.
E pau te aere.	The forest shall wither.
E pau te ai hia e te taata.	The food that man eats shall be consumed.
E pau te repo.	The land shall be scorched.
E pau te fenua.	The earth shall be obliterated.
E ore te fenua.	No more earth.

E ore roa'tu.	Never again.
Te parau maira Hina: atira.	Then spoke Hina: Enough.
Maoti ra ia oe iho.	So be it. As you will.
E ora vau i te marama.	I shall resuscitate the moon.
Ora atura ta Hina.	Thus what Hina created lived.
Pohe atura ta Fatu.	Thus were blotted out the works of Fatu.
Pohe o te taata.	Thus perished man.

The Tahitian Genesis has the thematic grandeur and poetic majesty of the Old Testament. In the animistic confrontation with the forces of nature these elements are the appropriate gods of a seafaring race of men. The dialogue between Hina and Fatu has the tragic beauty of a Greek drama. Yet I know no more implacable declaration of hopeless pessimism. The acceptance of a meaningless obliteration — resolute, lofty, and dispassionate — is hard to understand as the religious creed of this smiling and sun-kissed race.*

October 17, 1920

Since Sunday the wind has shifted to the north. The days are hot and the nights cool. The moon is near its full. This afternoon three women, dressed in black, their long skirts trussed well up about their thighs, stood fishing on the reef at the mouth of the Vaitipiha. Inside the reef Mari the Chief stood in his dugout, a ten-foot-long, five-pronged spear poised on his shoulder ready to cast. He was waiting for the great *hahavare* to rise to the surface.

October 18, 1920

Naipu and I have our meals on his gravel-strewn, pandanus-roofed veranda. At noon the faint buzzing chorus of the children, like the song of cicadas, drifts to us from the schoolhouse in the village. We have supper at five o'clock and take our coffee as the sun sets and the white cumulus clouds begin to billow upward behind the unscaled peaks of Orohena and the mountain ranges of Tahiti *nui*. In front of Naipu's bungalow is an ancient, curiously twisted mango. At this season the crest of the tree is freshly leafing in the palest emerald green. The vermilion and copper-red flowers hang above the dark blue-green of last year's foliage. About the garden are white and orange lilies, scarlet hibiscus, and the pearly blossoms of the *tiare Tahiti*.

When my work is going well I think I am more serenely happy here than I have ever been in my life.

October 19, 1920

Yesterday I began a large painting, fifty by sixty inches. I have primed the back of a Devoe canvas with fish glue and whiting. On this semi-absorbent surface I can get broader effects

*See *Vikings of the Sunrise* by Sir Peter Buck, an anthropologist of mixed European and Polynesian ancestry. He places the myths and legends of each particular island group into the over-all context of Polynesia.

and establish a rapid over-all color pattern with thin washes of turpentine on a heavily outlined linear design in black oil paint. As I continue to work I shall build up with heavier impastos, in the attempt to achieve greater textural richness. At the same time I shall work complementary color tones into the flat surface washes.

October 20, 1920

Recently a number of women have returned from the Tuamotu, where they accompanied the pearl divers. Nightly they gather at Amok the Chinaman's store for an *arearea*. Marama, Teha Amaru, Meri, Ani the Chinese half-caste, and Taoa, the *hihimata ore*—she without eyebrows. Pepe, who owns the only strong and well-fed boar hounds in the village, has loaned his accordion to his girl Terei. Like Uraponi, Terei is a *pupure*, sorrel-haired and light of skin. She has a rich contralto voice and sings the *ute* with abandon. These are improvised lyrics, gay and often salacious. Here is one, popular among the girls in Papeete:

I to matou moe raa e, to Tahiti e,	Shall we forget them, the women of Tahiti,
Ua rau hoi o te hure e, te vahine Tahiti.	They are all so different.
E au to ratou te mata, i *te unauna e;*	They have pleasing faces and they bedeck themselves;
Area ra hoi te vahine Tahiti, *te reira o te au e.*	They are indeed enchanting, the women of Tahiti.

On the other hand the *paripari* are very ancient, and forgotten now by all but the old people. There is every reason to believe that in another ten or fifteen years they will be entirely lost. Each valley, waterfall, or mountain has its own *paripari*. Often they are of great imaginative beauty. Here are two of them which I translated as best I could with the help of Afereti.*

E tii na vau ofati mai	Seeking, I break off
Te tiare rata no Tahuareva e.	The rata flower from the mountain of Tahuareva.
Tau fenua ra Fatutira nui e,	Fatutira, far-reaching, is my homeland,
Te peho Vaitia.	And the fruit-bearing valley of Vaitia.

E moua tei nia o Tahuareva e,	Tahuareva the mountain stands above,
E tahua tei raro Tiaraaopere.	Below the plain, Tiaraaopere.
E outu teitei Tatatua e	The high promontory of Tatatua
E hapu i te pape Vaitipiha.	Bathes in the waters of the Vaitipiha.

October 22, 1920

This evening Naipu and I strolled through the village. Nestling under the walls of the Temple stands the humble bamboo shack of old More, a cousin of Queen Marau. I have noticed this venerable gentlewoman slowly walking about the village, leaning on her *purau* staff. At other times she lies on her stomach weeding the small grass plot in front of her *fare*. With

*I subsequently showed these *paripari* to Frank Stimson, the brilliant anthropologist whom I had met in Papeete. He found a number of mistakes in Afereti's translation. I am using Stimson's version.

her live Vahio, her *tane*, and their daughter Huura. We came upon the old couple reclining on a pandanus mat, spread before their door. They begged us to join them. After a moment Huura went into the house and brought out a little sack, woven from palm leaves, which she presented to Naipu.

October 23, 1920

Recently I have become exhausted with my work on the large canvas. Everything seems to be going badly. Urari, my lovely model, has left for a week to work on her family plot in the *fenua ahieri*. Yesterday Moe came with her baby but posed badly. In the afternoon Teha Amaru. Finished the face and hands. All day it rained. I worked on the foreground. I must get away. Physically and mentally pooped out.

October 25, 1920

Last night a wild boar was driven down from the valley by Pepe's dogs. It appeared this morning on the spot of land opposite Naipu's bungalow. The animal swam across the river, toppled Naipu into the water as he was about to take his morning dip, and disappeared in the taro patch across the road. The boar emerged lower down in the village where Paea, the missionary, was at work in his garden. He was badly gored in the arm but finally killed the animal with an axe. Paea came to Naipu to have the wound cauterized. Naipu cleaned it and bound up his arm. We ate wild boar for supper. Very gamy and quite different from a roast of pork.

October 26, 1920

The language, like the people, is direct and democratic. I know of no words in contemporary use that suggest caste. *Arii vahine*, the word for queen, means literally a "chief's woman." The nearest approach to "Mr." and "Mrs." are *tane* and *vahine* following a given name. But the words are in no sense a polite form of address. They denote a relationship. So at l'Académie Julien in Paris the students spoke of *la femme de tel* – So-and-So's "woman." Nor is there any precise equivalent for "Thank you" or "I beg your pardon" as expressions of manners or courtesy. *Mauruuru*, the nearest word for "Thanks," literally means "It is agreeable" or "I am satisfied." Just so with equal directness our American small fry, in his genuine appreciation of the gift of a new jackknife, is content with "Swell!" – which comes from the heart, not the lips.

BEFORE coming to Tahiti I had seen a good deal of Jerry Blum and Lucile, his lovely wife, a sculptor of talent. Jerry was a Chicago painter of great promise. Among his many friends were Theodore Dreiser, Jo Davidson, Max Eastman, Boardman Robinson, Hunt Diederich, the Zorachs, and others of our younger, insurgent group. He had a small income from his family. Restless by nature he had worked and traveled in Europe and the Orient. Before leaving New York the three of us had sat up into the early morning hours, talking art, the Ecole de Paris, our own aspirations, and my intention of isolating myself for one or two years in Tahiti.

Jerry was a very stimulating companion. Lucile had deep understanding. Both shared my own romantic feelings about visiting unknown shores and living among primitive people. He was about my age but had started painting several years ahead of me. Owing to some physical defect he had escaped military service and they had both spent a year in China, working. His reputation was already established. I had suggested their joining me in Tahiti.

Jerry was short, broad-shouldered, ungainly, and almost humpbacked in appearance. His features and too often his demeanor were forbidding. At times he gave the impression of an irritable and bewildered gorilla. His childhood had been unhappy. This could explain his extreme sensitivity, his defensive attitude, and sudden violent outbursts.

Yet Jerry was generous, intelligent, and a fine critic. He was brutally honest, one reason why I loved him. His power of expression, however, was as muscle-bound as his frame. He was quite without mental poise or ease of manner. Groping painfully for the exact word, his face would become contorted in nervous spasms. I remember his once explaining to us the particular life-enhancing quality that a year's residence in China had given him. His voice rasping, his hands clenched till the knuckles were white, he blurted out in a sob of anguish: "The Chinese are the only people I have known who have given me serenity."

Jerry and Lucile arrived in Tahiti during the autumn of 1920. I saw little of them. Jerry hovered around Papeete. Tried to paint. Tried to settle down. His whole vital energy was leaking out of him: leaking out or bursting at the seams. He was beginning to topple over the edge. He came out to Tautira once. He approved of what I was doing, greatly encouraged me, but was ruthless in his criticism. In angry, disjointed words he clarified for me what I was feeling and groping after but had not yet been able to put into sharp focus. I shall always be grateful to him. Not just because he was one of those rare human beings who are never for one instant dead during their waking hours, but because what was important in life to him were its ultimate values. In our civilization this quality is rare.

October 27, 1920

Jerry and Lucile came out from Papeete to visit us. He genuinely likes what I have been doing; feels the change in direction. He promises to write to Marie Sterner of the Knoedler Gallery and try to arrange an exhibition for me next winter. But he was equally severe in his criticism. He felt that I have become too involved in detail and should simplify and strengthen my over-all design. We discussed and argued about this at length.

It is true that during these past months I have become more and more concerned with flat, compact, linear design. Consequently instead of the Renaissance masters and my heroes of the Impressionist movement I have been drawn more and more to my first love, the great Japanese printmakers, to the superb pottery design of the Hopi Indians, and to the earlier masters of the *quattrocento*. I keep recalling the admonition of that great woman Mary Cassatt, quoting Degas: "Il faut se plier devant les primitifs."

I have been aware of another influence since I came to Tautira, less consciously reasoned but more intuitively felt. Here nature is a gorgeous tapestry, rich in color and design. I feel no depth of atmosphere. There is no atmosphere. The distant mountain peaks, the copper-colored edge of the horizon, have the same weight and brilliance and formal design as the heavy scarlet leaves, the purple depth of shadows, the patches of vermilion and orange that lie at my feet and crowd in upon me from every side.

Ever since the Armory Show of 1913 I have been deeply intrigued by many of the artists and much of the painting of the Ecole de Paris. Untouched, too, by some of it. With interest and curiosity I have followed the various manifestos of the Cubists, Futurists, Suprematists, Vorticists, Synchronists, Dadaists, Surrealists, and the rest of them. Much of it has seemed to me verbiage. Often sheer nonsense. At its best the driest of dogma. Perhaps this is the necessary dust and turmoil that accompany every great revolutionary movement. Talking and arguing with Jerry it gradually dawned on me how the color and design of the tropics have opened my eyes to what is the true direction and meaning of modern art: to what extent I am and feel myself part of it.

Art uses nature as its raw material. For five hundred years it has manipulated nature with magnificence to its own chosen pattern. A cycle of history has run its course. The pattern is changing. Those dreadful, violent, suffocating, and empty war years in France may have marked a watershed in history. Art will once more manipulate lines and color and forms in a new idiom, in new designs, to interpret what lies ahead.

Recently I have been rereading Clive Bell. He believes that the creation of a work of art is so tremendous a business that it can leave no leisure for catching a likeness or even displaying technical craftsmanship. He goes on to say that every sacrifice made to the representation of nature is something stolen from art.

I ponder over what he says, but I cannot swallow all of it. He argues that to appreciate a work of art we need take with us nothing but a sense of form and color and a feeling for three-dimensional space. Over and over again he avers that art is merely the presentation of "significant form."

I heartily agree with his assertion of the significance of form – although for that matter he never clearly defines what *form is*. But I am convinced that in all art there must exist a relation – inexplicable and subtle – between the purely abstract in art and the presentation of life; what the Goncourts speak of as the human document. Otherwise it would follow that a portrait or a landscape is not a legitimate art form. That the drama of Goya, the poetry of Botticelli, and Rembrandt's deep insight into human beings are of no aesthetic significance; add no beauty to the abstract element in their paintings.

This I will not and do not believe. But I cannot yet explain this subtle relation in painting between the abstract and the human element.

Why in a great portrait or landscape are we profoundly moved by certain combinations of line and color? All that Bell has to say about "significant form" seems to me to beg the question. Is it not simply because to the artist the response to life itself is revealed most poignantly only through certain forms, lines, and color? Yes, that is very nearly it.

October 30, 1920

Princess Takao has met the Blums. She likes his paintings and has taken a fancy to both him and Lucile. She is organizing a picnic for them in the valley near Papeete which Loti has described with his nostalgic charm.

Papeete, October 31, 1920

We gathered by the banks of the stream well up the valley. The shifting wind carried to us the faintest spray from the waterfall above Loti's pool. Queen Marau joined us later in the morning. The old lady is enormously fat. A large wicker chair had been carried up by her attendants. It was placed beside a great slab of lava rock which served as a table. With some difficulty she was hoisted and squeezed into her chair. The food was substantial. She spared nothing. Raw fish, a platter of boiled shrimp, fried chicken, and roasted pig. She was then served the tender tips of taro roots stewed with salt pork. There followed a starch *poe* of banana and the native sweet potato.

We slept on pandanus mats stretched on the ground. Marau dozed in her wicker chair.

Ever since I was a small boy I have loved Pierre Loti's novels. Perhaps he is merely a second-rate Joseph Conrad. I have been told by his detractors that he spent only three weeks in Tahiti. If this is so then surely he had the reporter's eye – Hemingway's great gift – for the telling of detail. In his *Mariage de Loti* there is a charming vignette describing a similar picnic promenade of the last Queen Pomare; perhaps up the same deeply shadowed valley forest where we now were. The Queen's attendants, as they accompany her, strip from the overhanging branches of the *purau* tree the largest leaves, yet fresh and tender, so that at the propitious moment, absenting herself from her cortege, the old lady, unhurried and provided with an ample supply of nature's toilet paper, might in all comfort loosen her royal bowels.

It is of little consequence how the novelist during his short stay on the island, surely crowded with official and diplomatic banquets, had unearthed this one unimportant function among the many useful properties of the *purau* tree. A true artist, he knew how to place it most effectively in his over-all design.

November 1, 1920

In the afternoon Hall arrived. He wants to spend a few weeks here where he can work with more peace of mind. Nordy has returned from a visit to the States. I have arranged with

Moe to take him as a lodger at a hundred francs a month, some five or six dollars in American money. This will include his wash and breakfast coffee.

November 3, 1920

Hall and I have organized a *himene* among the children, to be followed by an *arearea*. This afternoon the little girls arrived. They wore clean, freshly starched white dresses. Their hair was plastered with coco oil flavored with mint. They perspired with excitement, for the *himene* was to be conducted with strict traditional ritual. We seated the *tamarii* – boys and girls – on the small grass plot before Tauire's house. We served them tea, boiled in an old kerosene can, and bread and jam from the Chinaman's store. This was in keeping with the formalities of the great religious *himene* when the natives gather from miles around and sing for eight and ten hours at a stretch with occasional breaks for refreshments.

Excited by the presence of Mari the Chief, Raiarii the Second Chief, and Tauire our host, the *tamarii* now began to sing. Huura, aged four, took up the lead part – *numera hoe*. Turere, who is perhaps eight or ten, excelled as a *marutete* – in free melodic accompaniment. A dozen of the boys, eight and ten years old, joined in the conventional rhythmic accompaniment of male voices. Little Roo, about three, was too young to sing. Sitting cross-legged with the rest, he bent and swayed his small naked torso and went through all the appropriate gestures of an old chorister.

It was an extraordinary experience. Little by little, attracted by the singing, older villagers joined us, to laugh and then to applaud. The *tamarii,* flushed in conscious awareness of the artistry of their performance, swaying to the rhythm, and cupping their hands to their mouths, put their hearts into the singing.

At length it was over. Hall and I distributed candy and an assortment of some forty small gifts which Nordy had sent down from the States. Our success was unparalleled. The *tamarii* all jumped up and ran to shake hands with us. Then maddened with excitement they rushed frantically through the village, blowing their tin horns. Little Roo was at first terrified with his jack-in-the-box and burst into tears.

November 8, 1920

I drove to Taravao with Mari's old nag, Rorotu. From there I walked twenty kilometers on to Hitiaa. At the edge of the village I suddenly came upon Jerry Blum. Naked to the waist, clad in a red *pareu*, he stood immobile, arms folded, gazing at a breadfruit tree. He seemed in a trance and was not aware of me until I called him twice by name. The native children, playing about him, seemed as little conscious of his presence as he of theirs. But the villagers obviously thought him mad and avoided him. They seemed surprised when I spoke to him as an old friend. Lucile told me that she had been unable to get any help and had to do her own cooking, washing, and cleaning. They both feel surrounded by a vague hostility. It is very sad, for he likes, or thinks that he likes and understands, the natives. Jerry told me that he has done almost nothing. They will return to Papeete and take the first ship back to the States.

The man has unquestioned talent and deep sincerity. Though an excellent critic he is so tongue-tied that at times I can hardly follow him or have the patience to hear him out. He is a sick man, frightfully nervous, argues with Lucile, and at times becomes deeply agitated. I wish I could help him.

November 14, 1920

Hall has left on a copra freighter for the Tuamotu and the Marquesas, or as the natives call it Nukahiva. It was here that Gauguin died. It will be an extended trip, stopping at the small atolls, and he may not get back until March. Nordy has come out with his girl Vahine and has taken over Hall's room, boarding with Moe. He and Vahine have been living together for some time and will get married as soon as they can procure the necessary papers. In the French colonies there seems to be much red tape in such matters. Both he and Hall are thinking of settling with us here next year. I cannot blame them. There is something corrupt and rotten in the atmosphere of Papeete.

Nordy brought with him a copy of their history of the Escadrille Lafayette. Among the photographs I recognized Julian and Charlie Biddle and George McCall, all three my cousins. Poor Julian disappeared in his plane, presumably shot down over the North Sea. Charlie had, I believe, a dozen German planes to his unofficial credit. I showed the photographs to the boys, who were of course impressed.

Nordy says of Tahitian girls: "In many ways I feel as comfortable with them as with Americans. In other ways they remind me more of the French or Russians than of Anglo-Saxons. They have such social tact that one feels immediately at ease in their presence." Yet I have often felt the primitive – sometimes the barbaric – lurking under the surface sophistication. Alone with American or European women they can become intimate, gossip freely, and sometimes form lasting friendships. But in mixed foreign company they at once lose their poise – pride? shame? – and will quickly retire on some trivial excuse. Nordy says: "When they hear the beat of a stick on a kerosene can they become intoxicated. They instantly revert to that moment in history since when, for five thousand years they have not fundamentally changed."

Vahine is a foster daughter of Madame Richmond, the mother of Nohorae and of Hall's little charmer Jeanne. She is an attractive girl, quiet, polite, and friendly. The family belong to that shadowy international society of Papeete – Takao, Pare, and the Salmon clan – who mingle with the literary celebrities, French officials, and occasional visitors who stop over for a few weeks between sailings.

November 16, 1920

Ueri tells us, objectively and quite without prejudice, that among the elders of the village we have none too good a standing. We have a reputation of drinking rum and wine. This has an unfortunate influence on the young people. The *orometua numera hoe* — the chief native missionary — in Papeete has forbidden the singing of *ute* and the weekly gathering of the *taurearea* to dance at night in the mango groves at the outskirts of the villages.

November 19, 1920

High up the Valley of Ataroa a perpendicular shaft of rock rises midway and almost to the level of the mountain shoulders on either side. This rocky tower is split down the middle as if by a stroke of lightning. Ueri tells us that in ancient times the *aito* — hero — Pae lived in the valley. One day to test his prowess he cast his spear at the mountain, splitting it in two. So powerful was his cast that after shattering the mountain the spear continued on its flight to the Island of Moorea before losing its impetus.

"And there it remains," added Ueri, "even to this day."

November 21, 1920

Yesterday we were all trying out tests of strength at Naipu's bungalow. Except for Timo, who is short, heavy-shouldered, and strong as a bull, I found that in the various competitions I seemed as strong as any of the boys. I could chin myself fourteen times; Timo, six. Naipu, who had been on his college football squad, could outrun all of them on a measured distance of about a hundred yards. Of course these were no real tests of strength. In carrying heavy weights Tahitians have an endurance that could exhaust our best athletes in short order. I have seen a dock worker in Papeete packing on his shoulders four sacks of copra, weighing about 450 pounds.

November 23, 1920

When a couple are formally married in Tahiti a ritual takes place, in which each is given a new, joint, identical name. And thereafter this also becomes a uniform manner of addressing, or alluding to either one, followed by *tane* or *vahine* to indicate the sex. Tauire *tane*'s family name was Tevi; Tauire *vahine*'s name was Valunetoi. The children, however, invariably take the father's family name.

November 24, 1920

To Papeete to obtain a passage home. The *Marama* is due to port here during the middle of December. She should reach San Francisco early in January. I have been working very steadily and feel that I need a vacation. I took a boat to Moorea, a three hours' trip. It is sixty-five kilometers about the island. I made the walk comfortably in three days.

Ahura, the daughter of the Chief of Haapiti, where I spent a night, told me this legend of the island. Long ago the men of Raiatea were jealous of Moorea and its beautiful mountain Rotui. So one evening two brothers and their sister came over from Raiatea to steal the mountain. In those days it stood in the center of the island. The two brothers attached a rope about the base of the mountain. The sister, more timid, remained far out in the lagoon holding the end of the rope. The brothers stood at the foot of the mountain swaying on the rope. Gradually they dragged it to the edge of the sea.

Now in Moorea there lived a *vahine tahutahu* — a witch woman. When she saw what was happening she began to crow like a rooster. And the brothers, believing that dawn was about to break, were filled with shame and panic. They feared that they would be caught in the act of theft. So they made haste to escape. But the witch woman was too cunning to let them get away. As they reached the sea she turned them into two rocks, and she turned their sister into a coral reef at the opening of the lagoon.

Walking along the shadowy path which circles the lovely little bay of Haapiti, I saw the two rocks standing up near the edge of the lagoon. Further out the silver water was breaking over the coral reef. Rotui, which once stood in the center of the island, now looms up like a shark's tooth by the edge of the sea.

I spent another night at the house of Tatamata *vahine*, to whom Pare had given me a word of introduction. She told me another folk tale — the sequel to what I had heard in Tautira of the prowess of the hero Pae. On Moorea there is another mountain, Moua Puta — the wounded mountain. Through the summit of the jutting cliff is what looks like the eye of a needle. Hence the name. Tatamata told me that Pae's spear, having split apart the rock tower in the Valley of Ataroa in far distant Tautira, continued on its flight and pierced Moua Puta, which casts its shadow over her small plot of coco palms. She asked me if I should care to see the spear. "It landed in my grandparent's garden, and my father left it to me."

It must be remembered that *tupuna* — grandparent — is a loose designation that might cover several generations. I have no reason to doubt that Tatamata considered the spear a genuine family heirloom. I examined it. It was made of very hard wood, almost black, and was about ten feet long, delicately incised with geometric designs.

Tautira, November 28, 1920

Worked all day on the big canvas. I think continually of the talks Jerry and I had together and of the advice he gave me. I owe much to him. The determination not to abandon a painting until I have put into it all I want to express, and eliminated all that hinders that expression. So now that the canvas is finished I select any part at random and work back and forth into it to the full extent of my endurance. To simplify, to emphasize the rhythm of line and design. To achieve the utmost vibration of color by weaving in complementary tones. Keep at it as long as I can without spoiling it. Every day it is a little richer in color, a little simpler in design. And I have developed a technique of my own which seems to meet my needs: starting in loose washes or glazes, and then working into the glazes with heavier impastos.

Rotui

November 29, 1920

I believe I may have cracked a rib a week ago boxing with Roo. I had bought a pair of gloves in Papeete. (Though a clumsy sparring partner, Roo is very powerful and aggressive. Younger than Raiarii, he spent a year with him overseas in the French army.) This morning I swam under water across the river. About thirty yards. When I reached the other side I spat blood.

November 30, 1920

Working again on the other large canvas of Moe and Paruparu: the banana leaves in the background, the mango tree above. It is uphill work and I suffer, trying to wrestle it from the commonplace; getting into it more solidity, simplicity, tension of line and color. Feeling pretty much like hell the whole time. These two large canvases have taken more out of me than I had realized. Sleeping badly. And at night I drink too much from sheer exhaustion. I don't think I have enjoyed a real night's rest since I started on the second large canvas on October 18.

December 2, 1920

There was an *arearea* last night on the porch of Amok the Chinaman. Terei, her sorrel hair falling to her waist, danced and sang facing her friend Tamaru. The eyes of both girls were clouded with a look of troubled ecstasy which seems to haunt Tahitians when they sing. Among Polynesians, more than any other people I know, music is an outlet for those hidden and mysterious emotions that we feel at times within us but cannot understand or bring to the surface. Happy are those who can dissolve their overcharged longings and anxieties in music.

Finally Terei nestled in the capacious arms of her friend. They chatted together in low tones.

December 3, 1920

The night was heavy and overcast. As Timo and I went up the Vaitipiha to spear eel and shrimp we came upon seven women crouching naked under the banks of the stream. Their smooth rounded backs glistened, emerging from the muddy water. Their dripping hair fused in the shadow of the overhanging bank.

December 4, 1920

In front of the temple stand four poinciana trees, under which the villagers gather on Sunday mornings, dressed becomingly in black. Two of the trees are already in flower. The vermilion blossoms against the dull pink walls and the rusty red of the tin roof. The indigo of the distant mountains.

Nature should always be painted as a background to man. How can we understand one

Women and children bathing in the Vaitipiha

without the other? Nature is the scale that puts man in his true perspective or gives him spiritual significance. I have in mind those two noble prints of Hokusai: "Fuji in a Storm" and another which I also own of his famous waterfall series. Below the perpendicular shaft of the blue cascade's weighty downward thrust can be seen, barely discernible in the artist's familiar splashes of dull reds and greens, the forms of men and horses; insects in the violent life and death struggle of survival; nature implacable, disinterested, omnipotent, sublime.

Yet in other great periods of art man and the physical universe were not always hostile or indifferent to each other. In Renoir's paintings man and nature sing together in sunshine and laughter. And in the finest Chinese landscapes they live together in perfect harmony, friendly and philosophic.

December 6, 1920

This morning at seven o'clock Mari's little baby died. For a month it has been languishing. The remedies of the native doctor at Paea were of no avail. This past week its feeble little hands became slowly paralyzed, its eyes glazed and purple, bursting from the sockets.

Yesterday many of the family and friends gathered in the house to offer prayers. This evening there is to be a *himene* followed by a wake. Pata has gone to Amok the Chinaman's to buy loaves of bread. Little Moo, sent over from Tauire's house, is boiling coffee in the *fare tutu.*

All afternoon Raiarii sawed and hacked at a tiny coffin. Mari sat on his porch in a rocking chair watching him. He wore a dirty white undershirt and red *pareu.* His wife did not appear. She stayed within, weeping. She loved her poor crippled baby.

December 8, 1920

For weeks the surf has slowly been choking up the mouth of the river. This morning it was barely ten feet across and no more than three feet deep in the middle. This afternoon the skies were loosened and the rain fell in sheets. Toward sunset the river rose with incredible speed, two feet in as many hours. It burst over the dike of sand and shingles which the sea has been piling up. Shoulder deep I could hardly fight my way across the channel which a few days ago had been isolated pools of stagnant water.

December 10, 1920

Each evening I pass Taaroa, the mother-in-law of Tetuanui, the *mutoi.* She sits in a scarlet gown under a pandanus tree near her little bamboo hut by the edge of the sea. She smokes her cigarette of native tobacco wound in a bit of dried pandanus leaf. She watches the sun as it dips into the lagoon at Ahui. She is dying of consumption. Like her daughter.

All afternoon the young people frolicked in the river opposite Naipu's bungalow. Teura and brown-haired Urari sported in the water, falling backwards into the river from the shallows, giggling and squealing.

Huura, the daughter of Vahio, stood on the bank under a mango tree. She divested herself of her wet and clinging dress. She drew from her basket a freshly ironed gown of pale blue with a flowered pattern. When she was freshly robed she shook out and combed her hair, copper tinted in the quivering light of the setting sun.

In the gathering darkness some thirty children continued playing in the breakers. Their brown naked bodies began to fade into the foam and black waves. Soon I could no longer see them. I still could hear their shouts and laughter.

December 11, 1920

I have finished another flower piece. This year I can work no more. I shall not paint again until I return next spring.

In the afternoon I walked for the last time about the paths and byways of the village. I stopped to say farewell at the houses of my friends. Tauire and his wife, Raiarii and Marai, Mari the Chief. Ori the grandson of Ori a Ori and his sister Tetia. Taura, the old father of Moe, where Hall and Nordy had lodged. Tetuanui the *mutoi* and Afereti the schoolmaster. Fareau of the *feefee* legs and his children, Paruparu the Impotent and Teha Amaru, the jolly ape-girl. Old More, cousin of Queen Marau, Vahio, and their daughter Huura; Tafaite, crippled by God for his impiety, and his withered old *vahine* Teata, who had cooked for Stevenson. Pepe with his boar hounds and sorrel-haired Terei of the slanting eyes. Nor did I forget the children who had sung so bravely in my *himene*: Turere the *marutete*, naughty Uraponi, matronly Tetuanui, little Huura, and the others.

December 12, 1920

In the evening Naipu and I were invited by Ori to a formal farewell dinner. He is one of the few in the village who shows an awareness of his background, of belonging to one of the great families of the island. He is serious, hard working, a man of weight among the elders of the village. The occasion was marked with the appropriate formalities.

Ori was the only member of the family who sat down with us to eat. The rest of the household stood about watching us or reclined on green and orange cushions spread about on pandanus mats. In a little speech Ori said that his sister Tetia wished to thank me and show her gratitude for the love I had shown to her baby girl Tehiva—"*Ua maururu maua na ta oe aroha na tona aiu na Tehiva.*" I expressed my appreciation of the honor.

Ori then asked if it would please us to receive new Tahitian names. Vahio and Huura, also of high social rank in the village, came in and settled down on the floor among the household help. Ori left the room. He shortly returned and placed before Naipu and me two bits of paper on which were inscribed our new names. Naipu received the name of Tetumatahio: "Tetu * with the observant eyes," because, said Ori, "he sits at his window daily and watches

*There is no such word in Jaussen's dictionary. It is presumably a proper name, but I am ignorant of the significance or allusion.

the passers-by." I received the name of Tetutamaiti — Tetu, the young man, "because I had come more recently to Tautira." Ori admonished Naipu that he must teach his boys from then on to address us by our new names.

Huura, his cousin, the daughter of Vahio, then arose and presented me with a straw hat, woven from *aeho* — a mountain grass — and a small satchel plaited of strips of pandanus leaf. Tetia gave me a long *hei* — a necklace of shells from the Tuamotu.

December 13, 1920

At eight o'clock I said goodbye to Naipu. I waded across the river and left on Owen's truck. Pata, Ueri, and Timo accompanied me as far as Ahui. There Tetua, Mari's wife, came out to wish me a farewell. Tears were in her eyes. She said that she was distressed that she had not been able to prepare me a *tamaa* — a feast — before my departure. She went back to the house and brought me a box of shell necklaces.

Papeete, December 14, 1920

For a week I have been low in spirits and torn at the thought of leaving Tautira. In the evening I walk alone along the quays under the black weight of the mango trees. The warm tropical nights are heavy with many odors: the sweet and wholesome odor of Tahitian women, the aromatic perfume of the *monoi* with which they oil their hair, and the ever present rich, pungent smell of drying copra.

Everywhere about me women. In twos and threes, alone on benches, strolling with their men. Shadowy as the whispers, the low voices and mingled laughter which float by me in the dark.

I am alone and can indulge in the fragrance of my memories: Pihia with the generous mouth and heavy somber brows; Ani of the Chinese eyes and twisted smile; the curving lip of Ave, wanton and depraved; sorrel-haired Terei with her songs and slanting glances; her friend Tamaru, smooth-shouldered, ample, and harmonious; Urari, of the adolescent breasts and slender waist, a dark-haired Venus risen from the waves.

The heavy, silent arms of many women.

And the fragrance of these memories is colored with orange and vermilion, gilding the terrifying fronds of the coco palms and the purple shadowed depths of the mangoes. Silver-crested waves as they break over coral reefs; the pale sky reflected in the rusty copper of the lagoon. Velvet-covered mountains, steel-ribbed, jagged; gloved with moss and ferns and hanging vines.

Warmth, luxuriance, opulence, fertility. Children lying among the dogs on the Temple floor, untroubled in their heavy sleep. Babies sucking at substantial breasts. The rise and cadence of the *himene*. The high nasal pitch of the *marutete*, and that last faint, plaintive, dying E-E-E-e-e-e!

December 17, 1920

At about five o'clock the island faded from sight. To the west the mountains slope gently to the sea. That must be Point Venus, Arue, and the docks of Papeete. And there to the east other mountains slope down to the sea and are swallowed in the sea's haze. There lies the eastern peninsula where the breakers roar against the cliffs of Te Pari and the tiny bamboo huts nestle under the bewildering fronds of the slender-stemmed palms.

Must the race die? Fatu said to Hina: "Man shall die." And Hina answered: "But I created the moon and the moon will live."

Fatu was right. In our world today no primitive race can endure. Even the highly sophisticated culture of the Mayan Indians could not contend against the "civilized" savagery of sixteenth-century Catholic Spain.

The Polynesians have not bequeathed any great legacy to man's development and happiness. No great sculptures; no painting; not even pottery — the humblest and most primitive of the arts. Nature was both too generous and too stingy: it provided abundantly of food and the like so that there was no challenge to ingenuity but it did not furnish the materials — copper, iron ore — necessary for serious creative growth. Their poetry and mythology are chiefly of interest to anthropologists. Their music — which has almost perished — is their only achievement of high artistic excellence.

The Tahitians have revealed to us, however, their one redeeming virtue, a way of life -- perhaps now lost to them for ever — that of harmony, symmetry and form. Early Greek civilization had it too. The archaic Greeks were close to the primitive. Every activity of the daily life of the Tahitians — work, play, music, and religion — is part of a whole. With them life has consistency, formal design: beauty.

But this is not the only reason why I love them. They have charm and grace — not merely physical, but "through-shining" from within. Their spontaneity and gaiety gilds their physical beauty with eternal sunshine.

The Tahitian is a child, with the unconscious grace of a child; impulsive and blithe. Shallow, without ambition, without depth of affection or of enduring sorrow. He lives in the moment; forgetful of the past, heedless of the morrow. "Blessed are little children and the lilies of the field."

NEW YORK INTERLUDE, JANUARY TO JUNE 1921

FOR eight months I had been living in comparative isolation. I had never felt a greater sense of tranquillity and happiness. Almost without interruption I had channeled whatever energy and creative activity I possessed into my painting. The excursions with my Tahitian friends, the study of the language, the moonlight evenings with the *taurearea*, the pulsing rhythm of the *himene* – all these were the necessary recuperative diversions to refresh my spirits and keep me going. They would also have a profound influence on my whole philosophy of art.

I was anxious to arrange an exhibition of my recent paintings in New York but there was another compelling reason for my return to the States. I was eager to obtain a divorce, the decree for which in Pennsylvania became final only after a two years' probationary period. My wife had an equal right to a final settlement. It was arranged through the good offices of a distinguished judge, a friend of both our families, in conformity with the customary perjuries and legal fictions. The procedure had been in accordance with the wishes of my wife and was equally satisfactory to me. I had spent three years at Harvard Law School studying the Euclidean theories and pragmatic hypocrisies of our common law.

"Love" is a persistent virus. Its aftereffects linger on as in a head cold, or are recurrent as with malarial fever. From time to time my sleep was still harried with frustrated longings. When I indulged in solitary drinking bouts I would lacerate what I imagined was an open wound, and wallow comfortably in self-pity. I have no shame in admitting this. We men inherit such weaknesses from our most remote mammalian ancestors.

In New York I was able to arrange an exhibition at the Kingore Gallery during April. On the whole it was well received. I was encouraged by the reviews and the moderate sales. Gerald Kelly of the Wildenstein Galleries – perhaps the finest in New York – promised me a major showing of my work when I should next return from Tahiti. All this gave me added self-assurance. Artists, even the most inspired and successful, have moments of self-doubt and uncertainty.

I had known Hunt Diederich ever since early childhood. We had met again in Paris in 1911. I was then a mere *nouveau* at the Académie Julien. Hunt had already a reputation as one of the coming younger sculptors. He had been commissioned by one of the Rothschilds to do a fresco decoration. Now in New York he and I became warm friends. He invited me to take an apartment in his house at 40½ Barrow Street in the Village. This small and dingy little tenement was a backyard appendage to the main house facing the street. The building was four stories high with a single-room apartment on each floor. Hunt's studio was on the top floor. My studio–living quarters were below him. On the second floor Hunt, his Russian wife Mariska, and their two adorable young children, Kuku and Sonny, all kept house together. The ground floor and the cellar were rented out to two other sculptors, Johnny Roberts and a young Japanese who could do a kabuki sword dance, but spoke no English.

Hunt had charm, wit, irrepressible vitality, and a touch of genius. Our slummy little Greenwich Village home became the occasional gathering place of a number of the younger sculptors, painters, writers, and others of the art world of the twenties. I particularly remember Bill and Marguerite Zorach, La Chaise, Nadelman, Man Ray, Rockwell Kent, Louis Bouché, Bob Chanler, and Harry Kemp the "Greenwich Village Poet." Sam Lewisohn, Léon Bourgeois, and Joseph Brummer would drop in on occasion. I remember, too, that once Van Wyck Brooks, whom I had not met since college days — we had sat beside each other in Economics 1 under Professor Taussig at Harvard in the autumn of 1904 — came in to see my paintings. Later that day we lunched together at the old Brevoort. I remember his saying to me that Heywood Broun, F. P. Adams, Bob Benchley, Dorothy Parker, and others of their group were fleas in his ear. This phrase stuck in my mind, for I had met some of them and considered them important persons. Dear Van Wyck. In his chosen field he could never tolerate standards below the highest.

But Hunt's taste, and mine, was catholic. A smattering of Park Avenue or Harlem intelligentsia would drop in, and such artist's models as the notorious Else von Freitag Loringhoven — the first of the Surrealists and contributor to Harriet Munro's *Poetry* — who later committed suicide in Berlin after her brief success among the perverts who frequented the Café de la Rotonde in Paris.

Mariska in her broodingly perceptive and inarticulate manner was herself a personality. In Paris where Hunt had met her, she had shown originality and distinction as an abstract painter, but after marriage she soon abandoned her career. In his more violent moments Hunt would grudgingly admit that she was his most intelligent and only truthful critic, but that without these redeeming qualities he would have thrown her out long ago. Mariska's tolerance in taking punishment suggested more than a little masochism, and Hunt could be brutal, as at other moments generous and sweet. Mariska had some silent, magnetic, and discerning essence which attracted men of talent. In Paris Albert Gleizes, Modigliani, Pascin, and Hermine David had been her intimates. In New York it was she even more than Hunt who brought La Chaise and Chanler and the Zorachs to 40½ Barrow Street.

Poor Mariska went through life in a daze, exuding an atmosphere of comforting and otherworldly Slavic mysticism. But she could not successfully cope with the demands of ordinary living. I cannot remember whether she could cook or make up the beds; they had a little colored girl who came in by the day. I distinctly recall that Mariska would occasionally lose her children. As she put it with a look of bewildered anxiety: "I cannot remember where it was that I last had them with me."

Some time before I returned to Tahiti Mariska and Hunt decided on a temporary separation. He felt that a vacation on the French Riviera, where she had many friends, would be good for her. A number of us celebrated her departure at a festive and what we hoped would be a propitious farewell party. We accompanied Mariska to her ship and gathered together on the deck to wish her a final bon voyage. The "all ashore" was cried and the gangplank about to be raised. The purser came up and asked to see her passport.

Mariska turned white. She was in a state of shock. She could not remember just where she had put it. It was a critical moment. By an act of hypnotic will we gently tried to relax and reassure her. Slowly it loomed up from the sunken depths of her subconscious memory. She murmured: "I think . . . perhaps . . . I sewed it to my underwear."

We formed a ring about her on the deck. In frantic haste, awkwardly and with bungling fingers, she undressed. Yes, it was there, fastened with many safety pins to her woolen undershirt.

It was the last time I ever saw Mariska. When I returned from Tahiti almost two years later she and Hunt were divorced. Perhaps it was true what he had said about her: that she was his only honest, objective, and perceptive critic. That winter and early spring of 1921 Hunt's creative force had already begun to disintegrate — as Jerry Kelly used to say, "dissipating into the act of living." He was then about forty years old. The last twenty years of his life were turbulent. His death was tragic. Today he is forgotten.

That winter at 40½ Barrow Street I met a group of artists many of whom became warm professional friends. Several of them had exhibited at the Armory Show in 1913. To all of us this had been an inspiration, an explosive force which turned our eyes from traditional nineteenth-century painting to a new world of line, color, and design.

The greatest inspiration to me was not the painters but the sculptors. I was deeply influenced, too, by the preoccupation among many of the younger artists in the crafts: ceramics, iron work, marquetry, batiks, textile designs, lettering, and so on. All this had an effect on me when I returned to Tahiti. Later in Paris I spent two years at sculpture. Ever since then I have from time to time executed and exhibited many of the crafts. I believe this interest in the crafts and the exploration of new techniques were important influences in the development of the modern movement in America during the twenties. Yet as far as I know it has never been seriously considered by the art historians and critics of the period.

Hunt Diederich with all his bombast was an intelligent and cultured craftsman. A client once questioned him on his ability and experience for undertaking a certain commission. Hunt answered him: "I don't think of myself as a sculptor, iron worker, or ceramist. I am an artist. If you have confidence in me as such, I feel professionally qualified to plan your house, decorate it with sculpture or frescoes, and design your furniture." Among the younger modern group in America at that time were others who had the same approach to their work.

There was nothing very original in this conception of the oneness of the graphic and plastic arts with the crafts. The Pre-Raphaelites had preached and practiced it. It was hardly new in Periclean Athens. In Tahiti I had seen it as a way of life – as it had existed among other primitive people since the dawn of history. In the Polynesian languages there are of course no words for the unity and the universality of art, or need of understanding. Their way of life makes art and life one.

Much the oldest of this modern group whom I like to think of as artist-craftsmen was Bob Chanler, no longer young when he exhibited his screens at the Armory Show in 1913. Former sheriff of Dutchess County, portrait painter, amateur muralist, he was, like Diederich, a Renaissance man. Yet both of them – in their physical appetites, their gusto for life, the innocence, sweetness, and generosity alternating with animal passion, brutality, and at moments sheer madness – had perhaps more in them of the Brothers Karamazov.

In New York I frequently saw the Zorachs. Both artists had an itch for the crafts in their fingertips. Marguerite had exhibited with the avant-gardists in the Salon d'Automne in Paris in 1912 and they were both at the time painting in a proto-Cubistic style. It was only a few years before I met them that Bill took up sculpture. Many years later he gave me a bronze replica of a small ten-inch figure of his young daughter Dahlov, which he had whittled with a penknife out of a small piece of wood, one of his first ventures into *taille directe*. And although Marguerite has remained a distinguished painter, perhaps her *magnum opus* is the embroidered bedspread which she took several years to execute for Mrs. John D. Rockefeller, Jr. I know no more intricate and subtly beautiful contemporary work of art in this medium.

At this time, too, Marcel Duchamp was experimenting, painting under glass. Man Ray, who considers himself primarily a painter, has supported himself all his life by his fine portrait photography. His many experimentations in this medium are not photographs at all but craft art done with a camera.

Henry Varnum Poor was the most versatile and many-sided of this group of artist-craftsmen. At the time he was supporting himself by his ceramics, but since then he has shown himself equally proficient in easel painting, watercolors, fresco mural decorations, and sculpture. He planned and built his own house and designed most of the furniture. He has shown the same sensitive and sympathetic understanding for each of these media. It would be hard to say in which he is best. And when he has occasionally written on art it is because he has strong convictions. How rare this is among art critics today! As with his design frugality and clarity are the essence of his style.

I have mentioned a few of the modern-minded artist-craftsmen whom I met during the early twenties. Their explorations in the various craft media culminated in an exhibition at the Metropolitan Museum in 1928. It was organized by Herman Rosse, president of the Designers Gallery. This group included Henry Varnum Poor, Joseph Urban, Donald Deske, Ilonka Karash, and other artist-craftsmen. I was invited to exhibit with them. The designs of the exhibiting artists were executed by different industrial firms. My own exhibits, metal furniture and block-printed linen, were done by Roman Bronze and Cheney Silk.

It was hoped by us that orders would roll in. But the moment was not ripe in America, as it then was in Germany and Paris, for the employment by industry of the creative artist. From then on the artist-craftsman had to make the choice between industrial design and his own creative expression. This brief, but I believe formative, influence of the crafts on American art petered out.

It was not until the late fifties and early sixties that current idioms of design – far different from those of the twenties – became acceptable both to architects and to industry.

Of the many talented artists I met that winter I have said that the sculptors were my greatest inspiration. Yet Diederich's preoccupation was more and more with iron work and ceramics. Zorach was still painting. I knew Nadelman only slightly. Although I immensely admired his work, he seemed to me sunk in a state of neurotic and self-imposed pessimism concerning the role of the artist in contemporary life. It was Gaston La Chaise who first opened my eyes to the meaning of sculpture – three-dimensional form.

Hunt had introduced me to him. We lunched alone together at a little French restaurant in the Village. In his threadbare black suit, flowing black tie, and black felt hat, talking more willingly in French, for his English was heavy, saltless, and without grace, his voice a little grating, he seemed at first a character out of Murger's *Vie de Bohème*. He was quite without humor, incapable of small talk, a dedicated man. Yet at this first meeting I was struck by his absorption in his work, his prophetic faith in his adopted country and the art that it would some day create, his boundless self-assurance, his idealism, and his intolerance of the second rate. All this made a deep impression on me.

Physically La Chaise was an unimpressive man. A medium-sized stocky build that would eventually put on too much weight. His complexion, unhealthy. His face round, and the features without bone structure or character. His lips were a little thin and pinched, the corners slightly drooping with the look of suffering one sees in small children who feel they have been unjustly treated.

I cannot remember whether it was that afternoon or a week later that La Chaise took me to his studio. It was small, cluttered up, and seemed hardly large enough to contain his heroic-sized figure of a woman, perhaps his masterpiece, which now stands in the garden of the Museum of Modern Art. It was still in plaster. He had never earned enough money to have it cast in bronze.

It was here that he first revealed to me the poverty, bitterness, and frustrations of his early career. He had had to support himself and his wife by working as an assistant to Paul Manship. It corroded his being that the other artist, whose work he despised, should have had such enormous success. It is improbable that under any circumstances either of these artists could have understood or felt much sympathy for the other's work. Yet they shared one approach in common. In their craft they were both *ciseleurs* — chiselers, filers, and polishers of bronze. This one trait in their artistic heritage descended directly from Benvenuto Cellini. I have often wondered whether La Chaise may not have picked up a trick or two in Manship's workshop. As early as 1912 Manship was recognized as a consummate and cunning craftsman. La Chaise, at bottom the most generous and pure-minded man, had through adversities been riddled with envy and self-pity.

It can be said of La Chaise that he created one masterpiece in many replicas. Enough for any artist to achieve enduring fame. This was of course the idealization of his wife. Into her image he breathed the bounty, exuberance, and nobility which he found in his adopted country, but could not express in his own way of life.

La Chaise's personal problem — tragedy is too strong a word — was that, as a human being, he never seemed to have developed from adolescence into full-fledged manhood. His art was cast in the heroic mold but he himself was without personal grandeur. His inner core — what was most authentic in him — dwelt among the clouds. On a more terrestrial plane he could never quite hold himself erect. Too often he was subject to small-minded vanities, to unnecessary doubts and petty jealousies. Instinctively generous but haunted by waves of persecution, he was untrustworthy in his relations with others. Sustained friendship with such a man was precarious, yet more than others he craved human sympathy.

All this, I think, is borne out by the relation between Gaston La Chaise and his wife. It is worth lingering on. As her husband became famous she clothed herself with all his prestige and authority. The "Mme." La Chaise was part of it — she was of course not French at all but Canadian. There is no question that he had — how I dislike such bloodless, desiccated terms — a mother complex. She seemed, especially when they were together, to be sucking and squeezing out all his pith and marrow as an adult male organism, leaving him in worldly matters ever more helpless and dependent on her. And in presenting herself as the wife of a genius she placed him in the role which she felt was due him, but which he was incapable of acting out on life's stage. I thought of her as a somewhat obnoxious and quite ridiculous person. But we got on well together. My very great admiration for him as an artist and my gratitude to him for his advice and friendship were the bonds that united us.

Perhaps I am unfair to Mme. La Chaise. He needed exactly what she offered him: a sublimated image of his aspirations and the ministrations of a nursery governess. I believe she gave him whatever happiness and serenity he was capable of enjoying.

40½ Barrow Street, January 8, 1921

La Chaise, looking at Hunt's group of two goats, remarked: "There is the artist who says, 'I shall do a decorative composition'; and his work will always remain self-conscious. And there is the artist like Diederich, who looks at nature and is so moved by what he sees that he achieves style. Style is unconcerned. Never premeditated."

He said: "One must start on a large composition with the ease and joy with which one paints a small canvas or models a little clay figure. I often feel the urge to begin twenty large group compositions. If eighteen of them are failures I can discard them and feel no loss. I must never approach a large work with the feeling that I am cramped. Attack it with the ease and joy of a small sketch."

January 18, 1921

La Chaise and I had supper together at Mrs. Perillo's at 20 Cornelia Street. Veal cutlets and red wine. Later Jerry Kelly joined us. Jerry said: "There are two sculptors in France, Maillol and Bourdelle. And there are two as good in America, La Chaise and Diederich."

I said that it was a tragedy that Hunt squanders his talent. Jerry said: "It is of no importance. Diederich's achievement is of such vitality and style that it is immaterial whether he ever works again."

Kelly is wrong. It does make a difference. But it was a nice compliment and I shall pass it on to Hunt.

It is curious how savagely critical the New York sculptors can be of each other's work. Yet one and all have nothing but kind words to say of Hunt. Paul Manship, one of Hunt's most loyal friends, feels that he has a touch of genius, and Paul is not lavish in his praise. La Chaise despises Manship. The other day Hunt brought Nadelman to see my work. Nadelman also thinks very highly of Hunt as an artist. This one can readily understand. They are both sovereign stylists. But when I ventured to mention my admiration for La Chaise he became incensed. "That sculpture! That style! It is as inflated as a rubber balloon. Without form, restraint, or grace."

Nadelman seemed angry and excited. I said nothing. He continued in bitter words: "The fact that La Chaise has experienced poverty and frustrations has nothing to do with the quality of his work. I too have suffered poverty. I have been a slave all my life, working like a slave. An artist should be free. Not a slave working for a living. Now that I am free I have no desire ever to work again."

February 4, 1921

Egmont Ahrens, who launched and edits *Playboy* on a shoestring, is bringing out a special number of the magazine with my English translations of Moerenhout's Tahitian myths. He came to my studio to select some of my linoleum cuts as illustrations. He shares my enthusiasm for the formal design of our American Indians. He said: "Primitive people took centuries to evolve a style. The son and grandson hewed the stone as did their ancestors.

Art, style, was slowly, unconsciously evolved. Today the artist in his short life's span must accomplish what the primitive did in a hundred, a thousand generations. He must acquire a new technique unknown to his immediate forebears. He must create a style which is not merely the expression of his civilization and period, but also something unique and individual. The creative artist today has set himself a goal far more difficult than that of the primitive artist-craftsman. No wonder that he has more failures."

February 10, 1921

Today I met Jo Davidson. We talked about Jerry Blum. They have been friends for many years. Jo said: "Jerry has no sense of color, line, composition or form. He has only a great yearning, a great tongue-tied desire to express himself."

I was not quite sure whether he said this in derogation or in praise. For Jo is a cunning craftsman and works rapidly. I think he is a little bored with Jerry's fumbling attempts and rough-hewn style. Two days later I happened to visit Jerry and looked again at his canvases. Davidson is clever and had analyzed his friend shrewdly. I could not help saying to myself: "I wonder if Jo would have said the same thing of the paintings of Van Gogh and Cézanne." And again I thought: "He is right. But a great desire is almost enough to create a work of art."

February 20, 1921

La Chaise said to me: "Clay, like charcoal, is fugitive. But with stone one cannot go far wrong if one proceeds tenderly. For one starts already with form, a slab of rock. The greatest sculptors, the Egyptians and Greeks, understood this. They carved directly into stone – *la taille directe*."*

La Chaise inspires me with such an eagerness to experiment in sculpture – wood, stone, or plaster – that I almost feel disloyal to my own chosen profession. As if line and color were inadequate to express form.

February 28, 1921

New York for the first few weeks intoxicates me. I feel bursting with ideas that it might take years to execute. But soon I become exhausted and my energy is dissipated without accomplishment. The hurry and noise affect me as if a hammer were beating at the base of my brain. The city – our whole civilization – seems fevered and unreal.

*La Chaise of course was wrong in what he said about Egyptian and Greek art. The actual stone carving was executed by master craftsmen from the artist's model. The use of wax, clay, and plaster was universally known from the dawn of history. It would have taken Egyptian and Greek artists hundreds of years to complete one of their great statues. But there is much more direct evidence. In the National Museum in Athens is a second-century heroic-sized marble copy of a bronze statue of Apollo, dating from the fifth century, B.C., possibly by Calamis. And the original bronze itself was of course made from a wax model! La Chaise was self-educated. The truth in what he said lay in his instinctive feeling. The *taille directe* which he preached – although in his own work seldom or never practiced – is the surest way for any student to achieve an understanding of form in sculpture.

I am in a bad state of nerves, as a result I suppose of too many drinking bouts of homebrew at Bob Chanler's late into the night. It is good fun and I meet all sorts of people,* old acquaintances and fresh friends: George Luks, Louis Bouché, Guy Pêne Du Bois, Paul Draper in the last stages of moral and alcoholic disintegration, and David Burliuk, in a red hand-embroidered waistcoat, who introduced himself to me as "der Vater des russischen Futurismus." He had gotten out of Communist Russia and had just settled in New York after a year's pilgrimage through China. But is all this conducive to serious accomplishment? I sleep badly and wake up early. I take long walks down along the waterfront; through Little Italy, Carmine, King and LeRoy streets, and across to the Yiddish markets on the lower East Side.

March 2, 1921

I visited Jerry Blum. He, too, seems disorganized and at loose ends with his work. He said to me: "Before I can paint again, I must obtain serenity. For without it art, which is the expression of life, would be meaningless and without form."

Jerry recently held an exhibition at the Boston Art Club. He was asked by the president of the Club, Mr. P., whether he was satisfied with the showing.

"Not exactly," said Blum. "You treated me like a prostitute."

"And just what do you mean, Mr. Blum."

"Well," said Blum, "everyone pats me on the back and says how lovely my things are and how much they are affected by me. That's the way you treat a prostitute. You send her flowers and feel her legs and tell her how much she excites you. But you don't behave that way with a plumber when he comes to fix your bathroom. If you did he might get sore. You just see that he does a good job and then you ask him how much. Painters like to be treated the same way."

Jerry is never dull. But Lucile's life with him cannot always be tranquil and harmonious. Will the poor fellow ever have the peace of mind he so desperately hungers for?

I SAW Jerry again in Paris three or four years later. By then things were going pretty badly. He had total instability and fits of paranoia. He kept accusing Lucile of trying to destroy him. More than once he threatened her. She was desperate and frightened. We all did what we could for him. I remember once — on her and his doctor's urgent advice — spending a whole morning arguing with him; begging him for both their sakes to separate for a while. To go to the country where he could settle down and work in peace; allow both of them a few weeks to see things in perspective. To give their hap-

*James Forrestal, with whom years later I became friendly, reminded me that we first met at one of Chanler's tumultuous midnight parties. Apart from the generous libations of homebrew Chanler provided, this gifted and disordered man had a personality and charm which drew to his home the most diverse and interesting people. Women often loved him. I don't remember, however, seeing any at his nightly gatherings with the exception of his two notorious paramours.

piness one last chance. He broke down and wept.

"George, I know you're right. I'll pack my things and leave for Giverny tomorrow."

He left my apartment, went straight back to Lucile in a fit of passion and told her she was engaged in a plot to ruin him.

I saw Jerry once again ten years later in my Croton home. He and Lucile were divorced. Jerry had remarried. He came to visit me. We sat and talked together. It seemed like old times. I took him around the house and showed him some of my paintings and others of my friends hanging on the walls. Over the years from time to time I had traded my work with artist friends whom I admired: Charlie Demuth, Pop Hart, Sheeler, La Chaise, Diederich, Maurice Sterne, Kuniyoshi, Diego Rivera.

Jerry said abruptly: "I don't see the painting I gave you." I had made an exchange with him, too, the head of a young Tahitian girl for one of his paintings.

I told him that my wall space was limited. I didn't have room to hang everything that I had collected. At that time the Philadelphia Museum of Art had very few of the Paris School and contemporary American paintings. I had made a gift to the museum of the works of several of my friends: Louis Bouché, Diederich, Bill and Marguerite Zorach, Jerry's painting, a fine Zadkine watercolor, and drawings and etchings by Severini and Chagall.

Jerry looked at me angrily. "So you don't like my work and got rid of it." There was no way I could reason with him. He left the house in a fury. I never saw him again.

Shortly thereafter his wife and doctor had him confined. He was later transferred to the State Hospital for the Insane at Orangeburg, New York. It was there that he died ten years later.

Jerry Blum was a Vincent Van Gogh incarnate. That is, he would have been if his very real talent and spiritual sensitivity had had a little something more: a touch of genius.

March 11, 1921

At the Coffee House Club Frank Crowninshield, editor of *Vanity Fair*, introduced me to the Russian artist Soudekine who has done some of the decorations for the Chauve Souris. I asked him how he likes New York. He said: "You cannot work here as in Paris. Paris affects one like a beautiful and enticing woman. *Admettons qu'il y a une belle femme à côté de vous. Vous avez le désir de la baiser* — to sleep with her. That is Paris. One is continuously inspired. But here there is no desire. New York gives me at best a series of premature orgasms. And as for your painters! They seem unable to digest and assimilate their environment. It all flows out in diarrhea. Look at Arthur B. Davies. If only he could have a good attack of constipation!"

All this angered me. It is the fashion now for foreigners who have spent a couple of months here to tell us all our frailties and deficiencies. But there is some truth in what he says.

March 19, 1921

Dinner with George Howe, who is in New York on a short visit from Philadelphia. He is, I suppose, my oldest friend. We first met in 1896 and two years later entered Groton School. We roomed together at Harvard. His conversation always delights and stimulates me. Although his thinking is not profound or deeply original he has a cosmopolitan education and a beautifully trained mind. It never plunges to the depths but skims and flits delightfully over the surface. I spoke to him of my frustrations in New York; of my fears that I am accomplishing nothing.

He said: "It is the leisure moments that produce art. When one fears that one must be working all the time then art becomes a matter of business."

April 8, 1921

Last night Gerald Kelly and I had supper together at Broad and Third Street. Later to Mrs. Perillo's where we drank Prohibition gin with Peggy O'Neil, well known in Greenwich Village society. Ended up at a speakeasy on Sullivan Street at one o'clock.

We talked and talked. Kelly insisted that either New York prostitutes such artists as Speicher, Bellows, and Luks or the sincere artist who must stay on in New York is crushed and withers.

I said to him: "But may not the artist find his inspiration in New York and work alone elsewhere under favorable circumstances?"

Jerry answered: "But does your work show New York's paternity? Rockwell Kent goes to Alaska and his work shows it. You fly to Tahiti and your paintings reveal the inspirations which you found in those islands. What original and significant art has New York produced? Surely not the Ashcan School, the Sloans, the Henris and the Glackens?" *

A load was taken off my mind and the depression of the last few months lifted. I know now that what has left me so weary and unhappy is the subconscious realization that I could never create freely in this city. New York is a great marketplace of art and of ideas. One must treat it as such: as the chicken puts to use the manure pile. Scratch for the grain in the fermenting mass and wander elsewhere to gestate and lay one's egg.

And when this afternoon I met Henry McCarter and Earle Horter and Arthur Carles at my exhibition and felt their genuine faith in me, I knew that my work – the artist's reaction to life – will some day find its audience.

April 20, 1921

La Chaise said to me: "If you are running away from New York you are losing the opportunity to express it in your art. But if you are running after something else, then I advise you to take the first steamer."

*These last two sentences of Kelly's reflected the attitude of our younger modern group toward the Ashcan School and other American realists whose style matured before the Armory Exhibition of 1913.

TAHITI, JULY 1921 TO SEPTEMBER 1922

July 12, 1921

What impresses me most on my return is the beauty of the island, a tapestry of colors, cardboard mountains jigsawed in irrelevant patterns, the massive bulk of the trees, blue-green-black edged with vermilion and cadmium yellow; the surface of the ocean washed in copper, pearl gray, madder, and jade green. The women stir me less but the bodies of the men are archaic Greek. Papeete fills me with abhorrence. It is the ulcer of civilization, festering in the rank deposit of tropical sensuality.

Here in Tautira on the cool river bank of the Vaitipiha my *fare* is almost finished. Naipu had it well started soon after I left for the States. The floor will be poured in cement under the supervision of old Taura, the father of Moe. Pau, the carpenter-missionary, has charge of the construction. I pay him seventeen and a half francs a day, although in Papeete a master carpenter gets as much as forty francs. I pay the other men ten francs and the boys five.

A large living room–studio in the center, eighteen by fourteen feet. At either end a kitchen and a bedroom, ten by fourteen. To give myself a minimum of privacy I shall design and block-print pongee silk curtains for my door and window openings. The walls are of unsplit bamboo, fastened together with native twine; the roof of *niau* – coco palm fronds which the women plait. This will ensure a watertight cover for at least three years. The height of my walls, eight feet; of my ridge pole, fifteen. From my open doorway I look out on the river, the strip of purple sand on the further side, the still lagoon, and the mountains of Tahiti *nui* drifting above the clouds.

Naipu had come in to meet the boat and bring me the latest village tidings. The most interesting item is that he had got himself a *vahine*. More and more, he told me, he became fed up with the waste, disorder, and laziness of his boys. He consulted Nordy and Hall on the matter. They strongly put forward the practical advantages of getting a girl to look after him. However, no self-respecting girl on the island would undertake such a job unless she came as his mate. Although Naipu seems very much a healthy male his attitude toward women is schoolmasterish rather than romantic. The thought of courtship must have seemed absurd to him and a little distasteful. He is the least practical of men, yet he prides himself on his rational and equitable conduct in his human relations. Since his essential purpose was to secure a competent housekeeper and laundress he decided to consult his friend Mau, the manager of the Tiare.

Mau is a character, a man of many parts. His body is heavy and well fleshed, his fingers long and slender. A layer of fat ripples under his velvety skin. But occasionally I have seen him show unusual strength and agility in handling drunken sailors. He has a lazy, friendly, and disarming smile. He has authority among the district chiefs. He will do anything to help a friend and as far as I know expects nothing in return. His background is shadowy. He speaks Spanish well. I asked him once where he learned it. He told me that he had spent several years in South America. There is something a little devious, a touch of the Levantine, about him. It is not surprising that with all these qualities he should stand in *loco parentis*, and on occasion offer his services as a gratuitous panderer, to many of his young friends or to visiting globe-trotters.

As we drove out to Tautira on Owen's truck Naipu filled in the essential details of his matrimonial venture. "Mau proposed to me that I should take on Nanai in a trial relationship. She is a young Chinese half-caste who has been working at the Tiare. Although she is not entirely what I want I think on the whole it is not a bad choice. She is young. Of course she does not know her age — or for that matter her parentage. I would gather that she is in her late teens. And then there is the touch of Chinese blood. Both these points are in one sense against her. I should have preferred a more settled age. And a girl of one of the old aristocratic district families would be more suitable to my standing in the village. As you know the Chinese are looked down on socially. On the other hand she has had some training as a cook. That seems to me the essential qualification. And the half-caste is almost always more industrious and dependable than the pure native stock. Then, too, in making such a choice there is the hazard of venereal infection to be considered. A virgin might seem the solution as far as physical contamination is concerned, but definitely not in acquiring an experienced housekeeper. Besides, I am a little aged to enjoy the thought of wooing a fourteen-year-old girl. As a wife she would be a damnable nuisance. Mau assures me that he has broken Nanai in. I have nothing to fear on that count.

"I have one favor to ask you, Tioti," Naipu concluded. "I am an inept linguist and the villagers seem to have some trouble in understanding my Tahitian. I feel that the success of my relations with Nanai will depend on her having from the start a precise understanding, not only of what I expect of her, but also of the conditions under which I shall provide for her in my will, should she bear me children. Tomorrow I should like you to act as my interpreter in making these points clear to her."

Of course I told him that I should be glad to oblige him. Naipu has considered everything. He is not one to rush blindly into an entanglement.

My first impression of Nanai after Naipu's meager description was favorable. It is not surprising in view of his brisk and businesslike courtship that I found her a little reserved.

But she was not at all intimidated. She seems shrewd and competent. I have a feeling that she will not have too much difficulty in sizing him up. Nor need she be unhappy with him. The Chinese are realists. In looks she is charming. Small, graceful, and lively. A square, kittenish little face — what the French call *minette*. If it were not for the slant of the eyes and the somewhat thin, determined line of her mouth she would pass for a native.

Today after lunch and the dishes had been cleared away Naipu asked Nanai to join us for coffee on the covered veranda. Here briefly and with no attempt at adornment is the substance of what he said to her, I acting as a halting interpreter.

He began by assuring her that he had heard well of her from Mau, and on his recommendation had decided to take her as his *vahine*. Since he had settled in Tautira for good he hoped that their relation would be a permanent and a happy one. She must realize that as his "woman" she would enjoy a position of privilege in the village and he was determined to honor it. Item 1: She was to have the entire management of the household and exercise authority over the boys, Ueri, Timo, and Pata — "whom by the way I am keeping on," he added as an afterthought. She was to report to him any lapses or infractions on their part. Item 2: As the *vahine* of a *popaa* — a European — he would give her credit at Amok the Chinaman's. This would cover current expenses and occasional feminine trifles: kerosene, bread, tea, cigarettes, ribbons, and eau de cologne. But not — definitely not — dress materials, silk shawls, or musical instruments without his express permission. There was a pause to let this sink in. Item 3: He would not bother her with a list of particular injunctions and prohibitions. He would leave such details to be worked out as they cropped up. But there was one absolute prescript. During his absence the large demijohn of rum which stood — uncorked but plugged up with a wad of newspaper — in the far corner of the living room was never to be touched. This was *tapu*. A direct command. And direct disobedience would mean that he would have to get rid of her. Another much longer pause.

I smoothed over this grotesque courting as best I could. The idea that Naipu's boys, who thought of themselves as grown men, should take orders from a girl — and an outsider — was droll enough. But that he should discipline her because his friends helped themselves from an open container of rum — which they probably considered they had a perfect right to do — was sheer nonsense. It was interesting watching Nanai's expression. What he was saying simply didn't make sense to her. She was trying very hard to understand him. Something evidently eluded her. She looked at Naipu and she looked at me, bewildered, but with growing concentration.

Unconcernedly Naipu continued: "And now, Tioti, there is one final subject that I think I should talk over with Nanai. I have always believed in complete frankness in the discussion of sexual relations. I am by no means impotent but after all there is a difference in our ages. Nanai may have an ardent nature. Although I think of myself as a healthy male it is quite possible that I shall not be able to satisfy her. Then again I shall have to return to the States in a few months to visit my sister. I have never been bothered myself by the thought of sexual infidelity as long as two people remain compatible in more important ways. I should have no objection if during my absence Nanai should indulge her normal appetites. In this case, however, I must insist that she confine her choice to one of the boys of my household. My only fear — and a legitimate one — is that venereal infection might result from promiscuity."

I thought he would never stop but I was determined, as best I could, to go through with it. I glanced again at Nanai. There was a sudden look of absolute incredulity, shock, anger. Then over that young, sensitive, yet self-disciplined little face a curtain slowly lowered. No longer bewilderment. She understood everything. There is nothing naive about Nanai. I fancy she takes life as it comes and is determined to get the best out of it. Obviously Naipu was laying a trap for her. First to test her honesty and now her fidelity. I don't think she was overly dismayed. I wondered, as I often have about Tahitians, whether she wasn't saying to herself: "These *popaa* must think us awfully innocent!"

ONE of my fellow passengers on the *S. S. Marama* from San Francisco to Papeete had been Dr. William G. MacCallum, professor of pathology at Johns Hopkins Medical School in Baltimore. Every summer he was in the habit of visiting some tropical island where he could study the various diseases and unique infections which thrive in these climates. His approach toward his branch of the medical profession fascinated me. As a good pathologist he was not primarily concerned with healing diseases and he was completely skeptical of all specific cures. His attitude toward epidemics, infections, contagions, pestilence, and plagues — even toward a simple head cold — was that of a gardener toward a bed of roses. He was only interested in studying the most luxurious blooms. "It is nonsense about 'curing' people," he would say. "The sick man gets well or he dies. We help and comfort him with advice. But the patient's own body is what turns the trick. During the past 2500 years since the days of Hippocrates medicine has only discovered three or four specific cures, '606' for syphilis, thyroid for cretinism, quinine for malarial fever, and salicylicate for rheumatic fever. What else?" *

Dr. MacCallum was anxious to study at first hand some of the diseases prevalent among the less accessible of the islands. Since I found on my arrival in Tautira that my *fare* would not be habitable for another week or ten days, I proposed to him that we take a walking trip about Moorea which I had visited the year before. He was a charming and intelligent companion and I could be of some help to him in ferreting out particularly interesting specimens for investigation.

From his point of view the trip — indeed his entire two months' stay among the various Polynesian island groups — proved to be a disappointment. He said to me later on leaving for New York: "Of course there is a good deal of tuberculosis. What can you expect? The traders brought rum and the for-

*This statement was made by an eminent pathologist in 1922. Since then with the discovery of antibiotics and chemotherapeutic agents, vitamins, endocrines, and so forth many hundreds of specific cures have been developed by modern science.

eign missionaries frowned on the natives' going about naked or wearing the *pareu* — much the most sensible clothing in this climate. At the very least they could have admonished them to change their wet trousers and 'mother hubbards' after bathing. There is too much syphilis and other venereal diseases. But their native cures are not ineffective, for they show very little of the secondary effects. There is the usual run of tropical yaws and here and there a case of elephantiasis. But on the whole they are as healthy a lot as I have ever seen."

The week's excursion with Dr. MacCallum about the island gave me a new understanding — in many ways heartrending — of the needs and plight of the people, something which hitherto their natural gaiety and vitality had hidden from me. On entering a village I would tell our host, in most cases the district Chief, that I had with me an eminent doctor from San Francisco — few of them had ever heard of New York, let alone Baltimore — and that he would be glad to help any who were ailing.

The next morning a dozen or more would turn up and patiently wait before our door. A man with *feefee* legs, so badly swollen that he had to be trundled about in a barrow; a young woman in the last stages of tuberculosis; boys with leg sores, running pus; others with cuts and minor infections. MacCallum would turn to me with a shrug of the shoulders.

"I think it's a mild case of flu" might be his diagnosis. "If I could submit a slide of his sputum for a laboratory test, I could venture an opinion." Or again: "This woman obviously is in the advanced stages of tuberculosis. She may live another year. A better climate, a different diet would certainly alleviate her discomfort. Perhaps prolong her life."

The eyes of the family were anxiously fixed on him. I felt that I could not let him down. Besides I had given him a reputation and I was determined to live up to it.

"The doctor recommends that, since you are running a fever, you should avoid a heavy diet. . . . Never plunge in the river directly after meals. . . . Stay in bed for a few days. . . ." And I would pass out a few simple remedies, aspirin, quinine, soda mints, a laxative. They would go away relieved, happy, full of gratitude. Later they would return and leave their offerings — a chicken, a suckling pig, breadfruit, oranges — in keeping with what they had on hand and the gravity of the illness. "This man," they seemed to say, "is not offering empty words. We trust him."

MacCallum impressed the Tahitians he met with his candor and with his disinterested honesty. He never made the least effort or concession to please or flatter them, either in picking up a few glib phrases of Tahitian or in wearing a *pareu*. Yet one and all during our trip around the island, and later when he visited me in Tautira, showed him a respect and gratitude bordering on reverence.

Temae, Moorea, July 17, 1921

All day the *maraamu* — the southeast wind — blew strong from Papara. In the evening to the *himene* with Tatamata. The Temple lies across a small stream which runs through her garden down to the Lake of Temae, circled by rice fields, swamps, and coco palms. The men, in crimson and indigo-blue *pareu*, sat cross-legged on the earthen floor carpeted with small shingles. Dogs crept in through the breaks in the bamboo walls.

At one end of the Temple the two *orometua* — native missionaries — sat behind a small kitchen table. The light of a kerosene lamp lit up their faces. The elder *orometua* leaned his head on the open Bible and covered his face with his hands.

July 18, 1921

About a hundred yards behind Tatamata's house is an ancient *marae* — a sacred burial ground. In one corner stands a *tii* — stone idol. It is smaller than the *tii* in the Valley of Ataroa, about two feet high and six or eight inches in diameter. From a distance it, too, looks like a phallic index. But on closer examination I could make out a face, eyes, mouth, and what appeared to be an ear. The arms were distinctly outlined, roughly carved in the stone.

One of Tatamata's neighbors, noticing our interest, offered to show us a much larger *tii*. He led us up a narrow *fei* path to a ridge about an hour's climb from the village. Here grew a very old *aito* — ironwood tree. Just beyond the tree and on either side of the *fei* path were two rocks about five feet high, obviously split long ago by lightning or some growing root. These, our guide told us, were *tii ofai maehaa* — twin stone idols. He added that the smaller stones that lay about their bases were *ofai fanau* — a stone litter of young. All about us and covering the ridge was an impenetrable growth of *aeho* — reeds, five or six feet high. From the village below they had seemed a grazing pasture.

July 20, 1921

I asked Tatamata if she could get for me some of the old *paripari* — district songs. In the evening a blind woman came with a nursing child, led by a small boy. She was the village bard. Later came two girls of the *taurearea*, wreathed with garlands of double gardenia. They also carried garlands for MacCallum and myself. They sat and sang *paripari* until late: the story of Pae who cast the spear through the mountain, the attempted rape of Rotui, other island legends.

July 21, 1921

The coastal road ends at Teavaro. We continued along the beach. Under a pandanus tree two men were gouging out a log for a dugout. The line of the hull had already been roughed out with an adz. The day was overcast. Tahiti lay like a black wall on the smudgy sea. When the gray clouds swept down over the Valley of Punuru the island was split in two by the weight of the sky.

At sundown in the villages the small children become intoxicated with the growing darkness. Like excited puppies they scamper about naked, uttering squeaks of excitement and rapture. They love nothing better than being chased and finally abandoned.

The writers on the South Sea Islands, Melville, Stevenson, and Loti, either dwell on the tragedy of a dying race or find their civilization the proper background for drama. Nothing, it seems to me, gives a more false impression of Polynesians. In this respect their character is utterly different from that of the Mexican Indians, of whom in other ways I am constantly reminded. The Mexican has the tragic view of life and a fine inborn sense of drama. But here there is neither drama nor tragedy in their makeup. Not because they are insensitive or incapable of suffering, but because their joys and their sorrows, like a child's, have no more lasting effect on them than April sun and April showers.

July 22, 1921

I asked both Tauire, the Chief of Aferehitu, and his cousin Teura about the fire-walking. Tauire had last seen it, and practiced it himself, at the horse races during the Fourteenth of July celebrating in Papeete in 1898. The lava stones had been heated for several hours on a huge pyre of timber until they were red hot. Cautioned by the *tahua* – the native priest – to look neither to the right or left, he had walked over the stones slowly for perhaps a dozen paces. The soles of his feet had been only slightly scalded. For several years now fire-walking has not taken place in either Tahiti or Moorea, but it is still done in Bora Bora and Raiatea. Teura, however, said that she witnessed it at Faaa in Tahiti five or six years ago. She herself had walked over the red-hot stones.

Tautira, July 27, 1921

Last night with Nanai and Temehau to the reefs after *maoa*. In the moonlight the girls' forms were silhouetted in deep purple against the sky and the luminous mauve depth of Tahiti *nui*. Nanai's slight, rounded adolescent figure. Temehau's ample and generous form which might have been directly taken from Michelangelo's ceiling in the Sistine Chapel. The girls' wet dresses clung to their bodies as they stooped in the white foam to gather the *maoa*.

I had met Temehau a Teae one evening a fortnight ago at a refreshment booth during the Fourteenth of July celebrations in Papeete. She was with her sister Moina. Moina reminded me that we had met the previous year. She asked me if I would buy them both garlands. We drank beer together. Later I accompanied Temehau home. I asked her if she would come and keep house for me when my *fare* was finished.

On my return from my trip to Moorea I took her to a Chinese store. For three hundred francs I bought her an embroidered white silk shawl, a guitar, and an assortment of brightly colored cotton material which we selected together, enough for seven or eight dresses.

Temehau tells me that her father was half-Tahitian and half-Tuamotuan. Her mother was half-Tuamotuan and half-French. She was born in one of the atolls of the archipelago. She came to Papeete when she was twelve or thirteen years old. Here she spent four years at the convent. When she left the convent she lived with a Caledonian from Nouméa at Makatea. She has only recently returned to Papeete.

Temehau a Teae

Temehau is broad in the waist and shoulders, heavily boned and well fleshed, the typical Polynesian. So, too, the beautiful brown eyes and the heavy jaw. The only touch of the Mediterranean is the almost too perfect profile.

I brought her to Tautira a week ago. She spoke little during the trip, but she seemed at ease. At Naipu's bungalow his boys and their friends were silent and watchful.

July 29, 1921

Four of the boys, Teamo, Ueri, Roo, and Nane went up the valley to gather more bamboo poles for my house. Toward sunset they came swimming down the river pushing their load before them. They have crowned their heads with garlands of *maere* – the mountain fern.

July 30, 1921

Temehau has been correcting my table manners. She tells me not to stare at people while they eat. It shames them. Also I must not ask: "Will you have more bread or tea?" This shames them too. I may pass the food, but should say nothing as I do so.

Tahitian women are voluptuous, but neither passionate nor lascivious – what the more sophisticated French speak of as *vicieuses.*

In the afternoons Temehau likes to drag a pandanus mat and two or three of my brightly colored cushions – red, mustard yellow, green – to the edge of the river. Here she contentedly sits under a small cluster of mangoes and gazes out over the lagoon. Sometimes she strums French or Hawaiian airs on her guitar. Tahitians are quite unself-conscious. But like cats they have an instinctive awareness of their own grace. They fall naturally into harmonious poses. Nor do they misjudge the setting and the background.

Her days are full. This morning she carried the wash upstream with Nanai. In the afternoon she sewed herself a red dress. In the evening when the dishes are washed she sits and gossips with Tauire *vahine*, telling her of the life at Makatea, the phosphate island, and of the shameful drunkenness at the July festival in Papeete.

August 3, 1921

My *fare* is almost ready. The roof is shingled with *niau*. Yesterday old Taura finished the walls, binding together the bamboo poles. Today he poured the cement floor. During the noon heat he would call on one of the boys to fetch him a glass of fresh drinking water from my kerosene can container. Before taking it he would strip a leaf from a *purau* tree, using it as a napkin lest he leave a fingermark on my glass.

This afternoon I helped Pau knock together some shelves and cupboards and I started painting them. My furniture – a couple of chairs, an unfinished table, and a kerosene stove – has arrived; everything but the bed which Nordhoff is having built for me at Bambridge's store in Papeete.

Tomorrow will be the *tamaa haamaururu* – the thanksgiving feast – for those villagers who assisted without pay in building my house, as well as for my more intimate friends. Temehau and Nanai have marinated the shellfish. The raw fish and shellfish will be packed into sections of bamboo and fastened with *purau* leaves. Ueri has gone to Naipu's holdings in the *fenua ahiere* after breadfruit, taro, *fei*, and the native sweet potato.

August 4, 1921

The *himaa* — native oven — was filled with suckling pig, fish, *fei*, breadfruit, and taro roots. It was then covered with banana leaves and packed down with earth, so that the entire mass of food would be thoroughly infused and saturated with the scents and juices. I have seen food cooked this way by the west coast Indians of Mexico. Indeed it must have been paleolithic man's only oven. It lingers with us today in the New England clam bake.

At five o'clock the *himaa* was opened. The guests had already begun to arrive, some fifteen in all. Since it was pouring rain we ate indoors. Banana leaves had been spread on the floor as a table covering. The guests sat on pandanus mats. Teha Amaru and Arai *vahine*, the mother of Uraponi, had woven garlands of gardenias for the guests. Timo and Ueri served them with generous portions. *Poe* of *iita* — papaya — had been dished out on *purau* leaves. The more substantial food was piled in wooden bowls. The guests helped themselves with their fingers to raw shrimp, boiled shrimp, raw fish, fried fish, fish baked in the *himaa*, chicken stewed in coconut sauce, and roasted pig. They drank hot tea. For those who desired it there was a demijohn of native rum and bottled wine.

As an elder of the church old Taura seated himself and offered prayers. He then emptied a straight tumbler of rum. In keeping with the island proprieties he ate steadily without talking. So as to show his appreciation of the food he sucked in noisily, after dipping choice morsels of raw fish into the bowl of *miti haari* which stood beside him. Taura is one of the few remaining "gentle and noble" Tahitians that one runs across in the pages of Cook, Bligh, and Moerenhout.

Some forty of the villagers stood outside peering in through the door and windows. The rain continued to pour down. Inside the party was getting out of control. Tetua had become very drunk. She was angrily abusing her husband, the Chief. She accused him of pinching Tuefa's behind and of carrying on an affair with her. Tuefa, a friend of Arai *vahine*, and one of the more notorious village matrons, had slipped into the house on the pretense of helping the boys replenish the empty platters. A few moments previously Mari had slyly whispered to me that he did not consider her a seemly person to be mingling with the guests. Finally goaded by Tetua's tonguelashing he lost all dignity. I was afraid he would come to blows with his enormous and outraged wife. Old Taura was the only one of my guests who had any effect in sobering either of them. He shook the little Chief by the lapels of his white starched drill uniform, upbraiding him for his loss of self-control. I finally persuaded the couple to leave the house. I kissed Tetua and warmly shook the Chief's hand. I felt that an impartial gesture of friendship was in order. Later I was told that the two continued their *peapea* —

wrangle — all night. Tetua went to sleep with her relative, Tauire *vahine*. Mari roamed up and down the village looking for her. Finally he stumbled into the house of Ori to sleep off his hangover.

Only old Taura remained unperturbed. He continued to eat heartily. From time to time he would exhort the other guests: "*Eiha maniania. Inu noa* — Don't chatter. Just drink."

August 6, 1921

Little spider-legged, freckle-faced Roti is one of the bravest choristers of my child *himene*. Today as I was planting ferns about my *fare* she came up and presented me with the half of a roasted *mape* nut. On other occasions she will bring me a rose or a yellow hibiscus. In return I offer her a slice of bread, spread with jam. Her dress is made of an old flour sack which she wears as an improvised *pareu* drawn up under her armpits. When she had finished eating she bade me a "prosper in the true God," and galloped down the road.

I could write a chapter on Tahitian chickens. They are only eaten on Sundays or feast days. They run wild in the bush, roost forty feet off the ground, and will take to the water if cornered. The usual way of catching them is to stone them to death after a prolonged chase. If one is taken alive the boys pluck out a tail feather and with it pierce the brain pan through the small opening below the skull. The chickens provide for themselves like wild pheasants.

August 8, 1921

Today I started painting. As the boys go by on their way up the valley to gather *fei* or fetch drinking water they stop and stare in silently through the windows. This gets on my nerves. I shall make block prints on my curtains — one from a sketch of Nanai and Temehau as they gathered *maoa* on the reefs.

August 9, 1921

Every evening she walks upstream to bathe where the water is clear and fresh. She wears a scarlet *pareu* wrapped below her breasts. Her back is massive and golden. After her bath she changes into a clean dress, perfumes her hair with *monoi*, and sticks a flower behind her ear. Supper finished, we lie on a pandanus mat, our heads on orange cushions. I watch the *veri* — harmless but stinking centipedes — crawl over the cement floor, attracted by the lamplight.

Tonight she and Ueri have gone to visit Arai *vahine*. It is against the village proprieties for her to go out at night without me. But I must have time to myself to work and read. I don't see why she should sit here alone and bored. I trust Ueri and Timo with her. I trust her, too.

August 10, 1921

This evening we fared well. Ueri brought us a bag of shrimp and a string of *orare* – a small fish of the mackerel family. For dinner we had *ia ota* – raw fish – and fried fish. Ueri, like many Tahitians, is sober in his habits. In the morning instead of coffee he takes water sweetened with a little sugar. In the evening only tea and bread. He neither smokes nor drinks. Yet I don't think of him as ascetic. He likes girls in a passive way. He is fastidious in what he wears and has a dry and caustic sense of humor.

August 12, 1921

Six months ago after I had left for New York Naipu's house was roofed over with pandanus. A pandanus roof will last from seven to ten years whereas a *niau* roof of coco palm leaves begins to deteriorate after three years. At the urging of the two *orometua*, Pau and Paea, the village decided to lay the roof by *tauturu* – communal voluntary help. This was a gesture of gratitude in recognition of the medical assistance he has given, but even more because they are proud to welcome him as a leading member of the community. The *tauturu* was debated for a month at the weekly *himene* and at the Temple, which functions as a New England town meeting house as well as a place of worship.

Naipu had contracted for two thousand strips of pandanus, plaited by the women at a franc a leaf. At the roofing the two *orometua* took precedence, seated at a table which had been carried down from the Temple. About a dozen men worked on the roof, each with two helpers below who passed up the plaited leaves.

There had not been a village *tauturu* for a private house in many years. Naipu was naturally very pleased. He declared that he would give a feast for the helpers. Two pigs were killed and forty kilos of starch were boiled for the *poe*. Detachments were sent up the valley for *fei* and breadfruit. It took two days to lay the roof. Each evening about sixty men sat down to dinner. It cost Naipu far more than if he had paid for the roofing.

Before the tidal wave in 1908 there were many native houses, some built in a circular form. Today his is the only pandanus roof in the village.

Sunday, August 14, 1921

I watch my flower seeds come up. I have never kept a garden. It seems a miracle to see the frail green sprouts burst their way through the black soil. These delicate struggling shoots, as much as any of man's creations, are the expression of life, of an idea, of whatever is the soul of man – or God.

This morning I was planting sunflower seeds by the edge of the road. Temehau and Nanai were both indignant. Nanai told me that seeds planted on Sunday would never grow. I answered her that since it was God's morning the seeds should grow better than on any other day. But she only threatened to pour hot water on them if they should come up. She added sententiously that on the day of rest I should be praying in the Temple rather than working in the field.

Temehau and Nanai seated in front of Tioti's home

August 15, 1921

Finished tonight block printing my window curtains. It has taken me a week to do it, using a kitchen spoon to press the ink into the pongee silk from the linoleum block. I have also started to decorate the two terra-cotta water jugs which I bought in Papeete.* They must have been turned on the potter's wheel somewhere on the Mediterranean coast. I have seen the same designs among the archaic Greek and Mycenaean earthenware in Roman museums.

In decorating these jugs I am conscious of the influence of the great Hopi Indian pottery designs. So much closer to the spirit of modern design than the classic or even archaic Greek.

August 17, 1921

Paddled with Nanai and Temehau to Naipu's bit of land in the *fenua ahieri* after oranges. One girl will climb up the tree and pull down the fruit with a long pole. The other stands below to catch the oranges lest they break. The girls are like monkeys in the trees. Perched sometimes forty feet above the ground – for the oranges ripen high up in the dense groves – they rarely cling and either stand erect or sit on a branch not much larger than my thumb. All Tahitians have a bit of the monkey in their blood. They climb, as they swim, seemingly without having to learn.

Coming home the wind blew strong. Dugouts laden with coconut drifted by. Some had raised a palm leaf as a sail.

August 21, 1921

Princess Takao came out for the day bringing with her MacCallum and a Fijian chief. Mari came down to invite Naipu and me to a formal lunch. The weather had threatened rain but the sky now cleared. Mari told me that many years ago when old Queen Pomare sailed out to Tautira to visit Ori a Ori the rain clouds would divide to let her pass through. It was her habit to send the escort on ahead so that the entire convoy remained dry.

*I used a confessedly meretricious technique which Hunt Diederich showed me: India ink painted on raw earthenware. Except to a professional ceramist this can easily be taken for an unglazed mat firing. Once in 1923 Sam Lewisohn came to my studio at 40½ Barrow Street to see my recent Tahitian paintings. He admired two large garden urns of Diederich's, decorated in this manner. He asked if they were for sale.

Said Diederich: "You can have the things for the price I paid for them. Faked glazes. Out of doors they will wash off in a couple of years."

Later I teased Hunt: "You spoiled a sale. Sam really liked them."

Hunt replied: "Not as dumb as you think. Lewisohn is now convinced that I am honest. He also believes I'm naive. I have reason to think that he is interested in my large group of goats in bronze, and I shall give him a damned stiff price." How poor Hunt enjoyed making himself out shabbier than he really was.

A year or two later a small plate of mine, similarly decorated, was submitted by the Ferargil Gallery that handled my work to a jury of the Chicago Art Institute. It was sold and received the Institute's Logan Medal for Decorative Arts. I mention this merely to indicate the general ignorance and low standards in the field of ceramics during the twenties. Curiously enough, notwithstanding the infinite greater sophistication today, both artists and critics seem to prize falsification and adulteration of time-honored media. I am referring of course to Pop Art, *et al.*

"She was a *vahine mea huru e* — a very strange woman," said the Chief.

During the past month or so Naipu has been troubled by painful swelling of his forearms. The villagers whisper that it is because he built his *fare* on a former sacred *marae* and that he has contracted *feefee* — elephantiasis. In a play on words, instead of Naipu, they now call him Maipu — the sick man — behind his back. He took the occasion of MacCallum's visit to show him his arms. MacCallum was puzzled but seemed interested. He suggests that when Naipu returns to America he stop at Johns Hopkins for a thorough clinical examination.

August 25, 1921

I cannot persuade Temehau or Nanai to clean eel. Nor will they eat them, asserting that they are disgusting animals. Yet they show no distaste in preparing and eating devilfish and *varo* — sea centipedes. Nordhoff tells me that formerly eels were *tapu* for women. Although this prohibition was forgotten generations ago the former *tapu* probably explains their repugnance for the eel.

August 28, 1921

An artist needs courage, intelligence, passion. But he must wait for inspiration. I have often felt that he is merely the unconscious medium for receiving Truth — the closest definition I can think of for the Absolute, the Godhead. I have been reading Anatole France:

"Jamais l'homme ne choisira. Il n'a pas le droit de choisir. Ce qui choisit pour lui c'est le milieu qui le pénétre, l'atavisme qui le soulève. Au fond vivre est sa fin et créer son moyen de vivre. Qu'il goute l'illusion divine d'une destinée définie ou l'ivresse de l'anéantissement dans la substance illimitée, il reste l'homme, le seul être qui ait le pouvoir prodigieux de projeter hors de lui-même pour son accroissement et sa foi l'image de son univers."

The artist should beware of wealth. The more intelligent he is, the more possessions and irrelevant diversions suck up his energy. This is too precious an asset for him to squander.

September 10, 1921

Naipu is shortly to leave for the States on a prolonged visit. Both Nanai and Ueri will take their meals with me. Nanai will continue to stay in Naipu's house, however, Ueri with his family. With the exception of native friends I shall be quite alone for many months. The nearest European is the old Corsican peasant Pietri, who lives with a Tuamotuan woman ten kilometers away. My nearest intellectual companion is a long day's journey distant in Papeete.

Recently Naipu negotiated the purchase of a new net. It will be jointly owned by himself, Mari, Vahio, Ori, Pau, and a half a dozen others. The net was ordered from the States at a cost of eight hundred dollars. It is four hundred yards long, nine yards in depth. The *taiate* — partnership — will pay two hundred francs for the truck haul into Papeete. Half the remainder will go to those who assist in the catch, half to the *taiate*. This year fish have been plentiful. In one haul Owen grossed four thousand francs. Naipu was recently honored with a feast, partly to wish him Godspeed on his journey, partly in gratitude by the members of the *taiate*.

September 20, 1921

The few starts I have made during the past two months in block printing, the decoration of jugs, above all in sculpture, have disturbed and modified my ideas. A greater insistence on flat, two-dimensional design? To wed sculpture and painting? I feel more adrift than ever before. Yet I had rather drift and experiment than continue down a path which I cannot follow with conviction. Probably during those five months in New York my approach to my painting changed more than I was aware of.

September 28, 1921

Uninterested, dissatisfied, depressed with my recent work. Yet fermenting, bubbling over with half-formulated and undigested ideas. Perhaps I have been wandering up blind alleys, probably attempting too much: colored block prints, monotypes, silverpoints, drypoints of Naipu and Nanai, four paintings, the head of Temehau cut in stone,* and a clay bust of Nanai.

October 1, 1921

It is the breadfruit season. Daily toward sundown along the black sand beach across the river the boys return from their holdings in Ahui. They slip down the steep bank carrying their heavy burdens on poles slung across their shoulders. Stripping off their clothes they lay them in their pandanus hats on top of the breadfruit. Crowned with hibiscus flowers or sweet mountain ferns, they come swimming across the river, pushing their green harvest before them.

October 5, 1921

Maria, the toothless, simple-witted sister of Timo, confided to Arai *vahine* that her father, the cringing, disreputable old widower Temeheu, has been cohabiting with her and her two sisters. Finally the girls had the gumption to leave his house and have been taken in by friends or relatives in the village. Maria is staying with Arai *vahine*. Ueri told us that the scandal was even gossiped about in Papeete. Of course there will be a ripple of indignation in the village. All will agree that it was *ohipa mea ino* — a bad business. But soon the incident will be forgotten.

Today as we sat at lunch old Temeheu passed by. He waved to us his "God be with you." I was taken aback when Ueri and Temehau both returned his greetings with the ha-

*I showed this sculpture to La Chaise on my return to New York in 1922. He persuaded Scofield Thayer, editor of the *Dial*, not only to reproduce it in the magazine but also to use the reproduction as the monthly poster announcing the next issue.

The stone head of Temehau

bitual "Come in and eat." I asked Ueri how he could lower himself by even nodding to such a disgusting old man, let alone inviting him to join us. Ueri answered that it would be *aita mea nehenehe* — improper — not to do so, and that he would feel ashamed — *haama* — not to answer the greeting. I asked him whether he did not consider it a greater *haama* to commit incest. Ueri seemed a little confused but remained stubbornly silent. I think both the girls agreed with him.

This attitude is revealing. Tahitians are very sensitive in their discernment of what is right or wrong under different circumstances. But since their reactions are instinctive and direct, never theoretic and abstract, they use one word — *nehenehe* — to cover many tangled emotions. Monseigneur Jaussen gives the definition of *nehenehe* as "beau, joli, élégant." An equally current meaning is fit or proper. And since there are no comparatives or superlatives in the language, Tahitians also use the word to mean the best, the shortest, the only, etc. For instance: The best, the shortest, the only way over the mountain is simply the proper — *mea nehenehe* — way to travel.

Ueri was quite aware that neither incest nor bad manners are elegant and proper. What was it, however, that caused his basic confusion about the relative degree of impropriety involved? I think this goes to the essence of the primitive's reasoning in sizing up what is right or wrong. He is not primarily concerned with the act itself but with the reaction of the community. An act is good or bad, but its condemnation is never a personal but a village censorship. Just so a child stealing an apple is cheerfully innocent until he is caught. And I suppose in this case the immediate shame of ignoring a greeting on a village street outweighed the more serious offense which was gradually dissolving into the impalpable murk of village gossip.

The primitive not only thinks and passes judgment, he makes decisions, commits himself to *actes de volonté*, on a mass rather than on a personal level. One can say that he harbors a personal doubt about his own adequacy and takes comfort in the strength of the crowd — the herd instinct of the adolescent. Often of an evening, while I am reading or working, a dozen of Ueri's or Timo's friends stop in on a visit. They sit about on the floor gossiping of the day's events. It will be getting late. Several of my guests are sleepy and would like to leave. Do they get up and go? Never. One of them will shyly murmur: "How about it? Shall we go?" Silence. Then a restless shuffling. They look round at each other to appraise the situation. After a moment someone else may suggest a little more boldly: "Well, let's go. Come on." More shuffling and side glances seeking encouragement. At length they subconsciously sense that the "ayes" have it. They arise in a body, wish me a goodnight, and troop together up to the village.*

* On this and the previous paragraph I quote a comment by anthropologist Robert C. Kiste: "One of the basic values of primitive man is usually a great emphasis upon the maintenance of good social relations between all members of the community. . . . It often appears to the European that primitives make impractical decisions in order to stay in line with the 'herd.' It is all a matter of values and the basic premises upon which the society is based. This is not indicative of a different type of mentality."

October 6, 1921

Each morning my bread is delivered from Amok the Chinaman by his three diminutive half-caste children, Asa, Pahero, and Tapu. They are never separate. Solemnly and in single file they enter my house and shake hands with Temehau and me. Asa the senior, aged six, has a Chinese name but is pure Polynesian. He is the knave of the three, up to any devilment, and will boldly ask permission to climb one of my trees after mangoes. Pahero and Tapu, proud of their Tahitian names, are in looks pure Chinese. Tapu, the youngest, wears a mask of frozen solemnity. He looks like some legendary warlord, dour and glowering.

October 9, 1921

She lay with her head on an orange cushion in the flooding moonlight by the edge of the river. "And is there moonlight in America?" she asked. "And is there snow?" And again, slowly taking it all in: "Is Amsterdam in America?" She stores up nuggets of information as a magpie gathers shining coins. She will gossip about all these things later with Arai *vahine*.

October 10, 1921

Old Taura, on his way by my house, complimented me on my ripening melons. "But do not show the boys the fruit," he cautioned, "for they will return to look at them, and if people are continually watching the melons they cannot ripen." Ueri also informed me that if you point your finger at a melon it will wither and fall off the vine.

October 12, 1921

Mary Cassatt once said to me: "An artist should work in drypoint to study line. The medium is so cold and tight and hard that one cannot cheat. It is either good drawing or bad." I feel the same way about a silverpoint. Its line is quite without color and atmosphere. Charcoal, on the other hand, is the painter's medium par excellence. No artists have used charcoal with the mastery of the great Venetians – Titian, Tintoretto, and the others – the first great colorists and painters of atmosphere.

October 14, 1921

From my beloved Anatole France in his *Opinions de M. Jérôme Coignard*: "Les vérités découvertes par l'intelligence demeurant stériles. Le coeur est seul capable de féconder ses rêves. . . . Si l'on raisonne, on ne s'envole jamais."

October 16, 1921

Temehau said of Nanai, who has become attached to Naipu – all the more since he left for the States: "Elle pleure pour lui. Elle en a tellement pitié." In using the expression "avoir pitié" she had inadvertently colored the word with the charming ambivalence of the Tahitian *aroha. Aroha* means to express one's love for someone – either in joy or in sorrow, for the child smiling in one's arms or the husband mourned in the grave.

Papeete, October 18, 1921

Aoni, the Chinese storekeeper who married Ueri's sister, is driving me back to Tautira. Waiting for him at the Tiare, I lay on the bed alongside dear old Mau. Brown-eyed Tatamata sat beside him. The two of them engaged in salacious reminiscences.

"Tatamata," said Mau, "is a beautiful woman. In the days of her youth she wasted no occasion which her many lovers presented to her."

Tatamata, still in her golden prime, enveloped Mau with the warmth of her brown eyes and gently stroked his enormous belly, "*Haavare* — he lies," she answered.

Mau asked me how Nanai liked the village life in Tautira. "You must never scold her or she will sulk for days. If she needed a correction I would give her a sound cuff, but later I would always caress and fondle her."

"A woman would rather be slapped than continually nagged," added Tatamata from the store of her experience.

Tautira, October 19, 1921

Naipu and I both dislike Roo, yet he is the idol of the *taurearea*. Like many of the young soldiers who saw action in France he is spoiled, overweening and ill-bred. He will enter my house as if he owns it, all unction and smiles. He affects a slick familiarity, a suggestion that he and the *popaa* — the whites — have a bond in common not shared by the others. He helps himself to my cigarettes without a by-your-leave, and, I fancy, to a swig from the demijohn when my back is turned. How different from the hearty, independent, and sincere greetings of the older generation.

Yet all Tahitians, even the most corrupted, though they have lost their dignity, have retained their charm. Only once have I seen a drunken native who was ugly. When the whores of Papeete drink they garland themselves with flowers, dance, and sing. As a race they are the cleanest, the most fastidious people I have ever known. They cannot bear to swim in the ocean without later washing themselves in fresh river water. Their strongest epithets of distaste or disparagement are the words of unpleasant odors — such for example as "He smells like an old man," or "a goat," or "a Frenchman." This last, I suppose, because the French are the only people they know who have actively interfered with their hedonistic enjoyment of life — having even enlisted them in their armies to fight the Germans.

October 20, 1921

The days and nights are so beautiful that the whole world seems to throb in a rhythmical cadence of heat and glory. Does beauty affect the soul of a people or are their senses deadened as they become saturated with it? The response to beauty should be an active creative impulse and not a passive reaction. The sailor becomes accustomed to the roar of the sea waves and cannot sleep without it. Nor are the peasants of Assisi or the guards of the Louvre particularly art conscious.

I remember once extolling the grandeur and beauty of our American landscape to a Russian lady exiled in Paris. She said to me: "We have little physical beauty in Russia. Our plains are monotonous and flat. That is why our people must seek spiritual beauty in their own hearts. Our peasants are poor and often hungry. But they never starve themselves of spiritual light."

October 21, 1921

Tu, the diminutive son of the late honored Chief Faanevaneva, has the reputation among his playmates of a buck and a *taata hauti* — a ragger. While I was at work this morning painting he appeared at the head of a delegation of little girls and boldly asked me for some of my zinnias. Uraponi had put him up to this. If she thinks it more discreet she will not ask for a favor herself, but loudly whispers in my presence to someone else to do it for her. Tu returned this afternoon, again followed by half a dozen small girls, and presented me with two green mangoes. I graciously refused to accept more than one. It was hard and bitter.

October 23, 1921

I have never known a people as moody as Tahitians. For two days Ueri has been sulking — *faa riri*. This time he is offended with Temehau who, he says, broke his shrimp spear. His *faa riri* follows an invariable pattern. He will not speak to either of the girls or sit down at table with us. He refuses to wash the dishes. As the ultimate proof of his misery he has now gone on a prolonged fast, asserting that he is not hungry. This self-mortification and gloom will last for four or five days. Then the *faa riri* is over for no apparent reason. Nanai, as a rule the gaiest and most sensible little person, is herself subject to similar morbid humors.

October 24, 1921

This evening as we sat down to supper Timo and his girl Maraia came to pay us a formal call. They are betrothed and are shortly to be married. I have given her a pale blue dress as a wedding present. Maraia is a *fetii* — relative — of Temehau. Like Temehau, Maraia is part Tuamotuan and lived in the islands when she was a child. Maraia sat cross-legged on the floor while we ate. Her long hair fell from her shoulders. She gently stroked the horny corrugated soles of her large flat feet with her slender pliant fingers. I knew that if I asked her what she was thinking about she would answer after a pause: "*Aita* — nothing." Yet she is not stupid and she has plenty of common sense.

Timo has been openly living with Maraia ever since Naipu left for the States. By Tahitian mores this is accepted as marriage, just as it is by the common law of Scotland and Pennsylvania. Here, as elsewhere, marriage in the church is merely a ceremonial ritual. But as a rule it is considered fitting only when the bride is a virgin. Occasionally, however, man and wife are remarried in the church.

One would think Timo and Maraia an admirably suited couple. Alas, Timo wants more than estimable qualities in a wife. "Yes, she is all right," he said to me the other

Ueri on the veranda of Naipu's bungalow

day, "but she never talks. I prefer a girl who can *paraparau* — make conversation — like Temehau. I like Maraia, but I don't want a wife at all just now. If I marry there will be no more *arearea* — merrymaking. This has not been my work — *Aita tau ohipa.* It is the old man's doing."

Poor Timo. Temeheu got word that he had been living with Maraia. That was the old man's chance. He would marry them, build them a *fare*, and Timo would have to leave the fleshpots of Naipu's household. But Timo was recalcitrant. Temeheu threatened that he would complain to the *pope* — the Catholic priest — in Taravao. The *pope* drove out to Tautira, told Timo that he and Maraia were living in sin, and finally frightened them into submission. So now they are both living in Temeheu's house while a new *fare* is being hastily built for them in the *fenua ahiere*.

I thought: "They will never have their wedding. But what difference does it make? And the church has had its gratification."

October 25, 1921

Pepe, a recent arrival from Papara, is staying with her cousin Arai *vahine*. She is popular with the youths of the *taurearea*, several of whom, it is rumored, have shared her charms. The women pronounce her *teoteo* — proud — and it is believed that she pilfers money. But her limbs are long and slender and her back is dimpled. Most Tahitians have large, flat, heavy feet, like all those who go barefooted from childhood. But hers have the sensuous delicacy of a Venus of Cranach. Her lip curves upward and her fingers taper at the ends. Her eye, however, is none too steady and the corners of her mouth are hard. Her body is as free and careless as a dryad's. But when our eyes meet there is for one brief flicker the calculated appraisal of the prostitute.

October 27, 1921

Although Tahitians are moody, easily hurt, and extremely sensitive to any slight, they are curiously indifferent about being personally discussed in a public gathering. The other evening Ueri and I were deliberating on the advisability of sending Maraia to Papeete for an examination by Dr. Cassiau. Might she have contracted gonorrhea from her *tane*? It happened to be Sunday evening. A number of friends dropped in on their way to the church *himene* — boys of the *taurearea*, Uraponi and her cronies, Maraia and her sisters. One would have expected someone to suggest postponing the discussion. But no one except myself showed the slightest embarrassment.

October 30, 1921

To bed last night at eight o'clock but wakened at six by the shouts from the *upea* — the net. The members of the *taiate*, their friends and family, were making their first haul. With two nets in the village now there is keen rivalry between them. Without waiting for coffee I swam across the river and joined the gathering. Two hundred yards up the shore hung the large black outrigger waiting for the fish to settle and begin to circle.

Now the men bend their backs to the paddles and drive the outrigger about the school of fish, as they drop the net. The net has been cast and the outrigger is coming in. Ueri sits in the stern, his head garlanded with a wreath of flowers. As the outrigger rises on the crest of a wave another comber rolls over the stern. The three boys leap into the surf and guide the great heavy *vaa* to the shore.

The old men and women are hauling at one end of the net, the *taurearea* at the other. A dozen swim about the perimeter of the net, diving below to see that it does not get entangled on the bottom. I am still cold from my swim across the river and work with them in the warm salt water of the lagoon.

October 31, 1921

It is still dark. In the full moonlight sixty of the *taiate*, men, women, and children—have gathered on the beach waiting to string yesterday's catch for the Papeete market. I rest on a mat spread for shelter to the lee of the large net, strung out to dry on *purau* poles. Some women and children sleep, their heads wrapped in towels. Others gossip. Temehau sits beside Tauire *vahine*, humming a Manihiki song which she had heard in Makatea.

The lights of the truck appear across the river. The men run down into the water, their backs and arms darkly silhouetted against the full reflected light of the moon. When the fish are all drawn from the small receiving net the women's work begins. They have stripped the bark of thirty *purau* saplings. They will string the silver *orare* in sixes and heap them in piles of ten. Three hundred strings for yesterday's morning haul to be sold at seven francs a string in the Papeete market.

The black sand. The gray clouds, "mackerel sky and mare's tail," a sweeping arabesque against the moonlit firmament. The dark bodies of the men as they leap about in the water. The women, as they bend over to string the silver fish.

Later the same day. The members of the *taiate* have spread a feast in celebration of the first catch of their net. The *taurearea* have gone up the valley after breadfruit; others of them to the mountain trails for *fei*. The girls have gathered flowers. On the plot of lawn, hedged with hibiscus and camelia, the women have spread banana leaves on which they will place the bowls of *poe*. Four men stagger under the weight of the wooden *umete* which carries the breadfruit, baked in the native oven. Four others carry a second *umete* with the sauce of *miti haari*. They will dip the well-seasoned dressing into seventy coconut shells, one for each of the guests. A hundred and thirty loaves of bread have been ordered from Amok the Chinaman. It is a pity that Naipu is not with us to take part in the celebration.

November 4, 1921

Raiarii has often spoken to me of an ancient trail that leads up the Valley of Ataroa and across the mountain divide down to Teahupo on the other side of the peninsula. "But there is only one man in the village who knows the way, old Punuari, who last year directed us to Teahupo along the sea cliffs of Te Pari."

Norman Hall and I have been long eager for the trip. So, too, Tauire, always ready for an adventure. We had more difficulty in persuading Punuari to guide us. The old man is well on in his sixties. Ueri and Nanai, agile and hardy as any of the boys, are also with us.

At six in the morning we started up the valley. The night rains had swelled the Vaitipiha. As we crossed the yellow current it sometimes wet our armpits. Suddenly high up the opposite bank, perched on a branch thirty feet above the ground, I saw little Uraponi. Her yellow mane swept about her meager form. She screamed and waved to a native, whom I then noticed further up on our side of the river. With a bound he was in the swirling current. In one hand he carried his long heavy *fei* machete. He steadied himself for a second, waist deep in the eddying water. In three leaps he reached the opposite bank, scrambled up the overhanging ledge and disappeared in the forest jungle.

It was only later that we learned that little Taniera, led on by Uraponi, had ventured up a dangerous *fei* trail. Taniera had slipped, fallen over the edge of the trail with a sprained ankle. There he hung and might easily have broken his neck if help had not arrived. Some of the *fei* trails are really wicked. Speaking of a particularly nasty one Pata once said to me: "I shouldn't venture on this one now. I haven't been climbing much lately and the soles of my feet are not yet *mea taratara* – roughened – like a goat's." Yet over such trails the men will carry *fei* loads of seventy pounds on a four-hour haul to the village.

At ten o'clock we paused to rest. Old Punuari and Tauire the indefatigable disappeared in the brush to find the footprints and traces of the *aito* Pae who had roamed through the valley. They scraped the moss and dirt away and showed us the marks in the lava rock. As the *aito* strode across the mountain with a tree in his hand as a walking stick, he had slipped and fallen. As he fell he drove his stick into the ground to steady himself. There in the rock was a hole the size of a great bowl. First the *aito* had come down on his heel. In the rock was the print of a huge "Kanaka" foot, long and splaying out at the toes. As he continued to fall he steadied himself with his right hand. The marks of his four fingers and thumb were pressed deep into the rock.

"It is all the work of the *varua ino* – the evil spirit," said old Punuari, who is versed in the legends of the island.

The stream was now shallow. We had long ago left the *fei* path and were stumbling over boulders in the river bed. At times we would leave the gorge and cut our way through the pandanus and *aeho* – mountain grass – which grew tall and thick as moss along the bank of the waterway. We had circled that fearful mountain, Te Ure – the Penis – which reaches up like a leaning tower. The Valley of Ataroa was far behind us. At noon we reached the divide. Here many years ago hibiscus and the *tiare Tahiti* had been planted.

Downward we plunged into a tall bamboo brake. The stream began to widen. We were again painfully slipping over wet boulders, clinging to *purau* branches and the roots of the giant ferns. It was dark before we reached the valley bottom. The moonlight filtered through the branches of the towering deep-groined *mape* which grow in the moist valleys and on the edge of the swamps. We saw a shimmering gleam ahead—the sea! We reached it in another hour. On we waded over the pathless coral flats, crossing another twenty shallow rivers and streams, trudging through the sand between the stems of the coco palms.

As we neared Teahupo the black silhouettes of the fishing outriggers glided by. They were starting for an early morning haul off the reefs of Te Pari. The nets were piled high in the bows.

At ten o'clock we reached the house of Paiatua, the Chief, where I had stayed the year before. He had been warned that we were coming. He had caught fish and killed chickens. We were not too tired to eat although with only a short rest we had been on the go for sixteen hours.

The next morning we hired a *vaa* to take us back to Tautira by the caves of Te Pari. There were eight of us in the big wooden outrigger. Soon the southeast trade began to blow heavily. The dugout was shipping water and we had not yet reached the gap in the reef where we must put out from the lagoon into the open sea. On a lee shore we never could have made our way around the perilous and sea-swept rocks of Te Pari. We put back and landed on the coral water front. Here the steep bluffs and boulders hampered our going. We continued on foot up to our waists in salt water. We had passed the last bamboo *fare*. The country was desolate and the mountains dropped into the sea. Between two shoulders rose the giant shaft of Te Ure which yesterday we had approached from the opposite side. The mountain descended sheer into the water.

We turned our backs to the sea and climbed the cliff, hand over hand, clinging to the roots of a *purau* tree. An hour's scramble brought us down again to the boiling ocean, for here there was no longer the protection of an outer reef. The waves tossed spray forty feet in the air. A gully ran inward between sheer walls of slippery rock. On the further side of the gully was a narrow shingle beach. Periodically combing waves swept in, covering the beach, and were swept back in an angry racing swirl.

Old Punuari leaned behind a boulder and scanned the crested waves. At the auspicious moment he roared out to each of us to run—"*A horo! A horo!*" One by one we jumped into the sucking backwash and made a dash for safety. As we reached the shingle beach the pursuing wave caught us about the knees and waist. So far Punuari had proved himself a trustworthy guide.

Beyond was the hardest and most dangerous stretch. Once again a wall of rock descended perpendicularly to the sea. In single file we crawled up and around the shoulder of the cliff, our bellies flattened on the wet clay and crumbling gravel. As we inched along we would feel ahead for a pandanus root, a bit of grass into which we could dig our nails. Old Punuari sought out the way and shouted encouragement: "*Faa itoito!*"

Toward sundown we reached the caves of Te Pari. We were without food and here there is no fresh water. The land provides. Nanai and Tauire, who had arrived first, were gathering *maoa*. Tauire, bounding about, a dynamo of energy, was off again and returned with bananas and young coconuts to slake our thirst.

We fed as the sun sank directly opposite the mouth of the cave. The darkness closed on an operatic setting. Overhead the vault of the cave. To the left the fronds of a coco palm silhouetted in black against the blue-black sky. To the right the delicate umbrella spokes of a pandanus leaf caught the reflection of our fire of coco husks. We lay without coverings on soft dry banana leaves which former wayfarers had gathered and left in the caves.

Punuari, schooled in island myths, narrated many of the legends of the districts through which we had traveled. Of the *aito* who drilled an opening in a rock as a drum. When he beat the opening with the stem of a palm leaf the sound was like the roar of thunder in the mountains. Beautiful women heard the drumming and came to the *aito* and danced.

Old Punuari is spare and sinewy, all knees, elbows, and bones. His hands are two enormous claws. I told him how I admired his strength and endurance. Over rough going, barefoot, he could outwalk any white man.

"When I was young," he said, "I was *itoito* — courageous — like Tauire. But now I am *paruparu* — feeble — and worn."

I slept badly. Twice I awoke to the boom of the old man's voice. Only Tauire the indefatigable still listened.

The next morning the wind was still blowing stiff. In the opening in the reef the waves rose ten feet high swept hither and thither by wind and tide, leaped and crossed each other in every direction. I doubt if a whale boat could have made the passage. We started home at sunrise and reached Tautira at two o'clock. Nanai, whose feet were cut and swollen, and Punuari lagged behind. His face had aged over night. He had cut himself a staff and crowned his head with a wreath of hibiscus. The rest of us dragged our steps along, every now and then sinking to the ground to rest. Tauire had rooted up two young banana plants and was carrying them for fifteen kilometers to plant in his garden.

November 13, 1921

The heavy sea breakers are gradually closing up the mouth of the Vaitipiha. In front of my *fare* what was recently a shallow stream has grown into a wide basin of fresh water, fifty feet in width and a quarter of a mile long. This has changed the whole character and rhythm of the village life. The women no longer go upstream after fresh water. In the morning while I paint I see a dozen of them kneeling at the water's edge below my window. Their vermilion, scarlet, and dark blue *pareu* are drawn up below their armpits. Kneeling, they pound the wash on the shingles and spread it over the sand to dry in multicolored patches.

The men no longer travel up the road in the rhythmic, jerky trot which eases the heavy load of *fei*, breadfruit, or water containers, slung on poles across the shoulders. Now they ride gaily in their wooden dugouts. In the evening the fishermen come trooping back over the hot stretch of sand and plunge into the cool river. As it grows dark boys drive the lean-flanked horses down the bank and splash water over their withers and backs and bellies. When school is over the children come racing down in a body, squealing and laughing. The little ones bathe naked in the basin. The older boys and girls ride the combers on boards beyond the reach of sand which has dammed the river.

November 16, 1921

In my painting I am always afraid of the slick and clever. Perhaps it is because my own technique has been so slowly and painfully mastered. Virtuosity is a danger that has blinded many to a true sense of form. One can forgive it in Leyendecker's Arrow Collar advertisements. But it was what sucked the blood and marrow out of Sargent, notwithstanding his extraordinary talent. Perhaps because we are a pioneer race we yearn for what is pretty in art. Maxfield Parrish is our American idol. Even in a great artist like Whistler the search for texture, precision of tone, and surface finish too often deteriorates into sugar coating. Of all my American contemporaries I most admire Arthur Carles. His meat is never on the surface, but close to the bone.

I am carried away by Van Wyck Brooks's *Ordeal of Mark Twain*. A great piece of literary criticism. Ringing words: "Moral freedom . . . the sole condition without which the creative instinct cannot survive and grow."

What is the ultimate meaning – spirit – of our world? I think I see in it life, art, and love. Life is art and love. Mark Twain wrote about himself: "What a man sees in the human race is merely himself in the deep and honest privacy of his own heart." He despised people because he despised himself. I have sometimes felt the same. How narrowly I escaped his view of life. Those early years roaming in California, cow-punching in Texas, riding through Mexico, later traveling in Europe were the years in which I developed as an individual, escaped from background and type. How narrow the escape. I thought at the time they were wasted years. I realize now that they were the only years in which I lived and grew. The rest was a painful effort to conform.

November 18, 1921

A week ago little Moerai, who lives at Arai *vahine*'s and is probably a relative, joined my household – after due deliberation on his part, much as a hermit crab will choose his shell. Little by little he began to make himself useful, lending a hand to Temehau in washing dishes, or helping me water the plants. Temehau was not disinclined to have his help and once or twice asked him to stay for a bite of bread and a cup of tea. One morning I found him sleeping on a pandanus mat in the kitchen. It seems that I have adopted him.

Moerai is perhaps twelve years old. His face is round and smooth. When he smiles his eyes are hidden in the fat of his cheeks. When he sits at table with us his head just rises above the board. Already he does most of the cooking.

Ueri enjoys teasing him in his dry manner. "Moerai," he says, "will never grow up.

When he is a *ruau* — an old man — he will be no bigger than he is now. You may think him ten or twelve years old. Not at all. He is perhaps twenty or even thirty. And he is hiding a woman up in the village."

Moerai squirms and grins. He makes great sucking noises of satisfaction as he drinks his tea and dips his fingers into the *poe* or platter of fried fish.

November 19, 1921

Anyone living alone will bulk large on his own horizon. But must not an artist isolate himself — go to the desert — to find himself and mature? How can one develop in New York where life is a continuous succession of external shocks? For me peace of mind and serenity are a more congenial atmosphere for creative work.

I admired Rockwell Kent's honesty when he said to me: "Every artist is an egotist. Each adventure or love affair is more important to me than the best of my paintings." Americans shrink from the expression of ego just as they consider expressions of emotion in bad taste. Christ was the supreme egotist.

The world has always been fashioned and usually governed by an aristocracy of the mind. The greatest danger that confronts our society is to equate egalitarianism with democracy — an unfortunate and unforeseen consequence of the Declaration of Independence and the French Revolution.

November 24, 1921

The sun glistens on the blue, laughing sea. Moo, the sweet young foster daughter of Tauire *vahine*, a white strip of cotton cloth bound about her slender waist, kneels in the water and pounds her wash. Her brooding eyes drink in the golden sunshine. This gentle, sensitive girl shuns her giddy playmates, who laugh and splash away the hours in the cool river.

November 28, 1921

Through the gray-green noontide leaves of the low branching *purau* tree drift the naked forms of sorrel-haired Uraponi, of Nanua, Teratara, Teura, and Aiunei. Their young bodies are chaste in line, their movements careless and free. Later they come clambering up the bank, wringing the water from their clinging hair.

November 29, 1921

About a week ago while Raiarii was out working in the *fenua ahieri* someone broke into his house and stole four hundred francs from his strong box. The money belonged to the *taiate*. Raiarii drove to Taravao to inform the French *gendarme* of the theft. Tomorrow Mari, who also has an interest in the *taiate*, will go to Papeete to consult Tirita who deals in cards. He has successfully visited her on other occasions.

December 2, 1921

Mari returned at sunset and waded across the narrow opening of the river.

"What are the *parau api* – the new words – from Papeete?" I asked him.

"Only that the thief is taken and is now in jail."

"And did you speak to Tirita?"

"Yes. And she truly foretold what would happen. She said that the thief would come to Papeete and drink much rum and that the *gendarmes* would capture him. *Ua parau mau ra.* These were true words. He did come to Papeete and spent his money on rum. They captured him at Faone."

The thief is a half-brother of Timo, a son of old Temeheu who bedded up with his three daughters. With the exception of Timo the family are a bad lot. Timo is having his troubles. He has been ailing and consulted the *tahua* – native doctor – in Teahupo. The *tahua* told him that he had ruptured a kidney. He treated him with native medicine and forbade his eating fish or drinking alcohol. Timo continued to languish. I sent him into Papeete to see Cassiau. He is suffering from a severe case of gonorrhea. His kidneys are affected. He is urinating blood. Cassiau is treating him at the hospital and I am paying his expenses. But will they ever learn?

December 4, 1921

During the past month I have finished nine canvases. I am exhausted and nervous. I badly need a change and a rest.

December 15, 1921

About a week ago something happened which upset and angered me. It has shattered my peace of mind and deeply shaken my understanding and affection for these people.

Temehau had just returned after a week's absence in Papeete, where I had sent her to see the dentist. A couple of missing teeth had been her only blemish. Now she looked lovelier than ever. I was happy to pay for this little extravagance. But instead of showing gratitude she seemed spoiled and moody. She scolded the others, Nanai and Moerai, and was often rude to me.

Almost at once she told me that she must return at the end of the week to Papeete. Her father was old and sick. She must visit him in the Tuamotu. The request was not entirely unreasonable. But I did not like her tone. Was I spoiling her?

One day Ueri stopped by to see me. He told me that Temehau had taken a *tane* while she was staying in Papeete with her sister. She was lying to me about her father. "When she walks up to the village on the excuse of buying bread and tea from Amok the Chinaman, she stops at the Chief's house and telephones to a man in Papeete." When I further questioned him he admitted that her sister had in fact telephoned her about their father and urged her to visit him in Makatea.

All Tahitians enjoy gossip and newsmongering. Like children they are easily offended

Paruparu and Ueri

and their grudges smolder. Temehau had a few warm friends in the village. But she was an outsider and had little airs and manners that might give offense and make enemies. At the evening *himene* at a villager's house the host would offer her a chair in deference to me, while the other women would gather up the skirts of their long gowns and sit or lie about on the grass. Others may have been jealous of her guitar, her white silk shawl, and her many dresses. Ever since Naipu had left for the States she had taken an upper hand with his boys and would scold them roundly for their laziness. A Tahitian has no defense against a woman's tongue-lashing. It festers and he does not easily forget it. For all these reasons I paid no more attention to Ueri's gossip and insinuations.

Two days later he and Paruparu came to me again. They said that they had further proof that Temehau had lied to me. She had been corresponding with her *tane* in Papeete. He had written her a letter which the *mutoi* – the postman – had personally delivered to her at the house of Arai *vahine*. She had hidden it in Arai's cedarwood chest. The same afternoon – Ueri insisted that it was the merest coincidence – he had stopped at her house to fetch some wash which Arai was doing for him. The cedar box was open. He had seen the letter and stolen it. He showed it to me. All this was told with an air of malicious and self-righteous satisfaction.

I read the letter. It was obviously from her former *tane*. The boys told me that he was a brigadier in the *gendarmerie* in Papeete, the son of an East Indian living at Hitia. Evidently he had met Temehau in Papeete and had made advances to her. He knew that she might soon return to Papeete. He hoped again to see her.

I recalled that Temehau herself had once told me that she had known this man. There was nothing, therefore, conclusive one way or another about the letter. I felt, however, that I was being slowly sucked into a tangle of intrigue, lies, and venom. I determined to have it out with her.

That evening I waited until she had washed and put away the dishes, and the others had gone up to the village. I then told her I wished to have a talk with her. She pretended that she was too sleepy to talk, began to scold, and finally burst into tears. Thereafter she maintained her proud and sullen bearing.

I asked her why she had been telephoning and corresponding with a man behind my back. She answered angrily that Ueri and Paruparu hated her and had lied. She added rather defensively that she was truly happy in Tautira and was as fond of me as ever. After a pause she said: "While I was staying with my sister in Papeete you told me that if I did not soon return you would take another *vahine*." I remember writing this to her as a joke. But her remark seemed to me beside the point and evasive. I said nothing and looked her in the eye. Again she declared with vehemence that she had not taken a *tane* in Papeete and that no one had courted her or made advances to her.

I said: "*Ua haavare oe* – You are lying," and showed her the letter.

She read it slowly. Then tossing it aside she asked me haughtily how I had obtained it.

I was dumbfounded at her duplicity and insolence. I was angry. I slapped her smartly on the face with my open hand.

She looked at me with proud and sullen eyes — the eyes of some wild creature, cornered, trapped, unafraid. Asking nothing, accepting life as it is, without regret or the hope of generosity.

After a silence she told me that she had lied in part. Her former friend had run into her in Papeete. He had courted her and had occasionally come to her sister's house. He must have learned from her sister that she would soon return to Papeete. He had written her, but she had not answered his letter. "He was not my lover," she cried. "*Ua parau mau ra* — These are true words."

She begged my pardon and acknowledged that she had misbehaved. I do not think as much was ever before wrung from those proud lips. She added in a low voice that she must return at once to visit her father in Makatea.

We were both silent for some time. Then she cried out: "You are the only man that ever struck me. Not even my father."

She said again that she would return to Tautira, but that the steamer for Makatea was leaving at once. She could not linger in Tautira another day. "I swear before God," she repeated, "this time he was not my lover."

The next morning she arose early and packed all her possessions, her dresses and her white silk shawl. She took with her her guitar. Her two friends, Arai *vahine* and Tamaru, accompanied us to the shore. Here Moerai sat in our dugout to ferry her across the river. On the further shore Owen was waiting with his truck, loaded with a catch of fish for the Papeete market.

Temehau wore a pale blue frock with white polka dots. She had made for herself a garland of pink and purple asters, gathered from my garden, which she wore about her straw hat. She had never looked more lovely. Her color glowed through her dusky skin. She had combed and oiled her long luxuriant hair with perfumed *monoi*. It fell below her waist. Before stepping into the dugout she offered me one of her pearls which she had brought with her from the Tuamotu. I told her rather stiffly that I could not accept it.

Arai *vahine* and Tamaru stood on the bank. Both women were weeping. Tamaru rested her head on her arm and leaned against a mango tree.

It is two days now since she has gone. As I was writing these lines little Moerai trotted in carrying a letter.

Papeete, December 14.

Dear Tihoti:

I wish to tell you one thing. I do not wish any longer to return to Tautira. I am leaving for Makatea. Do not count any more on me.

Goodbye.

Au revoir.

Do not answer my letter.

The letter was unsigned. Since she speaks no English she had gotten someone to write it for her.

I felt the blood rushing to my face.

December 22, 1921

A visit from Takao. She brought with her Williamson, a former student of Naipu's. He had come out to see his friend, not realizing that he was in the States. Takao invited me back to Papara for a Christmas celebration.

Papara, December 25, 1921

The party dragged in spite of several visiting celebrities: the young Comte de Noailles and the Marquis of Northampton, both on a world tour; Robert Service, the ballad jingler, pompous and dull; and the usual assembly of the Salmon clan, Mote, Hototu, Poma, Ina, and the others. The old dowager Marau, becomingly robed in a long empire gown of pale lavender, was in an execrable temper. She cast a damper over the festive family gathering. They are all mortally afraid of her.

Mote told me the following legend of Papara. In former days the natives of Raiatea were unacquainted with the spoon-hook — *matau umete.* Now an old man remembered once hearing of these hooks in Tahiti, and he was eager to test them. So he caught a great bonito fish and cut it into four parts. Three parts he cast back into the sea, but he kept the fourth part. He then bid his sons travel to Tahiti and bring him back a *matau umete*; his sons in their ignorance thought that he was referring to the *umete* — bowl — in which the islanders pound their *fei* and taro roots in making *poe.* When the boys reached Papara in Tahiti they met a fisherman and spoke to him of their errand. The fisherman gave them a spoon-hook and told them to go early the next morning beyond the reefs and fish.

"You will see a flock of black birds but you must not cast your line. Presently you will see a flock of white birds and then you must cast. But cast only once."

The next morning the boys did as they had been told. When they cast the line they hauled it in and on the end of the line was a part of the bonito which their father had cast into the sea in faraway Raiatea. This they brought back to him. He thus knew that the spoon-hook is superior to all others, and to this day they use it in Raiatea.

Tautira, December 26, 1921

I took the bus from Papara to Papeari. From here I walked the twenty-five kilometers to Tautira. Under the coco palms which edge the road thousands of land crabs scuttle hither and thither. At the entrance to their holes they stand erect, their claws raised threateningly. If I prod them with my foot they strike angrily back.

December 27, 1921

Today I finished another flower piece, "Dahlias and Zinnias." Perhaps a little sugary and wallpapery, but an effort to use flowers as a purely decorative design. I have in mind the late baroque Florentine iron work.

I have now completed a stage in my work, the experiments of the past four months. Some twenty small canvases: two still lifes of fruit, four flower pieces, eight landscapes, two heroic-sized, conventionalized portrait heads, and other small paintings. Now I must attempt something more ambitious. This afternoon I made sketches for a large composition.

December 29, 1921

Arai *vahine* had suggested that Uraponi's older sister Terae Hara join my staff and help Moerai with the cleaning and cooking. So now my household is established again on the somewhat shaky pillars of the three children. Terae Hara, the oldest and most reliable, is answerable for keeping the house clean and in order. She sets the table and serves the dishes. Little Moerai does most of the cooking. In Tahiti this is not below a man's dignity. Sorrel-haired Uraponi assists or desists as her wayward spirit moves her. She can be bland and matronly or an evil little trouble-making vixen. Of late she has not been helpful. She rarely obeys me. I threaten and cajole. It is useless. The excitement of my talcum powder and shaving lotion have gone to her head. Today as she finished sweeping the room in a cloud of dust she addressed me.

"Tioti, I don't want you to allow any more of the *tamarii* – the children – into the house. They bring in too much dirt."

"Uraponi," I said to her, "you have not made my bed or swept the house for three days. That is why there is so much dirt. Clean the *paepae* – the shelves. They are disgusting."

"*Ua ite vau* – I know how to do things." And then, as I seemed to be in her way, "*Haere!* – Get along with you!"

Uraponi rarely attends school on the somewhat flimsy excuse that she has too much housework. She is away all day in the brush with other truants, climbing trees after oranges or pawpaws. She comes in late for supper, disheveled and in rags. She eats everything with her fingers, spills coffee on her dress, and covers herself with jam. The other two tease her. Moerai remarks that she is a *vahine mea oviri* – a wild woman – and is probably a *taata amu taata* – a cannibal.* Uraponi rushes out of the room in a fit of anger and climbs up a mango tree. There she sits scowling and refuses to come down. Terae Hara calls out to her that the *tupapau* will get her. As it grows dark the child becomes really frightened. She climbs down and slips into the house. But she still sulks and will not sit down with us. Instead she crawls under the table. The other two hand her down tidbits of fish and baked *fei*.

*To be called a cannibal was a prevalent insult in Tahiti, and it got under the skin. It was widely believed that the natives of the Dangerous Archipelago were not only darker colored but practiced cannibalism.

Tioti with Moerai, Nanai, and Uraponi

January 6, 1922

I have been painting now morning and afternoon for ten days on my large composition. All is going well. Today finished the bank of black sand, the sea beyond, and the clouds. But I feel washed up, exhausted. In the afternoon I tried to paint again. It was too much for me. Instead I worked cleaning Naipu's land of brush on the further side of the road. Here he will plant taro, and line the road with *iita* — papaya.

January 7, 1922

It is in our moral strength rather than in any intellectual ascendancy that we differ from the primitive. He may be fundamentally as intelligent as we are, better bred, and more artistically gifted. But he lacks moral fiber. We can dominate ourselves and so we can dominate the primitive. The Tahitian may despise, deceive, trick, and evade us. He cannot face, as we can, a moral decision. In this he is like a child, or more properly — as Weininger would say — a woman. The child may not understand the difference between right and wrong. A woman should.

Once a woman left me because I spoke the truth to her rather than lie. Now another one because I trusted her. I don't think I deceive myself. I am not thinking now of love or of any deep affection. What is it that makes the hurt? Is it merely jealousy that I feel? Is it my vanity, pride, and self-esteem that are wounded?

I must draw on whatever energy and will I have. I feel drained and tired. I must not become twisted and sour.

January 12, 1922

This past week I have been working long hours on the large composition. All still going well. When I begin an important painting I feel in a fever to finish it in one sitting. I would paint every brushstroke with a concentration that would make it final, and the larger the canvas the greater and more fatiguing the effort becomes. Already I feel drained and tired. Or is it the loneliness at night in my little shack after the children have gone up to Arai *vahine*?

It is almost two o'clock but I cannot sleep. Perhaps it is the heat. The rats are scratching above my head on the *niau* roof. Through my window I can see the moon sinking over the black ridges of Ahui. Heavy rain clouds drift slowly westward.

January 14, 1922

Pau, the carpenter and missionary, told me that he saw Temehau in Papeete. She admitted that she would be leaving only next week for Makatea. She added that she had quarreled with me but that it was now over. As soon as she returned from visiting her father she would come back to Tautira. More subterfuge and lies? The good Pau, in his role of missionary, gave her a lecture on her behavior.

When a woman leaves you it is as if a limb were wrenched out. It takes time for the flesh to grow. I had become fond of her. I think she was fond of me. My life here with her was peaceful and happy.

January 15, 1922

Croce in his essay on Balzac writes that "Balzac inevitably begins with an energetic demonstration of what the Latins call *génialité,* the creative exultation of the artist." How descriptive this passage is of Balzac's prose. How characteristic of the French conception of the the creative process.

Weininger believes that genius is consciousness; that art is the power of giving form to chaos. My own philosophy that painting is the artist's reaction to life, expressed in line, color, and design, amounts to the same thing. The more I reflect on the meaning of art, the more I am convinced of this truth.

Does so-called modern art, notwithstanding its many pronouncements, convey the fullest revelation and expression of life?

The answer is No.

It gives us a new orchestration, a new synthesis, of line, color, and design. And this is significant form. The new movement is a Euclidean inquiry into the meaning of form just as the great Impressionist movement of 1860 to 1880 was based on an investigation of the laws of optics. The modern movement has created a new style but as yet has given us little new or significant perspective on the meaning of life.

For these reasons I can't entirely go along with the movement. Yet it has produced the only important art being done today. I am in sympathy, too, with much of what it asserts, as for instance that art is a projection from within and not, as the Impressionists believed, merely the eye of the camera, an objective transcription of the visual world. The paradox is that the Impressionists had a great deal to say about life notwithstanding their theories. Modern art insists on the importance of the artist's affirmation, but up to now what it says about life is not particularly significant, often depressing, and at times nonsense.

January 16, 1922

Taniera is one of Moerai's friends, but I am afraid that he is not too good an influence. Like many of the children he is self-assured and a little cheeky. He fancies that a glittering smile and high spirits can get away with murder. Lately I have noticed inroads on my cigarettes. I often spoil the village children but I will not have the discipline of my household corroded.

Yesterday Taniera disobeyed me three times. He had been making a *maniania* — a rumpus — beating an empty kerosene can with a stick. I told him to leave the house since I would not tolerate disobedient children. He gave the kerosene can one more whack and I cuffed him soundly over the head. He left weeping bitterly. This afternoon Uraponi came to me as his emissary, begging me to forgive him. "Taniera," she said, "is *mea riri* — filled with anger — and demands his wages for posing. He further says that from now on he will work no more for you."

I said to her: "Uraponi, you may tell Taniera that I, too, am nursing a *mea riri rahi* — a great anger. I consider him a worthless and disobedient *tamarii.* I shall not speak to him again until his *faa riri* has cooled down."

The comedy lasted for another three days, each of us growing angrier and angrier with the other. However, I held the stronger position. I could get along without Taniera but he could not get along without me. On the fourth day Uraponi casually mentioned that Taniera's rage was calming down and he was ready to apologize. I waited another day before I would see him. He reappeared, a little shamefaced but with his glittering smile. We shook hands as man to man.

January 18, 1922

About a fortnight ago Ueri confessed to me that he had contracted a severe case of gonorrhea. I treated him for ten days with a solution of permanganate. He came irregularly, often forgot to take the medicine which I had given him, and would not rest, although I had told him that physical exertion was the worst thing for him. His testicles and kidneys had become infected. I advised him that he must see Dr. Cassiau in Papeete and I offered to pay for the visit.

Dr. Cassiau has a warm heart and does what he can for the natives. But he is a *Marseillais* and has a blustering temper and he scolds them for their carelessness. They are all scared of him. Ueri stubbornly refused to see him. His infection rapidly became worse. At length he decided to see the doctor. Owen had come in with his truck for a haul of fish, but by now Ueri was too weak to walk down to the river crossing. He had to wait a couple of days for the small steamer for Papeete.

Cassiau telephoned me the next day that it would be necessary to send him to the hospital for treatment. I agreed to guarantee the daily charges of ten francs until I could consult with the boy's family. Temeheu, Ueri's father, is one of the wealthy men in Tautira. He has horses and pigs and sells copra, vanilla, and oranges from his outlying holdings. He could easily defray the hospital charges. I visited the parents the next day and explained to them the very grave condition of their son's infection. They both remained silent. The mother then said that she feared Ueri would feel lonely and frightened in the hospital. This was a subterfuge. They would come to no immediate decision. They must think the matter over.

Temeheu came to see me the next day. I explained to him over and over again the seriousness of Ueri's condition. Unless he took the treatment he might not recover at all and would remain an invalid the rest of his life.

Temeheu said: "If he is to die let him die in Tautira." I was shocked by his callousness. The more so when he further told me that his wife had already left for Papeete to bring her son home. The parents obviously feel that his recovery is not worth the price of a cow or a couple of pigs. Or am I misconstruing their motives? I am beginning to think that Tahitians are more complicated people than we realize.

Meanwhile it appears that Nane, a former member of Naipu's household, has also become infected from the same girl. Nane's family have no property and it would be extremely difficult for them to raise the money to pay for the treatment. I told him that I would cover whatever expenses there were, if he would visit Cassiau. He readily agreed but at the last moment he, too, lost his nerve.

January 19, 1922

I feel low in spirits. This afternoon a boy was carried by my house, I am told with two broken legs and perhaps a broken back. He had climbed high up in a mango tree and had fallen. Angry thoughts pass through my mind. They have been there before. "What difference does it all matter? Let it be. Beauty is complete in itself. It is eternal. I see it glowing in silver and orange in the great lily outside my window and in the splashes of gold and purple shaking in the fronds of the coco palm. Let it be. Unity and form are enough. His suffering or mine is of little consequence, a passing blemish which cannot affect the eternal and sublime."

January 22, 1922

Two days ago little Uraponi almost cut off the end of her finger splitting *mape* nuts with Naipu's large machete. The bone may have been severed. While I dressed it her lovely sister Urari and a number of the *taurearea* stood about laughing and teasing her. They told her that I would take her in to Cassiau and that he would cut her hand off at the wrist. Uraponi scowled back at them, but she showed surprising nerve and never whimpered.

I was determined to take the child to Papeete to have her finger properly dressed. I told her mother, Arai *vahine*, that I would pay the doctor's bill, but that she should contribute her share by borrowing a horse and cart to drive us to Taravao. She, too, thinks a visit to the doctor a quite unnecessary expense.

It is impossible to understand these people. Tahitians are fundamentally kind. Arai *vahine* is, according to their standards, a responsible parent. She is happy and flattered that I have adopted her children, and she shows me her gratitude in many little ways. With few exceptions Tahitians are not prejudiced against foreign doctors. On the contrary they have a deeper respect for and appreciation of them than toward the French officials and foreign missionaries. Does Cassiau's blunt manner frighten them? Does the likelihood of illness and suffering mean nothing to them unless pain is forcibly brought to their attention? A dog will yelp at a pinprick, but will run about unconcerned with an open festering wound.

Papeete, January 23, 1922

I took both children to Papeete, for I felt that Uraponi would be less frightened if she had Moerai along with her. She never flinched while Cassiau cleaned and bound up her finger.

When the good man scolded her for having such dirty hands she thrust out her lower lip and stared back at him resolutely under lowered eyelids.

Neither of the children had ever before been even as far from home as Taravao. They were particularly impressed by the electric lights, the size of the big ships, the ice which I ordered with my rum, and the watercloset at the Tiare. I had made it a point of showing this to Moerai as soon as we got there. Moments later he came to me to ask where he might urinate. They were both frightened when I pulled the chain. They thought the thing would flood the house and rushed from the room.

January 24, 1922

As I turned into the shabby lane back of the Restaurant des Poilus in Orivini, one of the outlying suburbs, I saw her stretching wash on a cord. I asked her if I could speak with her. She smiled, a little angrily, I thought. She asked me to come into the house.

It was a squalid little one-room shanty—a bed, a table, and soiled linen lying about on the floor. I talked with her for a long time. I said I only wanted to get the truth from her. This is, I believe, what happened—if it is ever possible to disentangle the truth from the prevarications, excuses, innuendoes, and lies.

While she was staying with her sister in Papeete visiting the dentist she met her former *tane*. By chance or connivance? I cannot tell. She may have resisted his advances as she affirmed. Perhaps she became troubled and hesitant. I have reason to think that on her return to Tautira she was of two minds. He continued to write and telephone her. She probably knew that she was being spied on.

Then came our quarrel. No woman likes to be caught in a lie. I struck her. She would not forget it easily. The touch of *Marseillais* blood. Right or wrong she had it in for me. Immediately on returning to Papeete she took a lover. But it was not her former *tane*. Naipu's friend Williamson told me that according to local gossip it was the young Comte de Noailles.

Had she really planned to sail immediately for the Tuamotu? Was the whole story of her sick father a lie? But why had she told Pau and the others that she was no longer angry and intended to return to Tautira? She repeated this to me now. She added sullenly: "But not at present. I shall only come later on."

I felt again that I was slowly being sucked into a mire of stalling, deception, and guile. I said to her: "Tell me the truth. If you care for someone else say so. Why do you continue to lie?" She remained silent.

I asked her: "Of what are you thinking?"

She looked at me darkly: "I am thinking of that slap you gave me."

I asked her whether all I had given her did not mean more to her than a slap. She shrugged her shoulders and laughed.

At that moment her sister Moina came in. I said to Temehau: "Since you will not tell me the truth I shall ask Moina." Temehau laughed again and went out.

I began to question Moina, who had started to iron the wash. She was silent for a while. Then she said: "Yes, I think she cares for that man."

"But why has she said to me and to Pau and others that she intends to return to Tautira?"

Moina said: "She will return."

"Do you mean," I cried, "that after the way she has behaved she will come back to Tautira and live with her friend Arai *vahine*?"

"No. She will come back to you."

"But you just said that she cares for another man!"

Moina shrugged her shoulders. "*E tau manao*—This is my belief."

After a few moments Temehau returned. Moina slipped away. I said to Temehau:

"Only tell me the truth. I will go away. You will not hear from me again."

Her face clouded. She said: "You will slap me again."

As I started to leave she asked me: "Shall I accompany you down the street?"

I did not answer and left without turning around.

Tautira, January 25, 1922

I have finished the large canvas which I started almost a month ago. I could exhibit it now, although it will need a few more days tinkering with it. I feel so nervous and washed out that I can no longer look at it objectively. At moments I believe it is the most important thing I have ever done. At other times it is no more than a large stretch of gray blotting paper seen against a gray wall. If it were burnt to ashes I could not care one way or the other. I am tired.

One reason why I feel this way is the state of mind I am in. Yet I lead a healthy life. Up a little after six. A swim before breakfast. A long morning's work and another swim. More painting in the afternoon. And a simple fare, baked beans from a can, bread and jam, and coffee for lunch. Lentils or red beans, fish, more bread and jam for supper. In bed by ten o'clock.

January 26, 1922

To a *himene* held at the house of old Taura. I lie under the black patchwork of a *purau* tree. Through the arabesque of the leaves the thin pale stars glitter against the pale blue-black sky. Gray clouds drift over the dark ledge of Tahiti *nui*. My flesh creeps with the thoughts of women. They obsess me. My head throbs and aches. Above the edge of a gray-black cloud the Pleiades coolly shiver.

January 28, 1922

Timo is the only boy whom we have helped who shows any gratitude or real affection. Before Naipu left for the States Timo's legs became infected with a nasty case of running yaws. We sent him in to Cassiau. Since he had no money Cassiau agreed to take payment in kind.

Every week Timo sends him bananas and oranges or an occasional chicken. And he brings me a string of fish whenever the nets are hauled. If I could feel that there were two or three others like him, I should feel differently about these people. And there are others — Pau, the carpenter-missionary, Tauire, and old Taura, the father of Moe.

I must keep objective and without rancor so as to understand them. I cannot expect to find sentiments in a primitive people which they are incapable of feeling. If I do this I suffer, and unconsciously I do them an injustice. I realize now that this is what has happened to me. Alas, it is not easy to regain my peace of mind. I suppose it is because I really love them that at times I think I hate them all.

January 30, 1922

I have two observations to make about my large canvas. I wish I had painted it in more direct and contrasting color tones. My color relations are harmonious but they are played in a minor key. This direct statement of color tones is what I so admire in Matisse's paintings. To the public his color seems crude, for he has created a wholly new orchestration of tonal relations. I remember Arthur Carles' bon mot: "Matisse was the first to put 'nigger pink' on the map." But his color tones are applied with the sureness of touch of a Manet drawing. One feels that he could not err by a hair's breadth. His color is *le mot juste* in the best French tradition of sobriety. Never in bad taste. It is only in his drawing, especially of the Fauve period, that he slops into the vulgarity of a pseudo-Germanic Expressionism. I remember Mary Cassatt saying to me ten years ago when I first met her: "Matisse could not draw. But he was extremely intelligent. He realized that his success must depend on shocking the public."

Painting the way I do, in successive washes, glazes, and scumblings instead of laying on the color directly, has advantages. In a large painting I retain an over-all color and tonal harmony as I work without the need of correcting, worrying, and overloading the canvas. I can also obtain a richer surface texture through the contrast of impastos on transparent glazes. The thing to remember is that although the artist's personal approach may be a constant source of weakness it is always his greatest treasure.

February 2, 1922

From a true friend who, though herself not an artist, has an understanding of the high purpose of art and its relation to life:

". . . You say this is perhaps the happiest period of your life. I think the happiest period of your life will be when you feel the power that comes from actually creating. You are feeling it more now than hitherto. When it comes it will be a positive rhythm like a song. Then you will do your best work and be a happy man.

"You said once that happiness was not your goal. You did not care about it. Can it be mere satisfaction you want? About your possible South Sea Island babies it doesn't seem consistent with your ruthless analytical mind not to know for sure, and surely you are mistaking the whole point if you are not a father. If the girls add tang to the adventure of being in Tahiti you alone know whether you behave well or badly. If real happiness results, then blessing on you. Happiness is important. Everything is important to the quality of life — the least thing — and an artist's work is but the ripened essence of his life. Do you agree a little?

"I like to think of you as a thoroughbred steed riding a noble cause well — very well. Max Weber says we are all stars with time passing through us gathering our contribution. But you need very much to be like the stillest pool which the better reflects the landscape surrounding it. You need to be very calm to catch the meaning of the universe. Give us causes in beauty and move our hearts.

"You really need very much to pause. Tahiti has called you for that reason. You missed it last year. From what I understand of your Tahitians their eyes are your example — deep untroubled pools."

February 15, 1922

What Weininger writes about art and genius has made a deep impression on me. I, too, am convinced that most men have moments of creative imagination, of genius. Yet even the most gifted have these moments rarely. There is no such animal as "a genius." Merely moments of intuition. We can only listen and wait for the word to come.

This is why every artist's work must be uneven. Just as the seed slowly forces its way up and finally breaks through the weight of the inert soil, so intuition, imagination, genius, the Godhead, Truth, must burst through the heavy crust of the negative, the already-felt-and-seen-by-other-men. No wonder that artists have moments of exultation, long hours of pain. Intuition is not a flame that can be turned up and down like a gas jet.

March 6, 1922

A small head of a young girl, Meri, twenty by sixteen inches, her hands joined in prayer. Perhaps the best of these heroic-sized portrait heads which I have recently done. Ideas to develop: (1) The element of portraiture rigidly sustained, shorn of all outside props, still life or landscape accessories. (2) The human likeness must be retained, yet if possible sublimated into symbolic type. (3) The line drawn with the severity of a Holbein or a Ming portrait. (4) Yet it must be painted in terms of modern color and form.

March 12, 1922

Sometimes I feel utterly alone in this laughing, sunny, crowded village. For hours at a time they sit about me and talk. Sometimes they discuss me among themselves, as if I were not there. As if I were merely a part of their experience, a distant hill, sunshiny weather, a gray day. The continuous hard, uninterrupted work, the heat and rain of the past two months, have sapped my vitality. I am drained, I don't think I could stand another month of it alone. Thank God Naipu will be back in another ten days. Then I must get away for a month's rest. A cruise among the Tuamotu and the Austral Islands. Rest and reflection. When I return I shall have time for five or six months of experimentation, and to paint one or two canvases which will sum up all I have learned.

March 23, 1922

The schooner *Parks* — captained by William Kemp, by looks a full-blooded Tuamotuan — put off from the Papeete docks at four in the afternoon. The sun sank in a splash of gold behind the purple mountains of Moorea and Tahiti. Something in that sunset gripped my bowels. Something deep down inside me turned round and round as on a spit, and was slowly drawn out as by a magnet. I felt myself flowing out and mingling with the universe. That same feeling of utter wild joy leaped up in me which I had felt as a boy in California in 1901 and later cow-punching in Texas and riding over the coast range in Mexico. An exultation that touched everything with romance and enchantment. So vivid are those memories, so precisely are they the feelings which now possessed me, that it seems impossible to believe in the passing of time, in the aging of spirit. If I could believe in their permanence I would doubt the need and purpose of art.

March 24, 1922

The summit of Orohena eighty kilometers away is still in view. The base of the island mingles with the flat white sea. To lie all day on deck among the native sailors. To breakfast before dawn in the gentle breezes of the Pacific. To sleep ten hours a night with only a pandanus mat between my body and the cabin boards.

March 29, 1922

Breakfasted at five o'clock as we lay anchored off Avatoru. Here is a small settlement at the opening into the reef of Rahiroa — the Very Great. The name is appropriate. The atoll is an immense ring of coral into which the entire island of Tahiti could be comfortably fitted. Standing on the inner shore one cannot see the opposite side of the lagoon.

As we slowly ran through the narrow pass the villagers gathered on the beach. Three women in scarlet seated on the pink sand. Behind them a man in a black *pareu*, a black cotton shawl wrapped about his shoulders. He held a naked baby in his arms. There is great beauty here but it is symbolic, not visual — what the scene suggests, not what it presents to the eye.

For four days we coasted about the inner shore of the lagoon, picking up copra at the different settlements — Fenuaroa, Hopiropiro, and Turuoe. The villagers are all out in the *fenua ahieri*, drying out copra. In each squalid settlement a few Chinese, a dozen miserable shacks with tin roofs and curtained *niau* walls to keep out the blistering heat. Occasionally

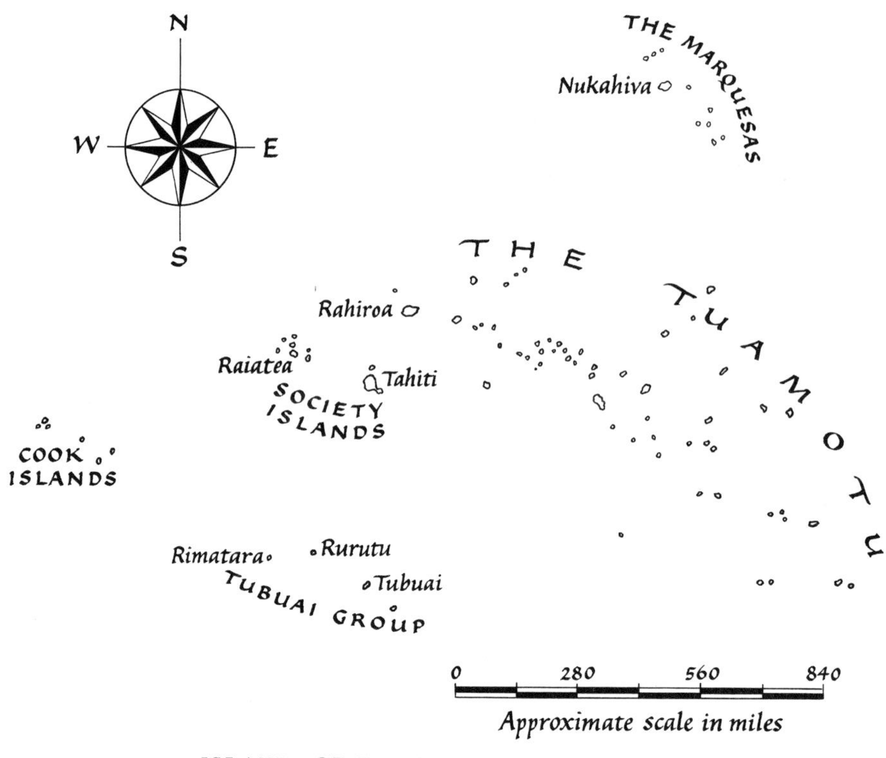

ISLANDS OF THE SOUTH PACIFIC

a water hole with a little dirty stagnant water, for the atolls are only a few feet above sea level and there are no springs. Avatoru and Tiputa where the *Parks* put in for only a few hours were the least forlorn of these hamlets. The semblance of a street marked with white coral blocks and lined with palm trees; a few wooden houses bordered with flowering hibiscus and gardenia bushes.

April 2, 1922

At noon we reached Ahui, a village of some importance, but we found it quite deserted. The copra had already been dried and shipped to Papeete. The inhabitants had moved in a body to Manihi. We pushed on and anchored off Manihi at sunset. The schooner was warped up to the coral quay. Here the entire village had gathered to welcome us. Among them three women in long scarlet gowns and a man in a bright yellow cotton suit. Although the only road in the village is no more than two hundred yards in length I saw three men gravely riding up and down on shining bicycles. A band of seven brass pieces greeted our arrival.

"C'est bien le genre Tuamotu. Qu'ils sont *kanaques*, hein?" snarled the half-caste supercargo. When he smiles he flashes two gold teeth on either side of a large blackened cavity.

As I stepped from the schooner on to the quay one of the villagers nudged his comrade.

"*Aue! tenei e Tioti.*" I thought to myself: When will I ever again achieve such notoriety? Arrive, a stranger, at a destination hundreds of miles from my village home and receive immediate recognition. The South Pacific is a region of seafaring men; of travelers having a wide knowledge of many ports, villages, faces, local gossip, and tall tales.

April 4, 1922

At six o'clock in the morning we pulled out, sailing between Arutua and Apataki the same afternoon. We approached Kaukura as the sun set.

April 6, 1922

Yesterday afternoon at about four o'clock we sighted Meetia, which I had made a fruitless attempt to visit a year and a half ago. It lay about thirty kilometers away. The base merged into the burnished sea. These terrible blocks and shafts of volcanic rock tossed up eons ago in the vast expanse of ocean by some shattering blast from the bowels of the deep. This morning at five o'clock, breakfasting on the deck of the schooner, I could still discern the peak hanging in the still air. Sixty miles to the westward lies Taiarapu and a cluster of small bamboo huts, nestling under the mango trees by the edge of a river.

April 9, 1922

We have left the Tuamotu and for three days have been running south with the trade winds. At sunrise Rurutu in the Austral group came into view, stretched out long and low on the horizon, its billowing hills tossed up like gentle waves at either extremity. After sailing for days the vast reaches of the Pacific in a schooner so small that one can reach over the lee rail and almost touch the surface of the water, the first sight of land, of a new port, strikes the imagination as an unknown and newly discovered vestige of a forgotten life. It is an intoxicating experience.

And what a gracious picture as we drifted through the *ava*—the pass in the reef—and the village of Moerai came into view. The long salmon-colored beach, the small white houses of coral blocks thatched with pandanus leaf, the red-tiled Temple and the scarlet-crowned, wide-spreading poinciana trees. The entire village was gathered on the shore. As we dropped anchor thirty small dugouts put out, skimming toward us, the men shouting, laughing, gesticulating. It had been long weeks since the last ship from the outer world had entered the little port.

We lingered here for three days while the supercargo unloaded his bales of bright cotton goods, his blue and scarlet *pareu* from the looms of Manchester, and other merchandise to be traded at the Chinese stores. I put up with Nee, a retired sea captain. He had made the run between Rurutu, Tupuai, and Papeete, eastward to the Tuamotu and as far south as Rapa.

Nee has sired sixteen children by the same wife, of whom twelve are still alive. With his earnings he built himself the handsomest and most imposing house on the island. It is a more stately and spacious dwelling than that of the *arii* — the former king — who still receives his pension from the French government. It is the only house in the village of two stories. The second floor is one large reception room about which runs a wide veranda. I was graciously offered this apartment during my stay. It held three shiny brass beds, a number of gilt mirrors, rocking chairs, and a table on which reposed the large *Pipiria* — Bible — the only book I know of translated into Tahitian.

Nee and his family sleep and eat in small bamboo outhouses, located in the rear so as not to mar the full effect of his mansion. It stands a little back from the grassy road that runs parallel to the beach a hundred yards inland. The road is lined with coco palms, acacias, and poinciana trees. The small white houses are well spaced, neat and clean, hedged with hibiscus and flowering gardenia. In contrast to the withering heat and pigpens of the Tuamotu the village is a cool and sunny paradise. We must be a great distance south of Tahiti and the other Society Islands for the land about is open, the hills covered with scrub fern and dwarf guavas, the sturdy *aito* crowning the summits. We are almost out of the tropics.

There are other differences that suggest — even today in our age of rapid travel and immediate telegraphic communication — the many changes in language, mores, and physical type which the immense barrier of ocean wilderness has built up during the stretch of hundreds of years between island and island. Although the Rurutuans all speak the language of the Society Islanders, I am aware of little differences in their speech. Here they leave out the h's and f's. Instead of *a hio i te fare rahi* — look at the big house — they say *a 'io i te 'are rai'i.* By an analogous law of phonetics Tahitians have dropped the *k* which occurs in Hawaiian and Tuamotuan — the Tahitians saying *'ai* for *kai* — food, *ma'ita'i* for *makitaki* — good, and *taata* for *kanaka* — a man or person.

I also notice a charming divergence of feminine attire. The women in their Sunday best for church service, instead of combing their perfumed tresses over their shoulders, braid them in long and modest pigtails and crown their heads with tall straw hats, fancifully woven in black and white patterns.

Although the Rurutuans are warm and hospitable to visitors from distant isles, they seem a more disciplined and less frivolous society than Tahitians. During the church service many small boys stood up to recite memorized passages from the Holy Scripture. As each young orator arose he would begin his recitation by announcing: "*Ua taviri hia te mau parau* — The words are now begun." And as he sat down: "*Opani hia* — They are closed (or finished)." The boys declaimed with youthful ardor, unprompted by their elders. All Polynesians — probably all primitive people — are born orators, impetuous and eloquent.

The village either lacks the money to buy a net or scorns such a newfangled gadget. As the fish begin to circle and approach the shore, perhaps driven in by sharks or other large game fish, the men gather at either end of the school and run down into the water, dragging with them pandanus leaves loosely strung together. They make a great splashing in the water. The frightened fish are driven into a narrowing enclosure of coral blocks. The women follow and scoop up the fish as they try desperately to make their way back into the open harbor.

Before I left Papeete, Moe, the daughter of old Taura, had asked me to bring her news of Pepe, her former *tane*. Pepe's father is by far the wealthiest man on the island. He owns a store in each of the three villages, Moerai, Averau, and Auti, and is a partner in a Chinese bank in Papeete. Last year he made a small fortune trading in vanilla. Yet the old miser lives in a small dark closet in the back of his store. Pepe told me that he will not allow him to marry. A woman would only eat up his earnings. She would be a useless extravagance. I think Pepe is fond of Moe. I told him that she had remained faithful to him. He shrugged his shoulders. "Let her take another man" was all he said. The Chinese are cold, practical realists. Or is the old man more ambitious for his son than I believed him to be? Perhaps he is thinking of sending over to Canton for a daughter-in-law. This would cost him a pretty penny.

There are plans afoot to bring down a motion picture outfit from Papeete. This is causing some excitement and much concern. The matter was freely debated at the *fare putuputuraa* — the village meeting house.

"But where can they install the cameras?" Nee asked me. "People will not allow them in their houses. They are afraid of them."

"Why not keep them in the *fare putuputuraa*?" I asked.

"That would not be right," said Nee. "These things are the devil's work."

During my three days' stay with Nee he fed me on roast pig and chicken. Yet he refused to take any money. I was his guest. I repaid his hospitality with various small presents for the six of his children — all of them grown men — who happened at the time to be staying with him. I made drawings of him and his wife, both of which he pronounced acceptable.

April 10, 1922

We approached Rimatara in the rain. My first impression of the island was unfavorable. The sailors were unloading bales of rice and boxes of merchandise for the Chinese stores. I spoke to a group of girls seated on a low mound beneath some giant slabs of rock. I had observed these with curiosity, for they stood out clearly, at a great distance from the shore. The girls informed me that they were memorial pillars or tombstones of the former rulers of the island. They themselves were the grandchildren of the last reigning Queen — the *arii vahine*. I read the inscription on one of the monuments: "*Tamaeva IV, Arii no Rimatara i pohe ai Novema 28, 1866* — Tamaeva IV, King of Rimatara, died November 28, 1866." The girls told me the present *arii vahine*, Himataura, was his daughter.

While we were talking the sailors had finished unloading their wares. Most of the girls went with them in the scow to take a look at the schooner. One of them, the youngest, lingered behind. Her name is Tamahareia. I asked her if she would accompany me to the house of the *arii vahine* so that I might make a silverpoint drawing of her. We found the aged Himataura taking her ease inside her dwelling. The room was bare. Pandanus mats were spread about the floor. The walls were of plastered blocks of coral. The roof of pandanus. The only piece of furniture, a handsome hand-carved settee of rustic design, stood in a corner.

Himataura lay on a pandanus mat, her head resting on a low stool. We talked for a while together. Her eyes were dim and her memory at times faltered. Yet she had the dignity of bearing, the serenity and low-pitched assurance that one associates with nature's aristocracy. When I asked her age she became a little confused but was quite certain that she was born in 1830. The date had stuck in her memory. Tamahareia added that her eldest boy is over seventy. Himataura said with evident pride that, although she no longer has control of the island, she receives an annual pension from the French government.

I asked the *arii vahine* where she had gotten the settee which I much admired. It was made, she assured me, *matamua* — many years ago — by her royal husband, who learned the carpenter's trade from the American whalers that in those days visited the island. This kindled my imagination. Had Melville in his wanderings ever been to Rimatara? Was I perhaps talking to someone who had known and spoken to the greatest of our writers? What then might have been the beauty of this old woman whose looks so captivated me now?

The *arii vahine* agreed to pose for a silverpoint portrait head. I seated her by the open door and hastened to draw her. Gradually her head sank on her breast.

Later that afternoon I returned. I had promised to make a drawing of little Tamahareia. Tama, as her cousins call her for short, is fifteen or sixteen years old. Her complexion is light. Her face is oval with the lovely slanting eyes of a Botticelli wood nymph. She tells me with pride that she is *Rimatara tumu mau* — of the genuine stock, more literally, of the very root of Rimatara. I teased her about her slanting eyes, saying that she was more likely *afa tinito tumu mau* — of half genuine Chinese breed.

It was getting late. I had some difficulty in finding the proper light for my charming model. I turned her head one way and another. "Now kiss her," said one of her facetious cousins, who sat on the floor weaving a pandanus mat. "Wait until I have found the right pose," I said. Then I kissed her.

During the four days the *Parks* rode at anchor outside the reef. I stopped at the house of Uua, the *mutoi*, grandson of the old Queen. Every evening my host brought me a pail of water and a freshly ironed *pareu*, that I might bathe and have a change of linen. After supper neighbors would drop in. The talk turned on the affairs of the great outside world. They were eager to know the prices of vanilla and copra on the Papeete market. I had dinner once at the house of the *arii vahine*. She presented me with a piece of the native cloth — *ohipa mahui* — which she had pounded herself from the bark of the *auti*. Today it is a lost art.

During those four days in Rimatara I had the haunting feeling that I was lingering in the Garden of Eden. In the afternoons when I had finished sketching, little Tama, gentle and possessive, took me in charge. Holding my hand she walked with me about the island paths. Nor did she fail to introduce me to the villagers we met.

"*Ovai tera tamaiti* — Who is that young man?"

"*O Tihoti* — It is George."

The answer seemed to satisfy their curiosity. "*A*," they would assent instead of "*E*," as in Tahiti.

April 13, 1922

Uua, the good *mutoi*, escorted me to the shore to bid me farewell. One of his sons accompanied us bearing parting gifts — a chicken, a sack of oranges, clusters of *fei* and bananas, a basket of coconuts. He and little Tama rowed out with me to the *Parks*. I presented Uua with a dress for his wife, and another one of a more sober pattern for his grandmother, the *arii vahine*. To little Tama, a box of scented soap. I would willingly have given her far more. I shall always remember her.

Why do they show such kindness to a stranger?

April 14, 1922

At sea. I keep thinking about the true meaning of "form" in art. It is not the mere translation of nature into abstract or geometric patterns. A drawing of Holbein has more form than any Cubist painting I have yet seen.

Max Nordau writes in his *Degeneration*: "To the weak-headed everything which is clearly, firmly defined, and which therefore has strictly only one meaning is flat. To them everything is profound which has no meaning and which therefore allows them to apply what meaning they please."

The art — the line — of the archaic Greeks, the Egyptians, and the Chinese was clear-cut and sharply defined. They were not afraid of clarity and vigor of statement. Today much of modern art shrinks from severity of line and form, and takes refuge in complexity, the impalpable, nebulous, and symbolic. And yet it is the only contemporary art that deeply impresses and concerns me.

April 15, 1922

Tubuai came into view about fifty kilometers away, a shapeless cloud under the rising moon. On our starboard quarter the Southern Cross — *fetia tatauro* — slanted into the ocean. Behind us hung Orion's Belt.

April 16, 1922

I borrowed a horse from one of the natives and rode about the island. In the evening I joined the sailors, bathing in an inland fresh-water pool — Aki, Paruru, Teina, Marama, Peni, and Tuerai.

April 20, 1922

The *Parks* is loaded. In the hold two hundred bales of copra, and the cockpit packed with more copra about the rudder box. In the aftercabin sacks of starch piled up above the level of the upper berths. The water tanks moved aft to either side of the cabins, so as to clear the main deck. Here stalls of *purau* poles have been set up and lashed together. A dozen cattle and forty pigs have been hoisted on board and herded into the stalls. In the bow are two hundred chickens in crates. A dozen turkeys wander about the fore deck. Others are lashed to the capstans by the leg. Forward of the cookhouse great piles of fodder for the animals, banana stems and grass; and, hung over the rail for the crew, clusters of *fei* and bananas, sacks of oranges, and drinking coconuts. In addition to the cargo we are carrying thirty natives from Tubuai back to Rurutu.

We took our supper on deck in the rain. There was no space in the cabin. Before eating there was a silence. The men uncovered. One of them prayed.

The supercargo nudged me. "C'est bien le genre *kanaque*."

I lay below on my pandanus mat in the dark. The black *popoti* — cockroaches — scurried over me. I meditated for a long time on certain aspects of art.

A year and a half ago when I first read Clive Bell I became deeply intrigued with his assumption that the aesthetic value of a painting hinges entirely on "significant form." If the reaction to life and nature has in itself no aesthetic importance are not the Cubists and other abstract artists justified in omitting it from their painting? Although I was convinced that they were wrong I was troubled by their dialectics. Nor could I understand or define the subtle relation in painting between the formal and the human elements.

The answer to the apparent impasse which has troubled me all this time suddenly burst upon me and became clear. *Painting is not significant form. It is the response to nature expressed in significant form: line, color, and design.*

And this must be also true of every art medium: sculpture, architecture, poetry, and the dance, all of which relate to and interpret life.

The substance, the raw material of each of these art forms is apprehended by a different sense: the eye, the ear, the mind, the touch, or the innate response to movement and rhythm. When this inert matter is infused with life by a personal vision it is sublimated into art.

My own twin forebears have been the Japanese printmakers and the giants of French Impressionism. In the main my art idiom is traditional and representational. Recently under the invigorating influence of Arthur Carles' paintings, of La Chaise's sculpture, and of Diederich's craft design much of my work has become more abstracted and conventionalized. Does this divergence in style imply vacillation or incertitude?

I think not. For if the *art form* governs the treatment of nature's raw material, then surely the degree to which an artist may vary his style, slide from the literal rendering to the highly abstract, will depend on the kind and purpose of his work. A portrait, a mural decoration, the design for a window curtain or a water jug, will impose a different degree of stylization on his work.*

April 22, 1922

Te po hopea no te haerea — the last night of the voyage. William Kemp, the Tuamotuan captain, crouched by the rudder box. He recited story after story of the *tau tahito* — the ancient legendary days.

He told of the two children who sat with nothing for supper but a bit of breadfruit in their hands, waiting for their parents who had gone out to the reef to spear fish. The little children waited and waited but their parents lingered on the reef and ate the fish. And the children grew tired of waiting and flew up to heaven. *Pipiri ma* they are called — the two who cling together — the constellation of the Pleiades. Their parents called to them in vain. *Pipiri ma* are still angry and will never more return. The legend has become a cradle rhyme which the mothers sing to their babies to nurse them to sleep:

"Pipiri ma e,	"Pipiri ma,
Hoi mai e."	Come back to us."
"Aita maua e hoi atu."	"We shall never return to you."
Tautai ino te ramarama.	Ill was the night fishing by torchlight.
Tautai faatii tamarii e.	The children were disappointed in the catch.
Ua riro aenei na pupa i ura	Ere now they have been changed into
i te rai e.	flower clusters, purple-flaming in the sky.

He told of the island of Meetia, which formerly was flat like Makatea. But an *aito* snatched it from the sea and turned it upside down. And today one can find fossilized eel and *maoa* shells on the summit of the mountain which rises like a great boar's tooth from the sea. "*E teie mahana!* — Even to this very day!"

He told of the tunnel which pierces Tahiti from one end to the other, from Marao on the west coast to the Valley of Papenoo on the north. So that if the leaves of the *mape* are flung into the current on one shore they will emerge on the other. "*E teie mahana!*"

He told of the *tahua* — the priest — who led the fire-walkers on Raiatea. Before proceeding barefoot over the red-hot stones he would wave a branch of *auti* and cry aloud: "*Haere atu te pape! Haere atu te matai!* — Let the waters fall back! Let the winds die down!" And

* The above — among other jottings — were the groping and tentative notes that I hastily scratched down the following morning on the deck of the *Parks*, a bale of copra at my back — my thoughts now momentarily arrested by the laughter and chatter of the sailors, now drifting with the wailing current of the Tuamotuan *himene*. These notes are the point of departure for the more carefully considered aesthetics which I advanced over thirty years later in my *Yes and No of Contemporary Art*. Today much is written about art, and most of it is indiscriminately swallowed down. Little, however, is digested by tough, sober thinking. I do not claim originality for my ideas. I can at least cite a worthy authority. Leonardo da Vinci once observed that what most stirred his imagination was to let his eyes wander over the cracks and smudges of a plastered wall. That is, *seeing an abstract form, he intuitively integrated it with an observed image of the visual world.*

the flames which licked up from the red embers turned and parted in either direction so that the priest and those who followed him walked boldly over the stones without even burning the soles of their feet. But if one should turn and glance over the shoulder he would be grievously scalded.

"Did anyone disobey him and glance around?" I asked.

"One man, and he was badly burned. But the *tahua* waved his branch of *auti* about his feet and the burns were cured." This fresh evidence would surely brush aside any doubts in the minds of his listeners.

William Kemp spoke of his grandfather, another *tahua* from one of the islands of the Tuamotu. His grandfather had the cunning to bewitch and kill whom he would. He would steal a few strands of the victim's hair, a shred of his clothes, and as he shook hands with him would scrape a grain of dirt from the palm of his hand. All this, together with a lizard, he would wrap in the husk of a coconut. And with this sorcery he could charm and kill.

He told of a man and his *tavini* – servant – who were swallowed by a whale and borne to a distant island of the Tuamotu. In this island there were no men and the women coupled with sea cucumbers. Now one of the women cut open the whale which was stranded on the beach and she prevailed on the man to have intercourse with her. Finding him more agreeable than a sea cucumber she spread the news among her friends. Eventually the two men had children from all the women on the island. But his servant's children all bore wings. So lest they fly away they were kept covered by a *peue* – a pandanus mat. Unhappily one day the covering was removed. The children flew away and were never more heard from. But the others remained and to this day their descendants inhabit the island. "*E teie mahana!*"

He told of the *aito* who was so enormous that when he fell he broke the island in two pieces. And even to this day it is cleft in the middle. The *aito*, when he fought, could hurl a rock from one end of the lagoon to the other. He could piss for the distance of a mile in a great waterspout and drown his enemies in the stream of his urine.

He told of the small cup worn into the rock on the summit of one of the mountains on Tahiti which is ever brimming with water. And though a hundred people drink from this small cup it is never emptied.

And of that other small bowl of water in the mountains, the surface of which shudders when a human soul is carried away.

By now the night was far gone. Out of his great knowledge of the islands William Kemp, the Tuamotuan half-caste, recounted the folk tales of the faroff legendary days. About us on the deck the sailors lay, half-naked in their *pareu*. Many listened. Some gossiped together, reclining against the bales of copra. Others slept.

The Captain further told us of the sirens who drag the sailors down into the *moana* – the deep. And how some Tuamotuan sailors came upon one of these sea women lying asleep on a rock. They bound her tightly down by her long hair which was her only covering. Then each of them ravished her and they left her bound by her hair to the rock.

Lastly he told of the island in the Tuamotu whose inhabitants will die four times in succession. For when a man dies his spirit, the *tupapau*, will go searching for a home, *apoona roto i te moana* — a hole deep down in the sea. And if he cannot find it he will return and enter his old body and bring it back to life. This miracle William Kemp saw himself, with upwards of a hundred others. After the body had quivered and come again to life for the third time the dead man told those about him not to bury him for another three days. Not until his body should become *mea pe* — a bit overripe. For this would be the sure evidence that his *tupapau* had found a new home in the depths of the sea. But the French Governor insisted on an immediate burial notwithstanding the protests of the islanders. When on the third day they returned to the grave they saw the earth shake and quiver. They knew then that the man lay below, scratching at the soil. It was *mea riaria* — a most terrible sight — to watch.

The eyes of the narrator shone. His back stiffened and he leaned forward as he crouched. His deep voice vibrated with emotion. The ship's engine throbbed. About us was the splendor of the night.

April 23, 1922

Eight A.M. About eighty miles away Tahiti *nui* is now plainly visible, lying pale and transparent on the edge of the sea. The highest peaks of Orohena are blanketed. The base of the island merges into the milky sea.

A few hours later Moorea and now Maia come into view. The lifeless heat beats down on the oily sea. Now the islands are hidden in the clouds. They fade away and emerge again from the cumulus clouds which swell and tumble on the edge of the ocean.

It is night and Tahiti is still many miles away. William Kemp and a *petania* — a Mormon missionary — from Rurutu argue whether Jesus Christ ever came to America. Both men are versed in the Scriptures. They exchange pithy and subtle arguments with frequent quotations from the Bible.

"How could Christ have come to America, since it was not yet discovered, nor for many years to come?"

"But America existed before it was discovered and Christ in his wisdom could have found it if he so wished."

"But why, then, is this not mentioned in the Gospels by his many disciples and friends?"

"But it is mentioned in the Mormon Bible. This indeed is the strongest evidence that what we believe is true."

"Because something is written in a book is no evidence at all. How can you show that this is not all a lie — *te mau parau haavare*?"

"But the only evidence that you give me that Christ did not come to America is your Bible. That, too, is a book. It well may tell a lie."

It is eleven o'clock. We are running by the lights of Paea. The cliffs of Punavia are dimly outlined against the blackness of the sky. I went below and slept. At two in the morning we dropped anchor inside the reef of Papeete.

I LINGERED for a few days in Papeete before returning to Tautira. After the month's sea voyage in the *Parks* with Captain Kemp and his Tuamotuan sailors it was a joy to see Hall and Nordy again. They were always curious about distant shores. Nordy to store up bits of information for a future story: the savor and features of the different islands, mannerisms of speech, dress, the flora, trees, and way of life. Hall, poet and mystic, perhaps dreaming of some distant cruise, alone in the crow's nest, to Rapa or Pitcairn.

At the Annex Pare mixed us his delectable rum punches. He was the perfect host in his freshly ironed white drill suit, powdered, scented – the Comte de Noailles had left him a bottle of really good French eau de cologne – gently coquetting in his stilted colonial French badinage or his exquisitely turned Tahitian obscenities.

Sometimes if we were lazy we would send one of Pare's boys to the Chinaman to bring us two or three Cantonese dishes in tin receptacles. Other evenings we wandered up for dinner to the Tiare. I loved the rambling, shabby, low-roofed, broad-verandaed old hostelry. The floor boards creaked, the mirrors were cracked, and the furniture in need of repair. But deeply shadowed mangoes and wide-branched poinciana trees kept the crazy corrugated tin roof always cool. There was no formal or cultivated garden but an untamed jungle of annuals and flowering vines, slowly encroaching on the paths and, as everywhere in the tropics, about to smother the old building itself; a disordered patchwork of color, zinnias, marigolds, red and white lilies, yellow and scarlet hibiscus, the multicolored croton bushes, bougainvillaea, and the flowering *piti* vines.

We might wait a long time for our dinner but there was always laughter from the kitchen. Mau was as jovial a host as Pare. We had good talk at the Tiare, with French wine and perhaps more rum punches after dinner. But in the tropics one rises and retires early. Now the cool season was nearing. About ten o'clock we sauntered down to the waterfront for a stroll along the silent quays before retiring to the Annex.

Nordy told me one day that an acquaintance of his at the Cercle Bougainville – as I remember it was rugged old Captain Jo Winchester who had threatened to horsewhip poor Freddy O'Brien – wanted to meet me. He had heard that I was a painter. He had acquired a sculpture by Gauguin. He couldn't make head or tail out of it, and wanted to know what I thought of it.

Nordy and Hall were both members of the Cercle Bougainville. I never went there. I knew the sort I should have to meet and have drinks with, and I wanted to avoid them; the occasional celebrities and globe-trotters who were put up for their few weeks' stay between steamers, and the thin-blooded French storekeepers, ship chandlers, and petty government bureaucrats who had lived too long in the tropics and spoke of the Tahitians as *kanaques* and hated the island. But I fancy one ran into some interesting characters, too.

Frank Stimson, the subsequently famous anthropologist, brother of Van Wyck Brooks's first wife and nephew of Henry L. Stimson, who served in the cabinets of three presidents, occasionally visited the Cercle. He had drifted to Tahiti a few years before and supported himself working in one of the big general stores. The natives called him *Taporo* – lemon. I never knew the significance of the byname. He was living with a native girl, Meri, and spent his evenings doing chess puzzles. He had just published a new Tahitian grammar and he had invented some sort of gadget which could register the day of the week for any date since the birth of Christ. But he never could raise the money to get it patented. "I couldn't persuade anyone that it had a practical value," he told me.

Then there were the three Smiths. There was "Borneo" Smith, a retired professor from the Massachusetts Institute of Technology, a friend of Hall's, who had brought with him a fine collection of sarongs from Indonesia, examples of which he gave his friends. He lived alone in a little house near Madame Butscher's at Taravao and did his own cooking and housekeeping. The second was "Whiskey" Smith. That pretty well describes all there was of interest to say about him. All the newcomers in Papeete were baptized with an identifying nickname. The third was "Seven Kilometer" Smith. He was such a completely faded, colorless, retiring individual that there was nothing really to identify him by except that he lived seven kilometers from Papeete. Joseph Conrad would have found the Cercle Bougainville grist for his mill. And O'Brien did – to his chagrin!

Of course I was tremendously excited to see Gauguin's sculpture and the Captain brought it to the Annex the following day. It was not a sculpture at all but a woodblock from which the artist had run off an edition of prints. Only a few years previously Somerset Maugham on a trip around the world had stopped off at Papeete and had bought for a stiff price a painted windowframe which still decorated the shack in which the artist had lived. And of course the recent publication of *Noa Noa* and O'Brien's books had put Gauguin on the map even in Tahiti.

I couldn't persuade the Captain to part with the woodblock. But he let me keep it for a couple of weeks. I was anxious to run off an edition of twenty prints for myself. I promised him one of them and assured him – although it was quite unnecessary, for the Captain was a guileless man – that I should not sell them but give them as souvenirs to my friends in Tahiti and in the States.

After I returned to Tautira I struck off about twenty prints on some soft Japanese rice paper which I had brought down with me. It is as fine a print as any by the artist I have seen. I wonder if it has appeared in any of the Gauguin catalogues. As with many of his South Sea Island paintings the subject matter is a mixture of esoteric and sentimental symbolism. In the foreground crouches a strange half-human, half-animal monster, *Te Varua Ino* – the Evil Spirit. Opposite is the figure of a Madonna and child, and in the background another image, *Te Atua* – God. Although Gauguin used a different vocabulary from the Pre-Raphaelites, he was closer to them in sentiment than to Toulouse-Lautrec. But as an artist his color anticipated the Fauves and the design in some of his prints is completely modern in spirit. Along with Degas's later work he was one of the precursors of modern art – that branch of it which by-passed Cubism and Abstraction.

The Captain's interest in Gauguin's art

was purely commercial. He owned another item by the artist in which he took no interest and which he was happy to give to me as a keepsake. It was a copy of *Le Sourire*, one of a series of hand-printed and illustrated brochures, violent and scurrilous political attacks on the French administration of the island, but more particularly on the local head of the Catholic Church, "Le Vicaire Apostolique de Tahiti." As self-appointed pamphleteer, champion and protector of the natives, Gauguin castigated all these worthies, in the most savage language, for neglect, inhumanity, hypocrisy, and corruption. By way of pseudonym he signed his articles *Titoi* – the Tahitian word meaning "Go masturbate." Paul Gauguin was all of a piece. But it is no wonder that he was *persona non grata* among the government hierarchy on the island.

After my exhibition at the Wildenstein Galleries in New York the following autumn I spent three years in Paris. Having no home or storage place in the States I left some of my treasures with a friend, among them the copy of *Le Sourire*. In the shuffle it disappeared. Perhaps somewhere there exists another copy. I hope so. For the brochure is of authentic interest to the art historian. It explains a good deal of what was genuine and what was meretricious in the artist. Gauguin found in Tahiti – as I did – beauty among the natives and an Arcadian purity of life. But he could only express it in the *M'en foutisme* and bathetic cynicism of the Europe of Oscar Wilde and *L'Assiette au Beure*.*

Gauguin was an educated man and his aesthetics was far more intellectualized than that of Cézanne or Van Gogh, whose approach to their art was more direct and intuitive. I find nothing in his makeup that suggests either a mentally unbalanced man or a neurotic. What urged him to the Caribbean and later to the South Sea Islands was the romantic and the rebel in him. He had an obvious identification with Tahiti and spent many years there and in the Marquesas. He was fond of using Tahitian titles for his paintings and many Tahitian words and phrases crop up in his *Noa Noa* † and in his letters. It has always surprised me a little that he had such a superficial knowledge of the language and wrote it so incorrectly. There is an amusing example of such a mistake, the title of one of his most famous and beautiful paintings, "Mahana Navenave." *Navenave* means beautiful or harmonious, but in reference to music or choral singing. The other use of the word describes the culmination of sexual delight, an orgasm. The word is, then, the exact rendition of the French verb *jouir*. I know of no other language in which the same word is used to describe the ecstasy which one experiences from great art and the supreme expression of physical love. I like to think that such a word is only

*A great French illustrated periodical, published between 1895 and 1905. Cynical, anti-military, anti-clerical, anti-government, and reformist. Although the Gallic offspring of Rabelais and Voltaire, it was in many ways comparable with *Simplicissimus* and anticipated the old *Masses*. It was the mouthpiece of such famous satirists as Forain, Steinlen, Naudin, and Poulbot.

† *Noanoa* means fragrant. This purely imaginative and charming idyl suggests a great deal about the author but little about the island, and the characterization of the Tahitian is entirely idealized. I see nothing in the title that seems at all relevant.

coined by a civilized and sensitive people. But the word in France, as in Tahiti, must be used with discretion. To talk of a girl, or of the morning — *mahana* — as *navenave* could only elicit, and often did, gales of laughter.

Tautira, April 28, 1922

Good to see Naipu again. After a six months' visit to the States he got back to Tautira just after I left for the Tuamotu. He has wound up his affairs there. Says he hates it more than ever and has no desire to return. What kept him there longer than he intended was a visit to the Johns Hopkins Hospital in Baltimore. Dr. MacCallum had him in the clinic for a week. They put him through every kind of test. But the results were all negative. "It's definitely not elephantiasis. MacCallum is cautious and won't express an opinion." The villagers here are more convinced than ever that anyone who has profaned an old *marae* by building on it will suffer. His left forearm is definitely more swollen. It doesn't give him too much trouble and he takes a rather morbid pleasure in talking about it. He seems to think the swelling has periodic cycles of inflammation. "Very much," he says with his strained smile, "like a woman's menstruation."

May 21, 1922

During the past three weeks working on my watercolors. I have now finished sixty-five.*

May 22, 1922

For the past ten days the cold *maraamu* has been drifting down from the mist-swept mountains. A week ago the river rose two, three, four feet in as many hours. The valley has been engulfed by the steady downpour. Great *mape* trees were uprooted in the valley, borne down on the current, and swept out to sea.

The villagers are salvaging the drying copra, their chief source of wealth. Others in their dugouts are as far out as the reef rescuing what they can from the drifting coco palms. My garden is submerged. The road is a riverbed as far down as Tafaite's house. In the taro patch and low land across the road boys splash about knee deep, rescuing drowning chickens. A dozen men, detached from the detail which work off their taxes repairing the road, strip down and swim across the river. "*Faa itoito*," they shout to encourage each other as they furiously chop out a new channel through the black spit of sand. Gradually the rising accumulation of water is discharged. In the evening Ueri brings me in a big pan of eels which had been stranded on the flats.

May 23, 1922

In June there is to be a triple wedding. Two or three times a week the members of the families gather at a *himene* to discuss the many details of the ceremony and organize the ban-

*One of these was bought by Sam Lewisohn from my Wildenstein exhibition. He bequeathed it with most of his paintings to the Metropolitan Museum of Art.

quet. After the meetings they sing and pray. I lay outside the house of Paea the *orometua* under the black patchwork of a mango tree. The rhythmic, asymmetric texture of the chorus, rising, galloping, wailing. Passionate, intense, purposeful, lamenting, dying, with that last, final, long drawn out E-E-E-e-e-e. Is it their music which carries the deepest, most meaningful and authentic spirit of the race? Or the laughter, the factitious smiles, and the prurient chatter of the *taurearea*, the drugstore-counter loafers?

I drink in the yearning, the passion, the sadness, and the fulfillment of the singing. Will it smooth out the wrinkles that eat away my peace of mind, my effort to achieve serenity in this Garden of Eden?

To sing. To pray: to accumulate.

In the faintly lit room of Paea's house, I can just glimpse his two daughters, Teura whose youthful curves and budding grace enchant me, and her gentle sister Toahite whose eyes in their innocence are not without a silent understanding. I suspect Teura of coquetting with me. When I meet the two sisters chaperoned by their mother on the way up the river for their evening bath, she sticks out her tongue at me, swaying her hips in the most provoking manner.

All day long about my house I endure the never-ending babbling, the screaming and bickering of the children. At times they drive me nearly mad. Each night I look forward to the moment when little Moerai, Uraponi, and Terae Hara bid me goodnight and slip up to the house of Arai *vahine*. At last I am alone.

On the way home from the *himene* I meet Teata, the ancient, lean, and wrinkled wife of Tafaite the cripple. Her black dress is trussed up about her thighs. Her pendant breasts catch the copper light of her lantern. What was she like in the vigor of her youth when she cooked and waited on Robert Louis Stevenson at the house of Ori a Ori?

She has been out on the reef after small *fee* — octopus. With her lantern she lures them from the shallow water to the surface. With one hand she snatches and pulls them from the shallow water. Their tentacles, loosened from the coral, twine about her arm. With her free hand she spears them in their one eye. She will chop them up, cook them in the *hima*, and serve them with taro tips in a succulent sauce of *miti haari*. She insisted on my taking home a portion of her catch.

June 4, 1922

Paruparu limped into the house today while I was at work and silently deposited at my feet a segment of bamboo covered with a *purau* leaf. It contained a starch confection of *ape* — a native vegetable — sweetened with honey. At first I thought the offering was in return for little favors I had recently done him, the loan of my machete which he has not yet returned and a letter I typed for him to send to a girl friend in Paea. I was mistaken. He stood before me a long time waiting, his eyes on the demijohn. But I was able to outface his cynical gravity.

Teura

June 8, 1922

When little Moerai is in the mood he helps Terae Hara with the housework. The floors occasionally get swept and my bed is made up at least every other day. He does most of the cooking, husks and fries the coffee beans, goes up the river after fresh water once a day, and climbs the coco palms to shake down the nuts. After all he is only twelve years old and when he smiles at me I know that between us there is understanding and shared happiness.

A few days ago he was playing with the heavy iron cart which the men use to carry shingles from the beach for the new roadbed. He crushed his thumb, breaking it in two places, and I have sent him to Papeete with Arai *vahine* to have it set by Dr. Cassiau. Without giving me a by-your-leave Terae Hara has gone along with them. Now I am quite alone and living like a poor white. The bed is no longer made up. I try to forget the filth and disorder. I cook eggs and tea for breakfast. Something out of a can and tea again for supper. At lunch time if I am lucky I corral a passing girl to help me out and wash the dishes. I need a woman.

Uraponi has the heart of a louse, unmindful of all my goodness to her, the blue and pink ribbons, the hair combs, the visit to Dr. Cassiau when she injured her finger, the heaping platters of rice, canned beef, bread and jam. She does nothing to help but hovers about the place like a little scavenger, slipping in at meal time. But I forget all her ingratitude in the joy of her presence, the copper-colored hair, golden skin, and red-brown eyes; the delicate limbs, the slim belly, and the flat modeling of her sphinx-like face.

June 14, 1922

I have been reading Albert Gleizes' *Du Cubisme.** What particularly interests me in this somewhat dogmatic treatise is his bold statement that since all painting is the decoration of a two-dimensional surface, "Prétendre l'investir d'une troisième dimension, c'est vouloir la dénaturer dans son essence même. . . . La peinture a deux mesures, la sculpture en a trois. La vie de la surface dépend de cette évidence."

This makes sense. When Clive Bell and the critics talk of the three-dimensional design of Cubism and the deep-spatial composition of Cézanne's paintings, they are talking nonsense. Last winter, without in the least convincing him, I argued at length about this with Tom Benton. Before starting to draw on a canvas Benton makes little clay models of his figures. These he groups to his satisfaction on a small set. He is then convinced that his painting acquires a three-dimensional design.†

I have never been quite sure what Berenson means by his theory of the "tactile values" of paintings. I suppose it is that he believes that the *suggestion* of solidity and space is in it-

* I met Gleizes a year later in Paris with a letter of introduction from Hunt Diederich. We became warm friends and he wrote the introduction to the catalogue of my exhibition at the Galerie Barbazange.

† Tintoretto also used small wax models for his paintings. But for a very different purpose. He was interested in drawing his figures greatly foreshortened. It is more convenient to do this from small wax models than hanging a man up side down from the ceiling.

self of great aesthetic significance. But whether you agree with him or not this is saying something very different.

In all this talk of three-dimensional design by the critics there is, it seems to me, a confusion between the design of a flat surface, which has two dimensions, and the *subject matter* of the design. Ever since paleolithic man first scratched his pictures on the walls of caves artists have used different symbols to record what they saw and what particularly interested them. For the Japanese printmakers a black band was evocative of night. The painters of the Renaissance used Euclidean perspective, Rembrandt chiaroscuro, and the Impressionists broken color tones to indicate atmospheric depth. Individual artists, as also alternating epochs and civilizations, have seen nature and responded to life with different visions. Some saw the world in sharp outline and in two dimensions. Other periods — the Greeks and the Egyptians — were impressed by its solidity and mass, and they best expressed it in carved stone. Still others were obsessed in breaking it up into radiant flecks of color or in symbols and abstract patterns — the Hopi Indians and the great periods of Moslem art. But the "significant form" of their paintings was of necessity phrased in two dimensions on a flat surface in terms of line, color, and design.*

My own inclination is with Gleizes that the highest form of painting should appear to remain on the surface rather than *suggest* a third dimension as do Rembrandt, Rubens, and the other artists of the Baroque School. I am of course biased, for I seem more and more to see things sharply outlined and in the flat. But how the French bore me with their passion for dogma, manifestoes, and isms. It is important for each artist to work out his own aesthetics and know what direction he wants to follow. But he should show restraint in laying down the law for others.

June 23, 1922

Nanai is a good little sport, a real tomboy. She would much rather leave the housework to the boys and join the men hauling the nets or climb to the topmost branches of the trees after oranges. But now she is three months gone in pregnancy. She has had one miscarriage. Naipu, who is as solicitous of her health as he is of her deportment, has explicitly forbidden such activities. She has disobeyed him. I am sure he feels that according to the terms he laid down when she first came to keep house for him this is grounds for getting rid of her and sending her back to Papeete. There are, however, mitigating circumstances. Here is what happened.

Yesterday there was a meeting of the *taiate* — the joint owners of the new net — to consider certain problems which had arisen. Since Naipu is the principal shareholder he invited the others for the discussion to his wide veranda and he asked me to sit in as interpreter.

* There is, however, one exception, pointed out to me years later by Diego Rivera. A mural painting can properly be said to have three dimensions since its color and treatment may alter one's apperception and impression of the hall or building which it decorates. I have treated this subject at greater length in my *Yes and No of Contemporary Art.*

Nanai, with the Valley of Ataroa in the background

Ueri had passed round cigarettes and coffee. The proper formalities had been exchanged. Things were moving along smoothly but without unnecessary haste. According to the accustomed ritual each member of the *taiate* was asked in turn for his opinion. He would get up and deliver it in carefully phrased rhetorical periods.

The discussion was interrupted by a commotion from the living room. Ueri came out and whispered loudly to Naipu that there was an important *popaa* who had driven out from Papeete to visit him. It was a hot day and we were all sitting about in our *pareu* stripped to the waist. Naipu got up, apologized to the *taiate* for the unexpected interruption, and we both went in.

He was an American regular army major in full uniform, overseas ribbons and decorations, stopping over on some mission or other on his way to Australia. He had a letter of introduction to Naipu from someone in the States. Naipu bowed but did not shake hands. He read the card of introduction without showing any particular cordiality. He dislikes anyone who barges in on him and violates his privacy.

"Major," he said, "I am sure you will excuse me, but I am engaged in a business talk with a number of my friends. I shall join you as soon as possible. In the meanwhile here are some excellent cigars. My boy will bring you a rum punch. We have no ice out here but I am sure you will make allowances for this. And now you will excuse me." He bowed again from the waist. The major seemed not so much ruffled as benumbed and thunderstruck.

We rejoined the *taiate*. For another hour the oratory rolled on. There was another commotion. This time from Nanai's *fare taoto* — sleeping shed. Several women were in there talking and wailing. Arai *vahine* came out and beckoned to Naipu. He again got up, excused himself for this second interruption, and went in to see what had happened. He was gone a long while.

Old Teata came scurrying out. "*Ua mirimiri vau e ua ite i te vavai* — I looked in and saw the kapok cotton." She had peeped through the cracks between the segments of the bamboo shed. We all knew what had happened.

Heedless of Naipu's injunctions Nanai had gone up the valley with the women after oranges. But she had felt sick and started back alone. The river was swollen with the recent rains. Crossing it she had been taken with cramps. Half-drowned she was able to drag herself to the bank where she fainted. When she came to more dead than alive she stumbled home. She had just had a second miscarriage and was bleeding profusely.

With all the to-do the major was forgotten. What had happened to him? "*Ua haere atu mea riri rahi* — He went away boiling mad," explained Ueri.

Later that evening I was sitting alone working on a linoleum cut. My children had gone up to the village for the night. Naipu appeared in the doorway. "You are quite sure I am not disturbing you, Tioti?"

"Heaven's sake, no. Come in and have a drink. You've had a rough afternoon and you must need one pretty badly."

Recently Naipu has been taking his main meal in the middle of the day, his drinks in the late afternoon, and nothing but tea and bread for supper. He is a man of habit.

He said: "No thanks, Tioti. You know I never drink in the evening. I just stopped in to ask you if you happen to have a wide-mouthed bottle which you could spare me."

"I have one, but I keep my varnish in it. What do you want it for?"

"It's not for myself but for Nanai. She would like to preserve her abortion in alcohol."

I said: "Jesus Christ, Naipu! You're not going to let her do it, are you? Is she going to have it in your living room as a decoration for the dining room table?"

He looked at me patiently as if I were an unreasonable child. Or was he just thinking the matter over? He has an exasperating way sometimes of giving the most trivial question careful consideration before expressing his opinion.

"No. It is *my* living room. But it is *her* abortion. If she wants to keep it in the cedar-wood box in our sleeping shed it seems to me she has a right to do so."

I said: "I'll empty the varnish into another receptacle and let you have the bottle to-morrow. You're sure you won't sit down and have a drink?"

He said: "No thanks. I'll be going." His face looked drawn and tired.

Sometimes I wonder if Naipu is becoming unbalanced. He has an active mind, intelligence, and, although his emotions are tightly disciplined, a genuine capacity for friendship. But he reads less and less. In fact many of his books are still in their unopened crates in the living room. More and more he sits there alone or out on the veranda doing nothing, occasionally tapping on the arm of his chair. I feel the tension, but it, too, is well under control.

A man living in the tropics, having cut himself off from his own background, determined to identify himself with the native way of life, can easily disintegrate. And the more intelligent and sensitive he is, the sooner he will go to pieces. With Hall and Nordy and myself it is very different. We all three came down here with a definite purpose, and I for a very limited time. Naipu had a clear-cut vocation in life. He was a born schoolmaster. Now his Socratic inclinations are centered on his boys. Is he beginning to realize the inadequacy of his relation with them? The futility of trying to reshape them after his own pattern?

Perhaps his trouble is something much deeper. He has often told me that he hated his father. Is there a hidden childhood obsession that an injury has been done him? — "Father, you're not fair with me. What you're doing is unjust!" And is his whole life a quixotic, irrational, desperate struggle to be equitable with other people? And also an almost neurotic puritanical resistance to anyone who interferes with his own way of life, as long as he leaves others strictly alone? He forgets that the world will not tolerate — and often persecutes — those who will not join the herd.

June 25, 1922

Punuari *vahine* owns a small strip of land between the river and the road bordering on Naipu's property on which my house stands. For a long time I have been anxious to buy it. I know that I shall never return to Tahiti. Why then do I want to acquire it? And yet, and yet?

Is it to ensure against a remote possibility? Or to ease what I know will be a painful farewell by the pretense of putting off an unalterable decision?

Today I found the old lady seated by the roadside surrounded by her grandchildren, pigs, and chickens. I broached the subject with her. She refused to sell on the ground that I was a *fetii* — a kinsman — and that I had helped Timo and sent him to the hospital when he was ill. She would not sell but she would give me the land. Knowing that this was a subterfuge I argued with her for an hour. At length she weakened but she refused to name a price.

The natives cling to the land and hate to part with it. Although in terms of capital investment the land has little value, yet for numberless generations it has provided the raw material for their livelihood. Their attachment, however, is far deeper than this. There is something almost sacred in their feeling toward it. Their beautiful district *paripari*, their myths, their proof of kinship and personal identity are based on the land — its valleys, streams, mountains, and promontories.

The Chinese also covet the land. With their frugality and cunning they know how to extract a tidy profit out of it, trading in copra and vanilla. They are the world's oldest businessmen and bankers. They are pleasant to deal with, too. They give the natives easy credit at their stores for all the things that make life pleasant — canned beef, sugar, coffee, and silk shawls for their women. They will do without a down payment and are satisfied running up bills with a mortgage on the land. Where I failed with my old friend Punuari *vahine*, they will be more successful.

July 3, 1922

Ueri has discovered a bit of ghost's excrement — *tutae tupapau* — coiled in a yellow spiral about a twig close to the ground. He was anxious to show it to us. Moerai and I accompanied him this afternoon high up the valley. We could not persuade Terae Hara and Uraponi to join us. Alas, during the night the ghostly excrement had been disturbed and trampled out of recognition by a boar or other animal.

The day was hot and we sat down to rest. Moerai gathered wild scented fern and wove garlands for us. To pass away the time he sang for us *ute*, little improvised verses on an old Tahitian air, celebrating or poking fun at the members of our household or other friends. The beauty of the setting — the tall, deep-groined *mape* trees, the sea below us, and the distant peak of Orohena on Tahiti *nui* — all this, and the purity and spontaneity of his childish voice gave me an instant understanding of what must have been the freshness and beauty of life when the world was young.

July 5, 1922

Peace and a semblance of order reign once more in my household. Sweet, sensible little Terae Hara has taken things under control. Uraponi for the moment is in one of her righteous and purposeful moods. Seized with a fit of energy she cut wood all afternoon. Nearby seated on a log Pata played for her on his accordion.

In the evening, grown coquettish, Uraponi bathes in the river. Wrapping her slender figure in one of my bath towels, she dabs herself with my shaving lotion before sitting down to supper. She eats with her fingers, picking at random from our plates. Her copper-colored hair hangs down over her eyes, sometimes falling into the jam or butter. Heedful of my comfort she selects for me tidbits of fish and places them on my plate.

This evening I read them all the story of Little Bob Thumb – *Tamaiti Iti Maiuu* – which I picked up in Papeete from the *Vea a te Hau* – Government News – a local publication. Later we all danced. I feel romantically inclined toward Terae Hara and give her the run of my Chinese perfume and talcum powder and the occasional gift of a comb, a cake of scented soap, or a blue silk handkerchief.

I do not think of myself as a *vicieux* because here in Tahiti I am physically attracted by young girls, often those who are of good families, well brought up, and carefully guarded by their mothers, such as Terae Hara and Teura the daughter of the *orometua*. Among primitive women the sex urge is immediately satisfied by the discharge of accumulated physical desire. They are, alas, normal and healthy, incapable of taking flight into the realm of the imagination. Only among the young girls emerging from adolescence is awakening sex sublimated for a brief moment into curiosity, the desire to stretch out and explore the unknown in other human beings.

July 8, 1922

This past week consumed with energy. Up at half past six. Six hours of painting a day. A swim before lunch and an hour's work in my garden during the afternoon. Reading three or four books a week. Baudelaire's *Journeaux Intimes*, Laforgue, Guillaume Apollinaire.

From Apollinaire's *Bestiaire*:

Admirez le pouvoir insigne
Et la noblesse de la ligne:
Elle est la voix que la lumière
fit entendre
Et dont parle Hermes Trismégiste
en son Pimandre.

"Bientôt, lit-on dans le Pimandre, descendirent des ténèbres . . . et il en sortit un cri inarticulé qui semblait la voix de la lumière. Cette voix de la lumière, n'est-ce pas le dessein, c'est-a-dire la ligne? Et quand la lumière s'exprime pleinement tout se colore. La peinture est proprement un langage lumineux."

Yes, that is it. Fine drawing is the bone and marrow of "the most noble art of painting."

And from the *Journeaux Intimes*: "Les nations n'ont de grands hommes que malgré elles, – comme les familles. Elles font tous leurs efforts pour n'en pas avoir. Et ainsi le grand homme a besoin, pour exister, de posséder une force d'attaque plus grande que la force de résistance développée par des millions d'individus."

Yet France in her hour of greatness honored and respected her artists – her great men. I remember during the war one evening at our First Corps G-2 mess discussing with the other officers what period in history we would have chosen to live in, had we been offered the choice. Among us was a Lieutenant Meade of Roanoke, Virginia, a distant cousin. He argued vehemently for the old plantation life of the South before the Civil War. I, too, had been brought up on this tradition by my mother's family who were from tidewater Virginia. But I maintained – and at times since then I have sometimes felt – that as an artist I would rather have lived in France between the age of Delacroix and the World War.

The three artists who have been the greatest inspiration to me are, first and foremost, Degas; to a lesser degree and because through her passion and integrity I had a better understanding of her master, Mary Cassatt; and for about three years after my student days, my friend Frieseke. Since then from time to time various artists of the modern movement in whose work I found something that I needed and that was helpful to me: Diederich, La Chaise, Matisse, to a lesser degree Gauguin – and Albert Gleizes' writings.

July 9, 1922

The only real human tragedy is suppressed desire, unspent energy, life frustrated.

July 10, 1922

In the shadow of a palm tree some twenty of the *taurearea* are waiting for the work to begin. Paruparu, Teamo, Roo, Pata, Ana, Teri, Tamaru, and the others are singing in the moonlight.

The children, overwrought, run zigzag on the black sand, laugh and squeal.

The babies sleep, their heads wrapped in shawls.

The men are stripping to their *pareu*, trussed up about their loins. They empty the fish from the receiving net, gently swaying between *purau* poles a few feet from the shore.

Teura, the grace of whose every movement entrances me, conscious of the air that caresses her, child and libertine, stretches wantonly in the sand, enfolding her head in her curving arm, darts into the salt water, flings small fishes at the boys, finally throws herself down beside Toahite and buries her head in her sister's lap.

As I return by moonlight down the sandy lane shaded by mangoes, old Tafaite the cripple calls to me from the dark. Too proud to parade his deformity he sits all day at his window and late into the night. He has compromised with life. Yet he still clings desperately to its intensity. Into his cheerful greeting he pours the yearning for youth, activity and conquest.

"*Hea oe?* – Whither do you come?"

"*No te tui raa mai no te ia* – From the stringing of the fish."

July 25, 1922

Some time ago I met Marc Chadourne, a young Frenchman in the government service, recently come out here from Paris. Unlike most of the French officials he is enraptured with the island, but his knowledge of the native life is superficial. He sees it through the eyes of Rupert Brooke, Pierre Loti, and the French Symbolist poets. With the help of Queen Marau he has been making translations of old Tahitian poems. He has asked me to illustrate them.

I made several small linoleum cuts for him: one of three naked fishermen standing in a long wooden dugout which cuts diagonally across the print, the raised fish spears forming parallel lines at a sharp angle with the dugout. The men are in the act of spearing conventionalized fish in a conventionalized sea.

I had been casting about for a theme for a large canvas which I am eager to paint before leaving—one which will sum up the essence of the island life and at the same time the new direction of my work. The little linoleum cut suggested to me just what I wanted. It will differ, however, from most of my smaller paintings in its decorative or mural approach.

Today I sized my canvas with fish glue and whiting. I worked all day drafting in the figures out of my head on a second canvas of the same size, fifty by seventy inches. This will serve me as a preliminary sketch. I like to keep the canvas on which I shall paint as clean as possible.

July 26, 1922

Copied the figures on the sized canvas from the preliminary sketch. Corrected the drawing, using little Taniera, Moerai's friend, as a model.

July 27, 1922

In the morning perfected my drawing and in the afternoon painted in the body of the figure to the left.

July 29, 1922

Worked on, and finished, the figure to the right.

August 3, 1922

Worked all day on the fish, using as models some red *iihi* and black *tare* which I had asked Paruparu to spear for me on the outer reef. But utterly exhausted and aching all over from a severe attack of grippe.

August 15, 1922

Still very weak from my recent fever. I have been lying all afternoon in the sun, watching the purple hills of Ahui, the copper sheet of water beyond the lagoon, and the little lapping waves as they chase each other in spiraling curves into the opening of the river. In the distance the summit of Orohena on Tahiti *nui* rises from the tumbling blanket of clouds. My body is still so weak that it is an effort to lift my hands or feet. But what a sensuous delight to lie back physically exhausted, drinking in new strength.

A fortnight ago I was taken down with a violent attack of grippe and ran a high fever for a week. I vomited everything I swallowed. Every muscle in my body ached, so that it was painful to move. Day after day I suffered from a blinding, torturing headache. I felt as if nails were being driven down in showers between and through my eyes. A dull lump fastened into the back of my skull. By the greatest concentration I could slowly move it round and round to the back of my neck, up and over my head and down between the eyes. But I could never shake it off and after the fever subsided it continued to drain my vitality.

By daytime the lizards seemed to rattle the very roof as they scurried about over the *niau*. At night the rats invaded the kitchen, jumped from box to chair to table, clattering the dishes. My body ached. I was exhausted but could not sleep.

Naipu had run out of aspirin and quinine and could do nothing to help me. The river was swollen by the recent rains and it was impossible to get medicine from Papeete. But good Arai *vahine* and Tamaru brought down their bedding and remained in the house throughout my illness. They mixed for me native drugs largely compounded from coconut, and bound my head in a poultice of starch and lime juice.

One day old Punuari *vahine* came down and massaged my head. After that I slept heavily. My muscles were still hard and stiff as if they had been crushed and bruised. Tamaru bathed me with hot water and massaged my body. Now I am better and in a day or two I shall be able to paint again.

August 17, 1922

In the morning worked over the three heads without using a model. All going well. But very weak and a bad cough.

August 19, 1922

All afternoon little Terai plaited many colored garlands of flowers, mostly from the pink and scarlet hibiscus and the yellow blossoms of the *piti* vine. She hangs them about the house and presents one to each of us before supper. Her lips protrude like delicate unfolding petals from her round, smoothly modeled face. Her eyes are really her only beautiful feature. But when her soft dark hair tumbles over the straight column of her neck and shoulders I feel that other features are unnecessary. The eyes illuminate her face which has the expressionless purity of a Kmer sculpture.

August 20, 1922

But yesterday reached the limit of my endurance. To bed and slept all day and again this morning.

August 22, 1922

Real friendship as we understand it is rare among Tahitians. Boys and girls, especially before puberty, form attachments in groups of two or three and they speak of each other as *tau hoa rahi*—my great friend. But such intimacies are easily dissolved. I believe a Tahitian is capable of an enduring friendship more easily with a European. Here the relation has something in it of respect, reliance, or hero worship, as that of a boy for his teacher or elder brother.

August 23, 1922

Perhaps it is because I am very tired that I feel uncontrollably blue about my work. It is only during the past year that I have begun to find myself. If it were not for the fact that I am stale and really need the trip to the States, I could stay here another year. I seem to have begun to paint too late in life. In another ten years the best of my working years may be over. Possibly, if my health stands up, another fifteen or twenty.

August 24, 1922

About three o'clock while I was still working Terae Hara, Teura, and Toahite clattered into the house like three young colts. They spent the afternoon writing imaginary love letters to their chosen sweethearts. They then read them aloud to each other with whispered modesty or sighs of wounded feelings. Here is one written by Terae Hara to Tauira, a recent arrival in the village. Toahite says that in another month the families will announce the engagement.

Tautira i te 24 no atete, 1922.

Na tau hoa here iti i te fare.

Te ani atu nei au ia oe e haere mai oe iau nei aunei ia po. E haere mai a oe. Eiha ia mairi. Mai te mea oe eita e haere mai tirara ia. Eiaha ia oe e maneo e haere faahou mai iau nei.

A rave a imi i te vahini api ia oe ei faanehenehe to tino e vaihoe noa mai iau te vahine hapaoraa ore. Amaa roti tei tau ooma tei haamanaoraa ia oe.

Tirara parau iti. Ia ora na.

Na Terae Hara vahine.*

Tautira, August 24, 1922.

To my darling friend in his house.

I beg of you to come to me this night. Come to me here. Do not delay. If you do not come all is over. Do not suppose you will then be able to visit me again.

* This is reproduced with Terae Hara's own improvised spelling—Tahitians are ear perfect but their orthography is chaotic since their language was never taught in any of the district schools.

Look for another sweetheart for yourself, get you ready and bedeck your body and cast me away, your worthless sweetheart. A twig of roses in my breast will be in memory of you.

My little words are spoken. May you prosper.

From the maid Terae Hara.

September 1, 1922

Moerai asked me if I had ever seen a *hee*—an ogre. They live hidden in the roots of the *mape* trees and in the evening emerge to attack and devour human beings. About four years ago one of the villagers was attacked by a *hee*. He managed to escape but subsequently died of the bite.

"I should think all of you would be afraid to go up the river at night after shrimp and eel?"

"O yes!"

"But why, then, do the boys do it?"

After a pause: "They go up just the same."

Papeete, September 2, 1922

X is attached to the French Consulate General. He shares my romantic involvement with the island. But he has little knowledge of the natives' life in the outlying districts. He told me with the greatest distress that a girl with whom he has been living is about to have a baby. He feels that his position here will be untenable and his career ruined. He would like to arrange an abortion for the girl and asked me if I could persuade one of the native doctors in the districts to bring it about.

There is something quite comic in this sudden foundering of his romance. Apart from the fact that illegitimacy is a meaningless word among Polynesians, any healthy child—and more especially one born with a light complexion—is generally considered an asset to an unmarried girl. And most of the best families in Papeete boast of some European blood. I have often myself felt that a child would be a more enduring and romantic way of anchoring my memory to Tahiti than a plot of Punuari *vahine*'s land on the banks of the Vaitipiha. Both would of course be the ideal solution. I was able to persuade X that his fears were groundless. Besides he expects soon to be transferred to another station.

Papeete, September 3, 1922

I have been reading Percy Smith's history of the migrations of the Polynesians. By a comparison of corresponding genealogical records—handed down by word of mouth and recorded in different island groups — he believes that he can trace the migrations with some accuracy from the Malay Straits and Indonesia across the Pacific Ocean. Some of the genealogies run back ninety generations. Allowing twenty-five years to a generation, their migrations would have started several hundred years before Christ.*

What particularly excited my wonder is his mention of Pae, an actual man, whose date he fixes at about 1250 A.D. Pae's name appears in the genealogical records of different island groups which had lost communication with each other for centuries: the same *aito* Pae who cast his spear from the Valley of Ataroa and transfixed the Wounded Mountain in far-off Moorea, landing it in Tatamata's garden.

This afternoon I called on old Queen Marau to pay my respects, for I shall be leaving for home in another fortnight. I asked her if she had known Percy Smith and had read his book. She remembers him well. He must have had many talks with her. But she had forgotten why he had come to Tahiti. I told her of his remarkable reconstruction of Polynesian history.

"He is quite mistaken," said Marau. "The Tahitians are indigenous to the island. We are all descended from a shark."

I let this one slip by and remarked that in his book Smith had spoken of the *aito* Pae and fixed his date at 1250 A.D.

"His version cannot be true," said Marau. "It does not at all correspond to the legends of my family."

Does the old lady really believe what she says? Or is she living up to the role which Henry Adams prepared for her in his life of her royal mother-in-law? What delights me in Marau is the blend of slyness and innocence. One finds it in all primitive people, in Homer's heroes, as among children.

September 6, 1922

The children have been correcting my Tahitian. Moerai told me that a word I had used, *ariana* — by and by — was *parau tinito* — Chinese Tahitian. After making a bet of a franc with him I showed him the word in my dictionary. When I asked to be paid he became furious. He hid outside and refused to come in for supper or say goodnight to me. Arai *vahine* told me the next morning that it was all she could do to get him to return. She threatened and scolded him, reminding him how much money I had spent sending him to the hospital in Papeete to have his crushed bone removed and the thumb healed. Even after he returned he refused to have coffee with us. For an hour he squatted at the edge of the beach, nursing his wrongs.

* Smith, like other earlier scholars of Polynesia, placed a great reliance on genealogies as they were remembered by Polynesians. The idea that one could trace the migrations from the Malay Straits and Indonesia with the aid of genealogies was current in the 1920's and 1930's. This is no longer the case. It has subsequently been found that Polynesians frequently reconstructed the genealogical record in order to validate the status of the existing chiefs, and for other reasons.

September 10, 1922

Today Moerai stole twenty francs from my purse which was lying on the table. He went up to the village with Terae Hara and Uraponi and bought four francs' worth of marbles at Amok's store. Terae Hara, as soon as she returned, asked me in feigned innocence if I knew where he had gotten so much money. I called Moerai in. He told me, unconcerned, that Arai *vahine* had given him the money. I met Arai later and she told me that she had given him nothing. I called Moerai in again. Once more he lied to me, this time saying that he had it from Arai's *tane*.

"Go up to Arai and repeat to her what you have just told me."

He slunk out of the house. Later in the day he returned from Arai with twenty francs. He admitted sullenly that he had taken the money. As a punishment I told him that for the rest of the day I did not wish to see him in my house and that he had better return to Arai's. This he did not do. Instead he hid under a *purau* tree where Uraponi found him crying.

Just as Terae Hara and Uraponi had at first hastened to peach on their friend, they now turned on me, saying that I was a *taata mea ino roa*—a very bad man.

As with children primitives steal and lie instinctively. The feeling of shame is born in the act of being caught. Otherwise deception is tolerated if not actually given consideration. Our ethical standards were first given us by the Jewish prophets and the Greek philosophers, not by the Old Testament or the Homeric gods. However, the double standard toward duplicity lingers on in our euphemism of the "white lie."

I suppose it is also true that the primitive's sentiments are rarely rational. His gratitude, affection, antipathy, or love is a spontaneous emotion. That is its charm. It springs truly from the heart. Never from a sense of obligation. As Anatole France somewhere writes: "Si l'on raisonne, on ne s'envole jamais."

September 15, 1922

For the past two weeks reworking on a number of old canvases and putting the last touches on my large painting, "Spearing Fish"—thirty-five sessions in all.

Deeply depressed. Of course I have not yet recovered my strength since I had the grippe. And the work I have been doing recently, although sometimes the most rewarding, is exhausting—trying to put more sparkle and color into paintings when the original impulse is dead.

But more than anything else I am sad because I am leaving this life, this village, and these children whom I have grown to love. No one of them can have the same feeling toward me. I shall pass out of their lives the day I step on the boat. They will remember me, I hope, as a sunny rather than a clouded day. But there will be neither regret, gratitude, or real affection.

September 17, 1922

These last few days Uraponi has vexed me beyond endurance. She makes no pretense of doing her share of the work without complaints, arguments, and, if I am at the end of my tether, a mild chastisement followed by tears. Whereupon there is a "*faariri* Uraponi – sulks and anger" or "*matau rahi ia oe* – you have scared her to death." She takes every occasion to create discord and ill feeling. She will pass the cracked bowl, a twisted fork, or the broken chair to one of the others. In the end she gets the worst of it. With hysterical sobs she rushes from the house and climbs her mango tree. Eventually I have to coax her in from the rain. She finishes her bread and jam under the table in a revengeful frame of mind.

September 19, 1922

I stepped into the scow which will take my baggage and rolls of paintings to the *Marama*. Naipu is accompanying me in to Papeete. On the beach a dozen of the villagers have come to see me off. Among them Paruparu, Ueri, Pata, Timo, Tauire *vahine*, Arai *vahine*, Tamaru, Terae Hara, Teura, and her sister Toahite. On the way down Moerai – characteristically – got engaged in a game of marbles and did not show up.

Among the dresses of the women I can still distinguish three, all recently bought at Amok the Chinaman's. That one in pale blue is of Terae Hara. The one in yellow with the black dots is of Toahite, the gentle daughter of Paea the *orometua*. The pale lavender one is of her sister Teura.

Now the colors mingle, dissolve, and fade away.

The Death of Teura

Faa rarahi te ura i te rai e.
E aha te matai e Teura i
maru iho?
I marumaru iho i nia iau nei
e Teura e.
Faa rarahi te ura i te rai e.

Unfold the purple of the sky.
What is that wind, O Teura, that bears
along with it the dark shadow?
That dark, dark shadow that bears down
upon me, O Teura.
Unfold the purple of the sky.

EPILOGUE

ONLY the author of *Heart of Darkness* could have done justice to the tragic and solitary end of my quixotic friend Naipu. I had the full account many years after I left Tahiti from both Hall and Nordhoff.

Naipu shared one quality with Gauguin, a thorough antipathy to the French bureaucracy of the island and an instinct for irritating and insulting the rigid sensibilities of the members of the Cercle Bougainville. There were those among them who swore *d'avoir sa peau* — to get his scalp.

At that time in the Society Islands homosexual relations might lead to many years at hard labor in the penal colony of Nouméa in French Caledonia. The fact that Naipu's household often was made up of teenaged boys was presumptive evidence to some that such relations were occurring. It would of course have been simple enough to obtain testimony that *seemed* conclusive from any of Naipu's young friends of the *taurearea*. This is not surprising considering the affection and social esteem for a *mahu* in the native community. Then too a boy from the outlying districts could easily be prompted on the witness stand to answer any leading questions in the affirmative.

In the tropics news — especially that of a squalid nature — travels rapidly by the grapevine. Naipu was quite aware, and probably warned, that there was a plot against him. Buttressed by his own inflexible moral code, contemptuous and arrogant, he remained indifferent — *au-dessus de la mêlée*. Hall and Nordhoff, most loyal of friends, determined, however, to save him in spite of himself. Rather than argue with him, they took direct action.

In Papeete, unknown to Naipu, they obtained the use of a small seaworthy power launch, captained by a trustworthy native. One evening they appeared inside the reef opposite Naipu's bungalow. That same night they spirited him away to the neighboring island of Manuiki, one of the Cook Islands under British sovereignty. His library and his other possessions followed him by slow freight.

Naipu had always been a lazy correspondent. I only heard much later that he had left Tahiti. The years rolled on. I was happily married.

On another far distant island, in another southern sea, by one of those fortuitous quirks that reunite the loose or broken strands of human relations, I once again ran across my friend.

He had changed little. His beard was as carefully trimmed and his manners as punctilious as formerly. There, too, he had become intimate with a small group of cosmopolitan, liberal, and cultivated friends. He lived in a one-room cottage in a remote spot on the island where he could lounge about in one of the sarongs given him by Borneo Smith. Many of his books were still unpacked or lay about on the floor. But occasionally he would turn up at a cocktail party in a carefully ironed white drill suit and Panama hat.

He complained a good deal of the swelling in his arms and the increased pain, "recurring in cycles like a woman's menstruations." But the joke was forced. When alone together we talked about those other days. At one time he said that Nanai had sent him a photograph of "her" baby, and added with his twisted smile that "It was the spitting image of my father." At other times there were long periods of silence. The look in the eyes was further beyond his own horizon, *à la recherche du temps perdu*. When I left he accompanied me down to the little steamer to see me off.

A year or two later I received a note from one of his recent friends. Naipu had been found dead in his cottage, the cause of death unknown. Of course if any of his Tahitian friends had heard of this they would have said: "We told you so. He built his house on a sacred *marae*."

PAINTINGS AND DRAWINGS BY THE AUTHOR

Drypoint engraving of Nanai

Mango and coconut trees

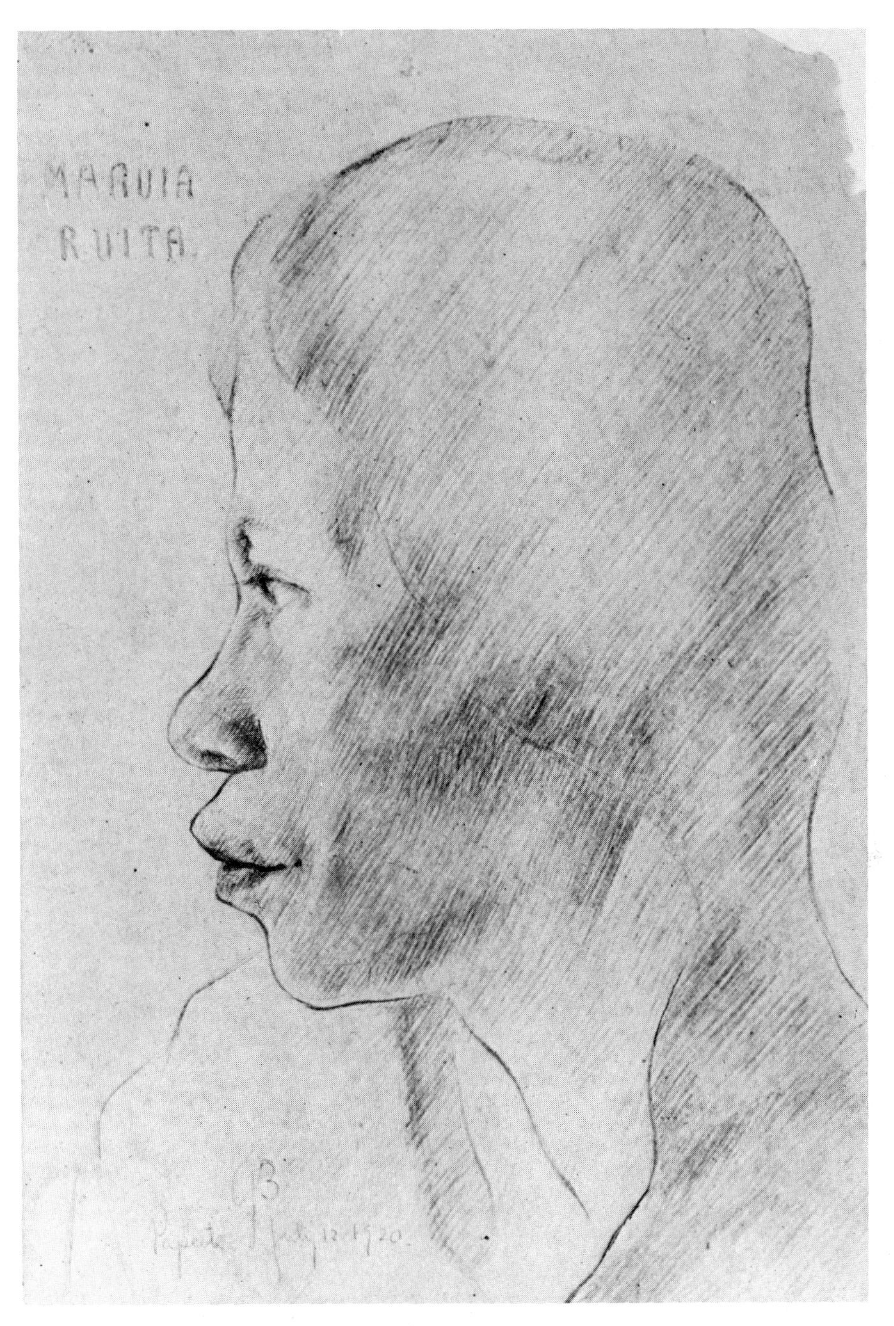

Silverpoint drawing of Maruia Ruita

Ana

The valley road

Meri

At the mouth of the Vaitipiha

The road to the village

GLOSSARY

GLOSSARY

THE structure of Tahitian is quite different from that of our Indo-European languages. Many words and phrases have subtle shades of meaning which cannot be more than approximated in English. I have attempted no more than this in my translation of the Tahitian phrases and sentences that appear in the journal. For the songs quoted in the journal, both the short, current, improvised songs and the very ancient ones, I have generally relied on the English versions – inevitably a free rendering – given me by Queen Marau or by my friend the anthropologist Frank Stimson.

In this Glossary I have scrupulously followed the spelling, definitions, and grammatical usage given in Jaussen's *Grammaire et Dictionnaire de la Langue Maori, Dialecte Tahitien*. It was printed in 1898 but is still, I believe, the best source available. All words or definitions which were not included in Jaussen's dictionary but were in common use while I was in Tahiti have been preceded by an asterisk.

A, interjection of surprise; designates the imperative of a verb; to be
Aeho, a tall reed, *Erianthus floridulis*
Aenei, had, were
Aere, firmament, the unknown
Afa, half
Afai, to carry
Aha, what (interrogative)
**Ahiere*, a wild grass. *Fenua ahiere*, open cultivated country outside the villages
Ahimaa, *himaa*, oven
Ai, to eat; food; then, so
Aita, no, not, nothing
Aito, hero; iron-wood, *Casuarina equisetifolia*
Aiu, baby
Amaa, branch, twig
Amu, to eat. *Taata amu taata*, cannibal
Ana, immediately, then
Ananahi, tomorrow
Ani, to ask
Ao, universe, world
Apatoa, south
Ape, an edible root, *Arum costatum*
Api, new. *Parau api*, news
Apoo, *apoona*, hole, grave
Ara, path
Area, to think, to conclude
Arearea, pleasure, merrymaking
Ariana, soon, by and by
Arii, king, chief. *Arii vahine*, queen
Aroha, love, compassion, sympathy
Ata, cloud
Ataata, emotion, laughable, pleasant, terrible, disgusting
Atu, far away; denotes comparative or superlative
Atua, god
Atura, then
Au, I, me, mine; charming
Aue, ejaculation of admiration or surprise, ah!
Aunei, today
Auti, native bush, *Cordyline australis*
Ava, a pass, channel

E, present, future, and imperative of verb to be; O, indicating the vocative; by; and; yes
Ehu, blond
Ei, for, in order to
Eiaha, negative imperative, do not, no

Faa, to do, to make
Faahou, again; to renew
Faaitoito, have courage, make haste
Faaora, to give back life, to resuscitate
Faatii, frustrated, disappointed
Fanau, to be born, to give birth; a litter

Fare, house, home. *Fare taoto*, sleeping house. *Fare tutu*, cook shed
Farerei, to come
Fee, octopus
Feefee, elephantiasis
Fei, mountain plantain, *Musafei*
Fenua, land, earth
Fetia, star. *Fetia tatauro*, Southern Cross
Fetii, parent, relative, family

Haa, used before another word denotes to cause, to make
Haama, shame
Haamanaoraa, memory, thought
Haamauruuru, to satisfy, to give thanks
Haari, coconut
Haavare, to lie; lie
Haere, to go. *Haere mai*, come
Haerea, voyage
**Hahavare*, a type of large fish
Hamani, to make
**Hapaoraa*, value, worth
Hau, government
Hauti, to vex, to tease, to be disturbed
Hea, where
Hei, necklace
Here, dear, beloved
Hia, designates passive of verbs
Hihimata, eyebrows
Himaa, oven
Himene, religious chorus; the singing itself (Gallicized)
Hio, to see, to observe
Hitu, seven
Hoa, friend
Hoe, one
Hohoa, drawing, painting
Hohonu, deep
Hoi, also; to return
Hopea, the last, end
Horo, to run
Hure e, strange

I, in, at; designates past tense of verbs
Ia, that, that one, it is; when, if, in order that; at, in, for; fish. *Ia ota*, raw, marinated fish
Iho, down, here, there. *Oe iho*, you yourself
Iihi, red; a small tropical red fish
Iita, papaya
Imi, to take
Inanahi, yesterday
Ino, bad
Inu, to drink
Iropu, the center
Ite, to know
Itea, knowledge
Itoito, courage

Ma, and his, or her, or their crowd (e.g., *Tu ma,* Tu and his gang)
Maehaa, twin
Maere, to admire; *a native fern
Mahu, homosexual, a pansy
Mahui, to disclose, to reveal
Mai, here, from, like; sick or sickness. *Mai te mea e*, if
Mairi, delay
Maitai, good
Maiuu, fingernail
Manao, thought, belief; to think
Maniania, noise, nuisance
Maoae, east wind
Mape, Tahitian chestnut, *Inocarpus edulis*
Maraamu, southeast wind
Marae, sacred ground, burial ground
Marama, moon, month
Maramarama, light
Maru, dark, gentle
Marumaru, sunset; shadow
**Marutete*, solo female singer in *himene*
Mata, face, eye
Matai, wind
Matamua, first, long ago
Mātau, to be accustomed
Matāu, fishhook
Mataū, to fear
Matou, we all
Mau, true; several, the following; *ancient
Maua, we two; mountain
Mauruuru, pleasure, thanks; agreeable
Mea, thing, matter
Metua, father, mother, parent
Mirimiri, to examine, to peer at
**Miti haari*, sauce of ground coconut flesh mixed with lime juice and salt water
Moa, sacred, sanctified
Moana, deep; the sea
Moe, lost, forgotten; to sleep
Moemoe, to dream
Monoi, scented oil, perfume
Moua, mountain
Mutoi, policeman, letter carrier

Na, adverb designating time or place, now, then, here, there
Navenave, harmonious, pleasant, delicious; to have an orgasm
Nehenehe, beautiful, suitable, proper. *Mea nehenehe*, better, best
Nei, here
Neia, printing
Nenei, to print
Nia, above
Niau, leaf of coconut palm
No, of
Noa, spontaneously, simply
Noanoa, sweet smelling
Novema, November (Gallicized)
Nui, great
* *Numera*, number (Gallicized)

O, article used before names of people or places
Oe, you
Ofai, stone
Ofati, to break
Ohipa, work
Ohu, to turn, to revolve
Oia, he, she, it
One, sand, beach
Onohi, to kill oneself; suicide
Ooma, heart
Opani, to close; door, window
Ora, to live; life
**Orare*, small fish resembling a mackerel
Ore, no, not, without
Orero, orator, talk, discourse
**Orometua*, native missionary or pastor
Outou, you all
Outu, cape, promontory
Ovai, who (interrogative)
Oviri, wild, savage

Pae, five
Paepae, shelf
Pai, to be consumed, annihilated, finished

Papa, rock
Papai, to write, to paint, to draw. *Taata papai hohoa*, painter
Paraparau, to talk; conversation
Parau, word, talk. *Parau mau*, truth
Pareu, native loin cloth
**Paripari*, ancient district song
Paruparu, feeble, impotent
Pe, rotten
Peapea, anxiety, vexation, quarrel
Peho, valley
Pereoo, wagon, carriage. *Pereoo uira*, automobile
**Petania*, Mormon missionary
Peue, mat
Pii, to call
Pipiri, to cling
**Pipiria*, Bible
**Piti*, yellow, flowering vine
Po, night
Poe, poi, fruit or vegetable boiled with taro root
Pohe, to die
Poipoi, morning
Poiri, dark
**Popaa*, foreigner of European or American extraction
Pope, Catholic priest (Gallicized)
Popoti, cockroach
Puaa, pig. *Puaa horo fenua*, horse. *Puaa toro*, cow, cattle
Pupa, flower cluster
Pupure, blond, light skinned
Purau, native tree related to the hibiscus, *Paritium tiliaceum*
Puta, a hole, opening, wound
Putuputu, to assemble
Putuputuraa, assembly

Ra, adverb of time or place, then, there
Raa, suffix to a verb changing it into a noun
Rahi, big; extremely, very
Rai, sky
Rama, *ramarama*, torch
Rarahi, very great
Ratou, they, them
Rau, several
Rave, to take, to seize
**Rehu*, blond, light skinned
Reira, then, this instant
Riaria, horrible, disgusting
Riri, anger, offense
Riro, to transform
Roa, long; very, entirely. *Ore roa atu*, never
Ropu, *iropu*, center, at the center
Roti, rose
Roto, in, within
Ruau, old; old man

Taata, man, person
Taha, coast, shoreline
Tahito, ancient, formerly
Tahu, *tahutahu*, to bewitch; sorcerer
Tahua, native doctor, priest
Tai, sea
**Taiate*, partnership
Tamaa, eat, feast
Tamaiti, son, small boy
Tamarii, child, children
Tane, man, husband
Taoto, sleep
Taporo, lemon
Tapu, tabu, prohibition
Taratara, rough, spiky
**Tare*, a native fish
Tatahi, shore, edge of the sea
Tatou, all of us
Tau, my; time, season
Taua, both of us
Taurearea, youth, young people
Tautai, catch of fish
Tauturu, to help
Tavini, servant
Taviri, to open or close (with a key), to turn
Te, the
Tei, *teie*, *teienei*, this, this one, this instant, today. *Tei nia*, above. *Tei raro*, below
Teina, younger brother or sister
Teoteo, proud
Tera, that
Tetei, to be seen above water
Tiare, flower. *Tiare Moorea*, double gardenia. *Tiare Tahiti*, single gardenia
Tii, stone idol, sculpture; to seek, to look for
**Tinito*, Chinese
Tino, body
Tira, *tirara*, enough, finished
**Titoi*, to masturbate
To, of, of you, yours
Toerau, north wind
**Tohuno*, a native tree, the odor of which attracts moths
Tona, his, her
Torea, a small native bird
Tuahine, sister of a brother
Tuana, older brother
Tuane, brother of a sister
Tui, stringing (of fish)
Tumu, root, tree, origin, foundation
Tupapau, spirit of the dead, corpse
Tupuna, ancestor, grandparent
Tutae, excrement
Tutu, to cook
Tutua, flea

Ua, designates past tense of verb; rain
Uaua, damp
Uira, lightning. *Pereoo uira*, automobile
Umara, native potato, ***Batatas edulis***
Umete, a long wooden bowl to hold food. *Matau umete*, spoon hook
Unauna, bedecked, splendid
Upaupa, dance; accordion, *mouth organ
Upea, net
Ura, flames, red feathers
Uri, dog
Uritaata, monkey
Uru, breadfruit, breadfruit tree, *Artocarpus incisa*
Uta, earth, land
Ute, song

Vaa, large dugout canoe
Vahine, woman, wife
Vai, who (interrogative)
Vaihoe, to remain alone
Varo, sea centipede, edible type of lobster
Varua, spirit
Vau, I, me
Vavai, cotton tree, ***Gossypium religiosum***
Vea, messenger
Veri, centipede
Vi, mango, *Spondias dulcis*

INDEX

INDEX